Ruxton:
The First Modern Murder

Tom Wood

RINGWOOD PUBLISHING
GLASGOW

First published in Great Britain in 2020

by

Ringwood Publishing, Glasgow.

www.ringwoodpublishing.com

mail@ringwoodpublishing.com

ISBN 978-1-901514-84-1

British Library Cataloguing-in-Publication Data

A catalogue record for this book is available from the British Library

Printed and bound in the UK

by

Lonsdale Direct Solutions

This book is dedicated to my father, Sergeant R E Wood, Edinburgh City Police, a detective of the old school.

And to the memory of Sergeant Robert Sloan, Dumfriesshire Constabulary – the hero of Gardenholme Linn, and all the other forgotten heroes.

"Red stains on the carpet
Red stains on the knife

For Doctor Buck Ruxton had
Murdered his wife

The Maid Servant saw it
And threatened to tell

So, Doctor Buck Ruxton, he's
Killed her as well"

After Red Sails in the Sunset

Bing Crosby, 1935

FOREWORD

When Bukhtyar Hakim arrived in Britain in 1925 with medical qualifications from the University of Bombay, it was his ambition to become a famous surgeon. Instead, he found a different kind of fame as one of the twentieth centuries most notorious murderers.

The trial of Buck Ruxton, the name he adopted when the General Medical Council authorised his qualifications, is a landmark case in British legal history. It's justifiably called the first modern murder because it marks a turning point in the role of science in the courtroom and the organisation of policing, as well as being a rare example of cross-border cooperation. Ruxton's conviction in an English court was only secured because of the evidence of Scottish forensic scientists, expert witnesses from a completely separate legal jurisdiction.

Ruxton, an apparently respectable GP with an extensive practice in Lancaster, brutally beat to death his wife and their maid in the family home in the early hours of a Sunday morning. Over the course of the next few days, he dismembered their bodies and finally dumped them in a river near the Scottish Borders town of Moffat.

Their badly decomposed remains were discovered by a family out walking. All identifying marks had been erased, which presented the police with a thorny problem. Who were the victims and where had they come from?

Thanks to a quick-witted local bobby and a group of scientists determined to develop new techniques and find new applications of existing knowledge, Buck Ruxton finally paid for his crimes.

Tom Wood, a retired Edinburgh detective with a distinguished record in catching the very worst of criminals, has had access to all the case papers, some of which have never previously been seen beyond the original team of detectives. They reveal the inside story of the murder, including lines of inquiry never before made public.

Wood tells his compelling story with the clarity and urgency of a thriller. He brings to life the Indian doctor and his charismatic wife in a vivid picture of their convivial social life in Lancaster. And he takes us on a painstaking journey through the complex tapestry of a murder investigation that is still relevant to forensic inquiry today.

Until now, the whole story of this fascinating case had never been told. Tom Wood's book fills an important gap in the history of British criminal investigation. And it's a damn good read.

Val McDermid
June 2020
Edinburgh

AUTHOR'S NOTE

When I joined Edinburgh City Police as a cadet in the late sixties, the famous crimes of Scotland's past were drummed into us as part of our training and, I suspect, our cultural indoctrination.

In the old training department in Chambers Street, hoary old sergeants, all bemedalled war-service men, repeated again and again the key elements of the most important cases until we knew them by rote. HMA v Chalmers, HMA v Manuel, the Moorov doctrine and the famous criminal investigations Burke and Hare, Peter Manuel and Dr Buck Ruxton.

The lessons were graphic, with no gory detail spared, and there were always two underlying but powerful messages. First, this is your legacy as Scottish police officers - step up or get out, and second, wear your uniform with pride, for better men have worn it before you. It was all done in the vain hope that this latest batch of pitiful recruits would one day fill the boots of previous generations – and it stuck.

I had always known about the Ruxton Murders. My mother spoke of them; she had been a teenager in 1935, the case had left a lasting impression and she could recite some of the street songs that sprung up to celebrate it. The murders had been famously bloody, brutal and a triumph of forensic science. So, when many years later I was given a file of old papers relating to Ruxton I was naturally interested.
The papers had come from the family of one of Edinburgh's legendary detectives, Lieutenant John Sheed, who had died some time before. They included original police statements, records of meetings, transcripts of telephone messages, documents and old sepia-tinted photographs, yellow, faded foolscap pages typed in a formal, old-fashioned yet familiar language that told a story that was more complex than – and sometimes different from – the long-accepted narrative of the case that is so widely known.

It was a remarkable story of new villains and forgotten heroes which deserved to be told.

Tom Wood
2020

PREFACE

The old high road from Edinburgh to Moffat runs south through the Borderlands of Scotland, winding round the Devil's Beef Tub then down through the old county of Moffatdale towards the county town of Moffat. Less than two miles north of the town boundary in the parish of Kirkpatrick-Juxta, the road turns across a narrow bridge over the River Linn, a spate burn that carries rain off the surrounding hills and down to the River Annan and the sea.

The place where the bridge crosses the road is called Gardenholme Linn, and as it straddles a tight bend on the road, most drivers hardly notice the bridge, or the river, let alone realise that Gardenholme Linn is notorious as the deposition site of one of the most infamous murders in British criminal history.

The ancient history of the Borderlands between Scotland and England is drenched in blood. For centuries, the feuding countries raided and slaughtered as the contested border between the kingdoms moved with victory and defeat. The Devil's Beef Tub, a vast hidden glen, earned its name as the hiding place of rustled cattle stolen in the Border raids.

For the people of the Borderlands this bloody history is alive – part of their heritage – but no one could have foreseen that this remote, unremarkable spot would become the focus of one of the most famous murder investigations of the 20th century. It was an investigation that brought together all branches of forensic science then known, broke new ground in the fields of anatomy and entomology, and culminated in the longest criminal trial in English legal history.

More importantly, the case forced a step change in the way that serious crime was investigated, and its legacy is still evident today. But like so many serious crimes, the investigation began with an observant member of the public and, after many twists and turns, ultimately rested upon the extraordinary teamwork of a remarkable group of professionals.

CHAPTER 1

STRANGEWAYS PRISON, MANCHESTER

11 MAY 1936

The condemned cell at Strangeways was small by any standards but relatively comfortable and furnished better than the usual spartan conditions of the old Victorian jail. Situated at the end of B Wing, in the central part of the prison, it was in fact a two-apartment cell with sleeping quarters for the prisoner and an anteroom. This is where the two wardens assigned to the prisoner sat and where meals were eaten together in the few days leading up to the execution. It had been purpose built in the mid-19th century, one of the few prisons in the country to have permanent gallows and an execution suite. It had been well used – hangings were a regular occurrence and the staff were well practised. The wardens were hand-picked old hands, chosen for their affability. They were there to make sure their charge did not cheat the gallows, but theirs was not to judge – Mr Justice Singleton and a jury had already done that, and the Lord Chief Justice himself had turned down the appeal.

The prisoner, Buck Ruxton, had time to reflect, for there was nothing else for him to do. "How had it all gone so terribly wrong in the last nine months. How had it come to this?"

Early next morning he would be woken, offered the meal of his choice, the chance to shave and change into clean clothes, then, just before 8 a.m., a group of prison officers led by the governor and the prison padre would enter his cell and, without ceremony, he would be pinioned, his hands behind his back, then ushered quickly through an adjoining door to the execution chamber itself. There he would be handed over to the Angel of Death himself, Thomas Pierrepoint, the famous executioner.

Pierrepoint had made a science out of execution by hanging. It was a family business, and he was a perfectionist who calculated exactly the drop required to sever the second and third vertebrae of the spine, causing instant death. The botched executions of his predecessors, the

1

struggling strangulations or the accidental decapitations caused by a long drop were not for him – speed and precision were the Pierrepoint family's hallmark. He timed his executions to the second and his reputation went before him. Later, he would be called upon to assist in the multiple executions of the Nazi war criminals at Nuremberg, but on this cold day in Manchester he had another celebrity prisoner to assist to eternity.

Ruxton knew his executioner was in the prison already; he had overheard the whispered conversation of the guards. He thought he'd caught a glimpse of the man at his cell door, sizing him up. From his time in the Indian Army, Ruxton could guess the drop would be roughly 7ft, maybe 7ft 6in. Perhaps not as much as that, for Ruxton was not the man he'd once been – he had lost weight and condition in the six months he'd spent in prison.

Dr Buck Ruxton

His once sleek black hair, his crowning glory, had turned slate grey during the trial and the small polished metal mirror in his cell reflected the haggard face of a man much older than his 36 years. Once an immaculately dressed doctor, he was now a shadow of his former self.

His prison clothes hung on him now as he contemplated his fate. Unusually for an occupant of the condemned cell he still slept well, welcoming the escape from his prison life. It gave him comfort, for in his sleep he revisited better times. In the brutal reality of wakefulness, he knew he was seen as a monster, a doctor who murdered.

2

While awaiting his appeal in Pentonville Prison he had even been put in the cell once occupied by Dr Crippen, which the guards had gleefully told him was haunted by the fiendish doctor. He was appalled at the comparison, Crippin had been a quack doctor and a premeditated murderer, he had not meant to kill – but he slept well in Crippin's bed, just as he always did, undisturbed by the terrible events that lay behind him and the bleak future that faced him.

He was certain that this was not his destiny. His beloved, frustrating, passionate wife, Bella, was dead, his three young children left without parents. Ruxton had worked hard to fit in – to be accepted by British society and but for the catastrophe of the previous September, he would have succeeded.

Now as the last few hours of his life ebbed away, he could only do one more thing, but it was important. He could brace himself and meet his end with the courage and dignity befitting the English gentleman he always aspired to be.

CHAPTER 2

THE PASSIONS OF CAPTAIN HAKIM

Ruxton's life really had started well. Born in Bombay in 1899 as Bukhtyar Rustomji Ratanji Hakim, quickly shortened to Buck Hakim, his father was a Parsi Hindu whose ancestors had fled persecution from Persia many centuries before, and his mother was French. He inherited his dark good looks from his father, his ambition and his excitable nature from his mother. His Parsi tradition taught him discipline and the dedication to cleanliness and purity so central to his creed. He was a natural fit for medicine and graduated Bachelor of Medicine from Bombay University before undertaking his obligatory military service as a doctor in the Indian Army. The Great War had just ended, and he found himself as a young captain back in the land of his father, posted to Baghdad and Basra, where his fluency in Farsi, the local dialect, was such an advantage.

Post-war Persia was the ideal proving ground for a young doctor, and his army service had allowed him to hone his skills as a surgeon. Without anaesthetic, speed and precision were of the essence. Cut boldly and cut precisely were the watchwords of a good surgeon, and Captain Hakim was a good surgeon.

The time in his ancestral home convinced him of two things: he wanted to practise surgery and he needed to spread his wings, and that meant a move to Europe. After qualifying as Bachelor of Surgery at Bombay, and still not thirty years old, he set sail for England with two ambitions; to be famous and to make a significant contribution to the field of medicine.

Although he knew he was handsome, his dark good looks had been unexceptional in Bombay, but in London Hakim noticed with satisfaction the sideways glances of the beautifully dressed English women who thronged the streets, seemingly without chaperones – so different from his homeland where women were hidden, covered, modest and subservient. His upbringing had been traditional and

4

conservative. No distractions had been allowed to interfere with his family's ambitions for him. There was a tradition of achievement in the Parsi community; to enter the professions was expected. The pleasures of life were secondary.

Now in the bright lights of London at the height of the roaring 1920s, Hakim knew these pleasures were his for the taking. His looks apart, his title of captain added lustre – ten years after the end of the Great War, military rank still meant something.

Determined to make the most of his assets he studied the latest London fashions and decided that regardless of expense, he would always be the last word in style – not gaudy but every inch the English gent. If he was to break into the upper echelons of British medicine, he needed all the advantages he could get. He was a good doctor and a good surgeon; he was confident of that, but as a man of colour he knew he would still face prejudice regardless of his abilities. In India, he had been a member of an exclusive sect. Parsis were well educated, sophisticated, but in England he was just another coloured man, an alien, seen by many as second class. He needed to fit in, to be accepted by British society to achieve his ambitions. He needed to make his name, so the pleasures that lay all around him would have to wait.

Edinburgh was the obvious place to burnish his career in surgery. Scottish medics were renowned throughout the world, and Scots surgeons were the best. A fellowship of the Royal College of Surgeons in Scotland would set the seal on his credentials.

The cold grey streets of Edinburgh in the 1920s were far away from the bright lights of London, but Hakim still found distractions.

He set about his studies for the fellowship exams. The practicalities of general surgery were easy for him; his experience in the army had honed his skills, but the written work was different. His English still wasn't fluent, and try though he might, he couldn't control his excitable nature. If he got frustrated or anxious, he could hear his voice rise and his English fail him. Time and time again he tried to control himself but failed. It was a serious weakness, and he knew it disadvantaged him against his confident, English-speaking rivals.

The fellowship exams operated on a strict three-strikes policy. No applicant, regardless of their abilities, was allowed to sit a fourth time, and for Hakim, failure was unimaginable. Yet fail he did, for the first time in his life. It would have been easy for him to blame his failure on prejudice or racism, but in his heart, he knew that wasn't true – he simply hadn't been good enough on the day, and the second time he took the exam, the result was the same. He had one chance left but his confidence was deserting him, though as it turned out, by the time he failed for the third and final time, his life was already starting to take a very different and unexpected direction. Between his long periods of work and lonely study he would often pass the time at one of Edinburgh's growing number of restaurants and one in particular had attracted him because of its striking manageress. Bella Kerr was not beautiful by film-star standards. She wasn't even pretty in the style of the day, with a large nose and protruding teeth, but all who met her spoke of her personality – a magnetism that Hakim found irresistible. The smartly dressed women he had seen in London were attractive but distant. Bella was completely different, unlike any woman he had met before, and for the first time in his life Hakim fell head over heels in love, and the feeling was mutual.

Bella fell for the dashing, beautifully dressed young doctor with such impeccable manners and prospects that promised the kind of lifestyle she had always hoped for. She had made mistakes in her life, including an ill-judged marriage to a Dutch seaman, who, it transpired, had a girl in every port and another wife in at least one. She had been just nineteen and the marriage had lasted exactly two weeks. It had been a blow to the young woman, and her older sisters had disapproved, but she had recovered her poise quickly. Bella had motivation, energy and a belief that she was as good as any man. She was an accomplished driver, rare for a woman in the 1920s, an ambitious businesswoman and a practised and successful gambler, particularly on the highly popular football pools of the day. Her goal was to run her own betting agency and her restless energy would not let her settle for less.

Bella Kerr and Buck Hakim were apparently a perfect match – both accomplished and ambitious, and also hugely attracted to each other – and they quickly became passionate lovers.

Living together in the Presbyterian Edinburgh of the 1920s wasn't an option, and as Hakim's dream of an eminent career in surgery was over, the couple moved to London. Bella's bigamous Dutch husband was quickly divorced, and the couple set themselves up as husband and wife. To complete the metamorphosis, Hakim decided on a final name change. He would drop the captain title and change his surname to something English and strong. He chose Ruxton. He would be known as Dr Buck Ruxton, and though they were never married, Bella became Mrs Ruxton.

CHAPTER 3

A COUNTRY PRACTICE

The new Dr and Mrs Ruxton set up home in London and Bella quickly became pregnant, meaning the Ruxtons had to make some decisions. The doctor's long-held ambition of a surgical career was shattered: three failures at the Scottish exams meant he was denied access to top jobs in Scotland and while he managed to pass the English exam system, the positions he was eligible for were no use now he had a family to support. Hospital work offered a poor salary and no real chance of advancement, but general practice meant he could build a business, work in a wide range of medicine and still practise minor surgery. Above all he would be the master of his own destiny, where his energy and commitment would lead to the professional success and recognition that he craved. But how and where could he establish himself?

In the pre-NHS days, general medical practices were private businesses often run by single doctors or partnerships. It was difficult and expensive to buy yourself in, and even when you did there were no guarantees. Doctors had to attract fee-paying patients. Young Dr Ruxton couldn't afford to buy himself into a partnership, and moreover he wanted to be in sole control. He needed to establish his own practice.

Lancaster in the 1920s was a very traditional, old-fashioned town. The county town of Lancashire had changed little since the 18th century. It was a conservative, prudish place, with a streak of northern puritanism running through it – a small town in every sense – and it already had two well-established general medical practices. It was an unlikely place for an unknown doctor to set up a new practice, but Ruxton saw the opportunities: there were more patients than the doctors could treat, the established medical practices were old-fashioned, property was cheap, and he was confident that with his skill and the charismatic Bella by his side, he could establish himself quickly and succeed.

He knew how important appearances were, so with borrowed money, he bought a substantial town house at 2 Dalton Square, right at the centre of the old town. Appearances were everything: Ruxton had to be immaculate, and so did his house and surgery. He supervised the redecoration personally in an exotic, oriental style – rich colours with gold trimmings. One of the public rooms had a dark blue ceiling decorated with gold stars. He filled the house with furniture and antiques. It was a statement and a far cry from the dowdy, austere décor of most of the other wealthy houses in Lancashire.

Success came quickly. Ruxton was the first man of colour many Lancastrians had met, but far from being a disadvantage, he found that his exotic appearance, combined with his skill as a doctor, attracted patients. Before long – and much to the annoyance of the town's established doctors – Ruxton had built a thriving practice of 4,000 patients.

Ruxton's success was a tribute to his skill but also his humanity, for in the days of strict pay-as-you-go medicine, he often waived his fee in cases where patients couldn't pay. His success in delivering healthy babies was the best in the county, and he was particularly good with children – frequently treating those from poor backgrounds without charge. This humanity was strictly in accord with the teachings of the Parsi people, but Ruxton was shrewd enough to calculate the effect. These were gestures that would win him friends and allies.

In a small town like Lancaster the word quickly spread. Not only did Ruxton attract more patients, but, as he had expected, he and his charming wife Bella became popular members of the establishment in Lancaster. Old-fashioned and stuffy the town may have been, but they took the exotic doctor and his bubbly wife to their hearts.

By 1935 the Ruxtons had three children and gave all the outward appearances of the perfect family: the hard-working and efficient doctor, his charming socialite wife and the children, and success had allowed them to enjoy some of the trappings of luxury, even in a time of economic depression. Ruxton and Bella had their own cars, and there was enough money to employ a number of domestic helps and a live-in nursemaid to help with the children – Mary Rogerson, a pleasant, young local girl who soon became one of the family, devoted to the children and particularly to her mistress, Bella, whom she worshipped. But beneath the perfect veneer there were tensions. Ruxton, though he gave all the appearance of style and modernity, was an old-fashioned man who expected Bella to be a housewife and mother first and to put her ambitions aside, to curb her restless and extroverted nature. He wanted to control her and became increasingly irritated by what he saw as her unreasonable behaviour. Like many men before and since, he found the very characteristics that had attracted him as a lover, worried and angered him in a wife.

In reality Bella had not changed at all – she had always been ambitious, energetic and outgoing. She still wanted to be a businesswoman in her own right, perhaps starting a football pools company, and she enjoyed visiting her sisters in Edinburgh or meeting them in nearby Blackpool, where they relished the latest attractions. Her irresistible personality continued to draw people to her, and amongst her wide circle of friends and admirers were several young men. There was and is no evidence to suggest a sexual relationship between Bella and any of her male friends, but Ruxton's jealous and possessive nature made him believe otherwise. His pride, his inability to articulate his feelings and his excitable nature combined in a toxic mix: there were rows, threats and several times Bella fled north to seek refuge in Edinburgh until things cooled or until Ruxton rushed north to implore his beloved to return home.

Gradually the word spread that all was not well in the Ruxton household. Lancaster was a small town and eventually the local police got to hear the gossip. There were calls about noise and disturbance at the doctor's home, and Bella was seen with bruises on her throat, but nothing was done, even when she called at the nearby police station to report being assaulted by her husband. As was normal in the day, no action was taken – it wasn't police or anyone else's business to get between a man and his wife, especially not the eminently respectable doctor and his wife.

CHAPTER 4

STAND, RUN OR COVER

14 SEPTEMBER 1935

By September 1935, tensions in the Ruxton home were running high. Dr Ruxton was carrying on his busy practice with all the energy and commitment he could muster, but increasingly he was finding life with Bella difficult. He had begun to wake in the middle of the night, haunted by nightmares about Bella's infidelity. He tried to rationalise his fears as he lay awake in the early hours, but as soon as he fell asleep, the dreams came back. Why could she not be satisfied with the life he gave her? Why could she not be content with her beautiful home and children? Why did she spend so much time away apparently visiting friends?

And there was the money. Despite his success as a doctor, Ruxton could not forget the genteel poverty of his upbringing; he was insecure about his finances and grudged the amount that Bella spent on clothes and travel. Of course, he wanted her to dress attractively for him – her style was what had first attracted him – but her extravagance troubled him. Why did she have to dress so well for these young men who seemed to flock round her?

He knew he was a jealous man, but perhaps he had cause. In his darker moments, he was sure she was having an affair, perhaps several. He had followed her to Edinburgh earlier in the month, expecting to catch her with a lover, but he hadn't. Yes, she had been staying at the Adelphi Hotel with a group of friends, but discreet enquiries with the concierge confirmed that she had slept in a single room. Even so, he couldn't suppress his suspicions. He knew they were irrational, yet every time there were cross words between them, out would come his jealousy, his anger, his frustration.

He could hear himself jabbering incoherently, unable to form words – all sense lost in his passion and his hurt. And he had laid hands on her – several times he had lost control and gripped her by the neck or shoulder. He knew it was wrong – such behaviour was shameful against the teachings of his religion and his culture, he loved his family and he was devoted to his children, but sometimes the passions that Bella aroused overwhelmed him.

It was getting worse – a pattern was starting to form; their friends could see it. There would be a minor row, about the children, the housekeeping – nothing important, but it would spark the deeper issues – his jealousy, her need for independence. He would lose his temper, and she would storm out and off in her car or the train to Edinburgh. After his anger had cooled, the children would be farmed out to friends or left with little Mary, the nursemaid, and Ruxton would begin his search to find Bella and get her back.

When the reconciliations came, they seemed complete. Ruxton and Bella had always been passionate lovers and the rifts between them seemed to heighten the excitement they both felt. Though much had changed in their relationship, their mutual physical attraction remained undiminished. Ruxton knew enough about psychiatry to realise that their relationship was complex, the love-hate dynamic was strong. But he was a solitary man isolated by his pride, he could not discuss his feelings with Bella or anyone else, his only friends were little more than professional colleagues.

On the other hand, Bella seemed surrounded by admirers and confidantes, loyal and devoted friends. People were drawn to her. He knew that while they tolerated – even respected him, they loved Bella and if it came to a choice their friends would side with her. Despite all his efforts to fit in, look the part, in the end he would always be the outsider.

The weekend of 14th September 1935 was sewn with tension from the start. Earlier in the week Bella had told her husband that she was heading to Blackpool on the Saturday to meet her two older sisters, who were making the journey from Edinburgh. Ruxton wasn't sure whether to believe her or not; he had recently found out that she was going swimming in the local baths with some new friends, including a young man. All of his fears and suspicions had crowded in on him again, and he would wake in the night imagining her having sex with him in changing cubicles, or in her car, or in his lodgings, wherever. He remembered all too well his own early encounters with Bella, how sexually uninhibited she was. If she was like that with him, why not others? If he found her irresistible, why would other men – younger men with the ready wit to match hers and the social skills that he would never possess – not feel the same?

The glamorous Bella

He pleaded with her not to go to Blackpool. Who would look after the children? Why could her sisters not visit them in Lancaster? He knew the answer to that one – her sisters knew of their domestic squabbles. They had never liked him, never thought a man of colour worthy of their family.

For her part, Bella was well aware of her husband's moods and feelings. She wasn't interested in other men, but she did love life and enjoyed the company of others – the wit, the conversation. She liked to be seen as desirable and treasured her independence and ambitions. She remained hugely attracted to her husband, and she loved her children and her comfortable lifestyle in Lancaster, but she couldn't be a prisoner, and she worried about Ruxton's increasingly violent and unpredictable behaviour.

She had thought about leaving him, had even tried moving back to Edinburgh, but it hadn't worked. In her heart, she knew she couldn't go through with it. She had heard him joke that, 'we are the sort of people who can't live with each other and who couldn't live without each other,' and she knew it was true – she would just have to manage

13

their relationship, at least until the children were grown. Then she would have more options and could face her family in Edinburgh knowing that she had tried her best and wasn't responsible for a second failed relationship.

That weekend she knew Ruxton was tense, but she was determined to visit Blackpool with her sisters. She would have liked to stay the night there, but she knew that would cause trouble and decided to take her car and come home on the Saturday night. That way she was only away for the day, and there would surely be no rows about that. She would leave the children with Mary, who would be at home to cook and keep house while she was away. It was a good compromise and it would have worked on most days. But Saturday, 14 September 1935 was anything but an ordinary day.

It started well enough for Bella. She was up early with the children, full of life as always. They had an early breakfast before she drove away, heading for Blackpool, excited at the prospect of the day. Back home, Mary got the children dressed and took them out to leave the house quiet for the doctor to work. When she came back, she was struck as she always was by the change that occurred when Bella wasn't there. It was as if a light had gone out, and she wasn't looking forward to a day in the company of her dour employer, Dr Ruxton.

Bella's faithful maid, Mary

If the day had started well for Bella, the same could not be said for Ruxton. He hadn't slept well and had tried to convey his displeasure at Bella's planned day trip by turning his back on her in bed. She hadn't seemed to notice, and then the nightmares had come again, so vivid that when he woke unrested, he couldn't quite distinguish between reality and those imagined hurts. He hadn't joined Bella and the children for breakfast, and when he got up and dressed, he was tired, irritable and the house was quiet. He knew Mary was out with the children, but he also knew that when they returned, she would creep about quietly, to avoid him as long as she could.

The house at 2 Dalton Square was a large stone-built Georgian building with the imposing frontage befitting a doctor's surgery. Ruxton's consulting rooms were on the ground floor, while the family's accommodation was on the first and second floors. There was a large, luxurious drawing room together with Ruxton's private office on the first floor, the family's bedrooms, bathroom and nursery, together with the nursemaid's room, on the upper floor. The kitchen and scullery were on the ground floor at the back of the building adjoining two spacious outside yards with coal cellars and outbuildings. Within the house, the floors were linked by an imposing semi-circular staircase. The public rooms and staircase were carpeted and lavishly furnished, with some fine antique pieces on display.

Overall the house gave the impression of an affluent upper-middle-class home as befitted a family of consequence. One obvious sign of upper-middle-class status in 1930s Britain was live-in staff, and although Mary Rogerson was employed as a nursemaid, she frequently acted as cook, housekeeper and even receptionist for Ruxton's busy practice.

It was Bella who had employed Mary, and at first sight she was fairly unprepossessing – just twenty years old, small in stature, with a bad squint in one eye, plain in appearance and very quiet. At first, Ruxton thought she was of low intelligence, but he should have known better, for Bella, with her experience of managing staff, had a good eye for people. Mary Rogerson may have been a simple country girl, but she was loyal, honest, clean and hard-working. The children loved her, and she was devoted to Bella, who, much to Ruxton's chagrin, she openly admired. Moreover, Mary had no vices – she neither drank nor smoked, had no boyfriends and spent what few days off she got visiting her parents in Morecambe.

In the time before labour-saving devices, Mary epitomised the legions of domestic servants who, by their hard work and diligence, kept middle and upper-class houses working.

She also held Ruxton in awe and often marvelled at the dozens of medical books in his study, though she could not read the titles, let alone the text. And then there were the specimens he kept in glass jars above his desk. They looked revolting, but she dusted them carefully – like his books, they were testimony to his brilliance.

Respect him she might but Mary did not like Ruxton. She was wary. It wasn't his race – she hated the way he sometimes treated her mistress. Several times Bella had come to Mary's tiny room, weeping, with marks on her neck or face where the doctor had hit her. While Mary took a strange pleasure in the shared confidences of her mistress, she worried about the future. The last thing she wanted was the family to break up. She was determined that she would do all in her limited power to protect her mistress and keep the peace. That Saturday morning Ruxton had appointments to see several patients in his consulting room. He often booked appointments with difficult patients or awkward cases for a Saturday. There was more time to deal with them, and usually this worked well, but on that morning, tired and irritable, the difficult cases were yet another vexation. Ruxton knew they were his bread and butter, but it was a long way from the career he had envisaged. He still felt he had something bigger to contribute to the field of medical science and dreamt how different his life could have been had he fulfilled his destiny and become a famous surgeon. Even now in his study in Dalton Square, he carried out limited experiments, and he still gathered what interesting samples came his way, preserving them in formalin for future examination. But for all his aspirations as he struggled through his Saturday appointments, Ruxton was weary and worried about Bella and what she was doing behind his back.

The day dragged on, Ruxton endlessly watching the clock. After his morning appointments there were no distractions. He tried to play with the children, but he didn't have the energy. Six p.m. came and went and Bella had not returned, so he ate a cold supper that Mary left for him in the kitchen. At 8 p.m. there was still no sign, and the children were put to bed. Ten p.m. came and now his suspicions were aroused. What could keep Bella and her sisters this late?

He was exhausted by then, tired by a day of tension, so he decided to go to bed and escape into sleep, but he could not – he heard every noise in the quiet of the old house. Eleven p.m. then midnight. It was then he knew that all his fears had been realised – she had to be with another man; she was betraying him, humiliating him, and he lay rigid in his bedroom, his fury growing by the minute.

In reality, Bella had enjoyed a relaxing day with her sisters in Blackpool. She had intended to drive home in the early evening, but they had persuaded her to stay for the famous illuminations. She had driven them all along the long promenade, past the famous tower, taking childish pleasure in the lights and the gaiety of the holiday resort. It had been a day that she could relax, enjoy the company of her family and put the troubles of home aside.

It was past midnight by the time she left Blackpool to drive the 17 miles home to Lancaster. She hoped that her husband would be asleep by the time she got back. She would let herself into the house as quietly as possible and go to sleep in the nursery, hopefully without confrontation, then the next day would be another where all would be well.

After a pleasant night drive, she got home about 1.30 a.m. The house was in darkness as she quietly let herself in and, taking off her shoes, padded up the flights of stairs to the top floor. As she passed her bedroom door, she saw a movement in the dim light and felt strong hands grip her neck. In the few seconds of consciousness left to her she would have known the hands strangling her were the healing hands of her husband – the love of her life and father of her children.

In the small room just across the hallway, Mary Rogerson had also been lying awake waiting for her mistress's return. She would get up and make her a cup of hot milk and perhaps Bella would come and sit on her bed and confide in her, tell her about the day.

Mary heard the front door open and close gently then the sound of Bella quietly climbing the stairs. She was about to get up when just outside her door she heard a noise – a struggle then a sickening thud and a small scream that instantly turned to a whimper. She had no time to calculate her response, consider her actions or think about her safety. Instinctively she knew her mistress was in trouble and, leaping from bed, she rushed from her room on to the hallway landing and oblivion.

Till the day he died, less than eight months later, Ruxton could not recall exactly what had happened that night – he could never distinguish between his nightmares and reality. In his dreams, he vividly remembered Bella coming back late that night and meeting her at the top of the stairs. She had mocked him – dismissed his pleading to change her ways; he could feel her utter contempt; then, she was lying at his feet. There was blood; little Mary, had attacked him with the ferocity of a wild beast, pummelling him with her fists. Then she was lying at his feet too, her body across Bella's.

It was his most vivid nightmare yet, but when he woke the horror was real – he was holding the poker from the bedroom fire, it was matted with blood and hair, and his hands and clothes were bloodstained too; he must have gone to sleep fully dressed. In the awful reality that many killers face he realised he was awake; it wasn't a dream and his beloved Bella and Mary lay dead or dying on his bedroom landing.

Ruxton's medical training instantly kicked in, giving him some respite from the awful consequences of his actions. Mary was already dead, but though Bella wasn't breathing, he thought he detected a flutter of a pulse. He knew that to move her would be fatal, and when he tried again to find a pulse it was gone.

Over the next hour, he tried again and again, hoping his diagnosis was wrong. It wasn't. Bella, the woman of his dreams, the only woman he had ever loved, and the mother of his children, was dead, and poor little Mary with her. He knew he was responsible, although he had no waking memory of his actions.

Like all accidental murderers, Ruxton now faced a choice: to stand, run or cover. It is always the same choice and it must be made in the minutes after the crime. Once made, there is no going back, and the consequences are unforgiving and final.

To stand is to admit the crime, tell the truth and face the consequences; to run is just that – disappear, try to hide and hope that you won't be caught.

To cover is the most difficult option of all. It takes planning, determination, nerve and resolve; there is no rest and the pitfalls are many.

Whether Ruxton consciously weighed these options is unknown but they are always the only options open and, given his nature and circumstances, his choice was logical.

He could not stand, give himself up, explain about his nightmares, his jealousy, his weakness. His pride would not allow it. Neither could he run; he was easily identifiable, and he had no plan, nowhere to go and there were his children – he couldn't abandon them. No, his only option was to cover his tracks, and as a doctor he had distinct advantages. His intelligence, his medical and surgical experience and his knowledge of forensic medicine gave him the edge. Never lacking professional confidence, he believed he could outsmart the police.

His decision made, Ruxton embarked on one of the most elaborate and determined deceptions seen in British criminal history. Ultimately, it was to lead him to the gallows and to the unique status of monster in the cultural history of crime in the twentieth century.

But that weekend in September 1935 he had more urgent matters on his hands. He had two dead bodies to dispose of, a bloody mess to clean up and the need to maintain a pretence of absolute normality. He had children asleep in their nursery a few feet from the bloody ruin that faced him; he had them to look after and a busy medical practice to run, all while executing his deception. And despite having no other acceptable options, as he formed his plans, he had every confidence he would succeed.

CHAPTER 5

GARDENHOLME LINN: SERGEANT SLOAN'S STORY

SUNDAY, 29 SEPTEMBER 1935

The late summer of 1935 had been wet in the lowlands of Scotland. The days of constant rain had chased the last of the tourists home early and by late September. With the peak of the grouse shooting past, the hotels and guest houses in the Borders were quiet. It was the time for special deals – holiday breaks arranged with the coach companies and the railways.

After the long economic depression, there was at last some money about; people were starting to spend carefully again and for the hotels of towns like Moffat, it was a lifeline.

Like many small towns, Moffat had been hit hard by the ten years of depression, that on top of the loss of so many of its young men in the Great War and the awful Spanish flu epidemic that followed. The weaving and spinning industry had not recovered from the downturn and never would. Even agriculture had suffered, and many farm hands hadn't returned after the war, though the new motor tractors would have made them redundant if they had. Many of the old farmhouses and steadings lay empty and desolate, falling into disrepair or rented cheaply to sportsmen who came for the rough shooting and fishing.

It was on a short holiday break that the Johnson family and their friends came down from Edinburgh to Moffat for the weekend of 29th September – to enjoy the hospitality of the Buccleuch Arms Hotel, to take the air, enjoy the beauty of the Borders and relax. After lunch on Sunday, Miss Susan Johnson and her mother decided to take a walk and set off north on the Edinburgh road. After a steady climb out of the town for nearly two miles, they rested at the bridge running over the Linn Burn at Gardenholme. Susan leant on the south parapet gazing down 40 feet to the stream bed below. Then as now, it was a steep gorge lined with birch trees and strewn with boulders. On that

Sunday, the flood water of the recent rains had passed, leaving the rocky stream bed with barely a trickle of water.

As she took in the scene, something caught her eye and she saw what looked like a human hand and arm raised from the stream bed, almost as if summoning help. She looked again and couldn't be sure, then asked her mother to look. Still, they couldn't be sure but were alarmed enough to cut short their walk and make their way as quickly as they could back to the town.

At the hotel Susan told her brother Alfred who, with a family friend, quickly made his way back to the bridge. The two young men managed to scramble down the ravine next to the bridge but stopped halfway as they took in the scene. Beneath them in the bed of the burn they saw not only the arm and hand that Susan had reported but what was obviously a human head wrapped in some kind of cloth. Even from a distance they could smell the unmistakable stench of putrefied flesh.

The two young men had seen enough. Retching with the awful smell they climbed back up the bank and ran as fast as they could back to the town. They were city dwellers but were not unfamiliar with the countryside. They knew that dead animals, sheep or deer, smelled bad and were often found decomposed in ditches and streams, but they were in no doubt as to what they had found – the rotting flesh they had seen in the burn was human remains.

Sergeant Robert Sloan –
the right man in the right place at the right time

The call to the police was made at 3.40 p.m. and was answered by Sergeant Robert Sloan, the officer in charge of Dumfriesshire Constabulary's station in Moffat. He was on duty that day as most others, for in a small station with few men, rest days were scarce.

In many ways Sloan was a typical county sergeant of the day; in his late 30s with 20 years' police service, his early career had been interrupted by war service in the Scots Guards. Like many serving policemen he had been excused the first draft of conscription in 1916, but by 1917 the slaughter of the Somme had created severe shortages and previously preserved occupations were called up. Sloan was desperate to go, and as many policemen did, he joined the Scots Guards. It was a natural fit. The height, bearing and ability to carry a uniform made policemen ideal Guardsmen.

Robert Sloan joined his regiment just in time for the desperate fighting of 1917-18. Ypres, Cambrai, the Somme, the Hindenburg Line then back to Cambrai. By the time he was demobbed and rejoined the police in 1919 he had seen and done things most men don't encounter in a lifetime.

The grainy photographs that survive of him show a sandy-haired man, lean and fit with a strong jawline. He looked as if he could have been hewn from granite, and in this case, appearances were not deceptive. For the county policeman had to be tough, resilient and utterly self-reliant. Unlike in the bigger towns and cities, there was no backup for the county men. They were on their own to face whatever came, and they knew it. But for Sloan it was more than that, for he was the officer in charge – Moffat was his town and he was personally responsible for its law and order.

Sloan quickly made his way to the Buccleuch Arms, met the two shocked young men and listened to their story en route as the three men made their way back to the bridge at Gardenholme Linn. There were no police cars based at Moffat, so the sergeant wheeled his pedal cycle as they walked.

At the bridge, Sloan left the two young men on the parapet and alone made his way down the steep ravine and into the bed of the Linn Burn. Although he did not know it, the scene that met him was what would now be recognised as an organised crime scene, carefully planned and executed. Scattered down the bed of the burn were dozens of body parts. Some wrapped in rags, some in sodden newspaper, some lying exposed. If the sight was unfamiliar to Sloan, the smell was not. It was the same clawing stench of flesh that he had lived with during the war. The maggots and bluebottles he saw covering the body parts were familiar too, his old companions from the trenches of Flanders.

As he surveyed the scene and calculated his next actions, the sergeant was at first sight ill-prepared for taking charge of a complex crime scene. He had received no training in crime-scene management for none existed. He had no experience of major criminal investigation, and he had no forensic awareness but his native wits. He had no protective clothing, no scenes-of-crime specialists to call on, no CID backup. He didn't even have tape to cordon off the scene, and as the afternoon faded, he had no lights to illuminate the ravine.

Yet for all this he proved to be the right man in the right place at the right time. His long police and army service had given him a coolness under pressure; he was unflappable, and nothing would faze him. His attributes were sound common sense and the self-confidence of a man who had proven himself in the hardest of times. Sloan, like many of the generation that survived the Western Front, was toughened psychologically and physically in a way that later generations could never really understand or match. The old adage, 'cometh the day cometh the man,' was never truer than in the case of Sergeant Robert Sloan of Dumfriesshire Constabulary.

Thinking quickly, the sergeant sent the two young men back to Moffat with clear instructions as to what help was needed. He then used the only equipment he carried, his notebook and pencil, to make notes and sketches of exactly what lay before him. Even read today these notes are a model of clarity, his sketches pinpoint accurate:

About 66 feet from a point in a straight line with the parapet of the bridge and downstream from the bridge, I observed the right forearm and hand of a human being, also a human head, lying amongst the rocks in the bed of the stream. I descended to where these objects were lying.

I then observed another head, a large number of pieces of flesh with skin attached, a left forearm with hand minus the top of the fingers and the thumb, two bundles each wrapped in a piece of what appeared to be a cotton bed sheet, one bundle wrapped in a part of a pillow case or pillow slip, and one bundle wrapped in a lady's blouse.

From one of the bundles protruded the lower part of two legs (feet included) tied together with a piece of what seemed to be the hem of a cotton bed sheet.

One of the heads was only partly exposed at the crown, the remainder of same being covered with paper and a child's woollen jumper or knickers, secured at one end with a piece of elastic and tied round with a piece of hemp twine.

The various parts were spread over an area of about 20 feet.

While waiting for help he measured and sketched the area, pinpointing the exact location of each of the body parts. Sloan knew that when help came he would lose control of the scene – his crime scene. Senior officers would soon arrive and take charge, but for now at least this was his job. Moffat was his town, his responsibility, and so he made sure that in the brief time he had alone he recorded everything of significance.

At about 5 p.m. reinforcements arrived in the shape of two local doctors and Sloan's senior officer, Inspector Strath, who had rushed from Lockerbie in one of the few police cars in Dumfriesshire. The doctors depending almost literally on a head count confirmed that what lay on the stream bed was the remains of at least two people. They could only see one torso but from the other limbs the two medical men agreed that two bodies were most likely.

By this time dusk was falling; it was important that the body parts were moved to a safe place. Today this crime scene would have been floodlit, screened off and secured for days while forensic scientists carried out meticulous examination, but none of these sophistications were available in 1935. Instead Sloan carefully carried the dozens of rotting body parts up the ravine and placed them in the police car, checking as best he could that everything had been recovered before the two policemen and two doctors made their way to what served as Moffat's mortuary.

The mortuary still exists, much as it did in 1935, a small stone building at the corner of the town cemetery. It is now used to store garden tools for cemetery maintenance, but in 1935 it served as a temporary resting place for coffins awaiting burial. There was no proper post-mortem examination equipment, just stone slabs on which the numerous stinking packages were laid.

Securing all the keys to the mortuary in his personal possession, Sloan returned to the police station, removing his uniform coat, jacket, trousers and boots before entering. He knew the smell of The Gardenholme Linn would stay in his nostrils for days, perhaps weeks, but he did not want to contaminate his station, which in the next few days would certainly become the hub of a large police operation.

In the late evening the sergeant finalised his statement and made arrangements for the next day. Inspector Strath had already briefed the senior officers of the force and the call had gone out – all available police assistance was to converge on Moffat the next morning. Sensing the onslaught of tomorrow, Sloan made sure his paperwork was complete before heading slowly upstairs to the sergeant's house above the station, where he told his wife and young son absolutely nothing of what he had seen and done that day.

MONDAY, 30 SEPTEMBER 1935

At first light Sloan, in his spare uniform, was back on duty and, with a dozen of his colleagues, had returned to the ravine, but the word was already out. The news had spread like wildfire – a local roadman had found an arm with hand attached near the bridge – and before the morning was over dozens of locals had made their way to the Gardenholme Linn.

Speed was of the essence and before he lost control Sloan organised a structured search, finding part of a thigh and more small pieces of flesh and skin.

Later, the entire course of the Linn Burn would be meticulously searched by other policemen and even a pack of bloodhounds, and other body parts would be found, but for the moment, satisfied that he had recovered all he could Sloan returned to the mortuary, where he met the two local doctors and Inspector Strath. Together, they carefully opened the numerous bundles of putrid flesh for the first time and tried to make some sense of what lay before them.

• One bundle wrapped in a lady's blouse containing two   upper arms

- Bundle wrapped in a piece of a pillow slip containing two upper arm bones, two thigh bones, two lower leg bones and nine pieces of flesh and skin
- Bundle wrapped in what appeared to be part of a cotton sheet containing seventeen pieces of flesh and skin
- Bundle wrapped in what appeared to be part of a cotton sheet containing the upper part of a human trunk and the lower part of two legs, including feet
- Bundle wrapped in what appeared to be part of a cotton sheet which contained a human pelvis

The two human heads, wrapped in scraps of old clothing, were also unwrapped to find that they had been hideously disfigured, almost beyond recognition.

In all, there were nearly seventy pieces of what was believed were human body parts, including a strange unidentifiable lump of fibrous material. Later this find was to feature significantly in the trial.

Sloan and the local doctors had done all they could with the body parts – further expert opinion would be needed. But the wrappings were another matter. Sloan felt that they were the key to the investigation, and he was determined to keep control of them. In his statement, he recorded:

The various parts of newspapers found being in a wet condition were carefully laid aside, as were the various pieces of cotton sheet, lady's blouse, child's woollen romper or knickers.

This terse summary does scant justice to the extent of Sloan's efforts. Carrying the stinking and sodden papers and scraps of cloth back to the police station, he carefully dried the pieces of newspapers, borrowing his wife Annie's flat iron to assist the process. Mrs Sloan's feelings about this are not recorded but a fair guess would be one of stoic long suffering. Later she would hand-wash and preserve the maggot-ridden articles of clothing which wrapped the body parts. Such was the lot of the county policeman's wife.

Having pressed and dried the newspaper fragments Sloan noted:

The various parts of newspapers found were portions of *Daily*

Herald dated, 5, 6, 7 and 31 August and 2 September. The *Sunday Graphic and Sunday News* dated 15 September 1935, serial no. 1067, and *Sunday Chronicle* dated 26 May and 8 September 1935.

This was vital evidence and Sloan knew it. The *Sunday Graphic and Sunday News* was particularly significant. Its date, 15 September, meant the body parts could not have been dumped before that. The establishment of a time parameter is crucial in any investigation, but there was more. Sloan later found out that the *Graphic and News* was a Lancashire local Sunday paper and the copy he had was a limited 'slip edition' distributed in small numbers.

Later in the day the sergeant visited an old contact, a local who lived beside the Linn Burn and who kept a rain gauge with which he recorded the height of the water. Consulting his sketch of the positions of the body parts up the riverbank he concluded that they had been in the river when the water had been at its peak on 18–19 September, following several days of heavy rain. He had narrowed the angles further; the body parts had been dumped on his patch between 15 and 19 September, so he was at least ten days behind the killer.

But time was running out and for Sloan. The brass hats would soon arrive from Dumfries, Glasgow or Edinburgh and the press would descend in hordes; he would be sidelined as the investigation gathered pace and developed a life of its own, unstoppable, and almost unsteerable.

We don't know if Sloan had a moment of reflection that Monday night, but if he did he should have been quietly satisfied, for viewed now at a distance of 80 years and with all the wisdom of hindsight, this ordinary county policeman had done an extraordinary job. In the first 'golden' 24 hours of one of the most notorious criminal investigations of the 20th century, inexperienced, untrained and ill-equipped – he had almost single-handedly secured the crime scene, recovered, and preserved the evidence and, recognising the importance of the timeframe, he had established a chronology and identified a vital piece of evidence that would eventually point directly to the culprit.

It is not the differences between Sloan's actions and later sophisticated responses to major crime that are so striking, but the similarities.

Monday morning, 30 September 1935 found Moffat a changed

town, a hive of activity. All the senior officers of Dumfriesshire Constabulary had arrived at the police station and a press pack was arriving by train, bus, and car, sensing a sensational story. The print media in Britain was at the height of its power and influence, before the television age. Circulations were enormous and nothing sold copy more than crime, the more gruesome the better. That day was the start of a steep learning curve for Dumfriesshire Constabulary in both major crime investigation and media management.

At the same time, arriving to take charge at Moffat that day was Chief Constable William Black of Dumfriesshire Constabulary. Black was one of a new breed of county chief constables – professional, experienced and, importantly, with a background in criminal investigation.

Traditionally county chiefs had been drawn from the minor squirearchy, often retired army officers, appointed by the patronage of local landowners to protect their interests and rigorously enforce draconian poaching laws. But times had changed; the coming of the railways had brought real crime to the most remote parts of Scotland.

The big cities had always had professional police officers in command, and from the end of the nineteenth century, gradually the county forces did likewise. Black had risen through the ranks in Glasgow and served as a detective lieutenant before moving as chief to Dumfriesshire. He had managed major criminal investigations before and knew his force now faced its greatest challenge.

Dumfriesshire Constabulary comprised just seventy men to police a huge county. Apart from the handful of towns, there was a vast landward area which required a police presence. There was no criminal investigation department in the force; nor were there any specialised services to aid the investigation of crime. There were a handful of motor cars available to the force to augment foot and bicycle patrols, but in some of the remotest county areas horses were still used.

As Black read Sloan's reports, he knew he faced one of three scenarios. Natural deaths were out of the question, even to a layman's eye. The marks on the limbs pointed to deliberate dissection; these were unnatural deaths.

He knew from experience that most murders were local, and that the probability was that this case was no different. There were numerous farms and country houses across the county, many rented by strangers to the area. They would all have to be visited and checked for missing occupants. The towns and adjoining counties to Dumfriesshire would likewise have to be checked.

There were, however, other possibilities. It could be an elaborate hoax. Medical students were known for such gruesome pranks – perhaps it was an ill-judged joke or even the careless disposal of unwanted specimens. This theory was not as incredible as it now sounds – the dissection and mutilation of the body parts added weight to this option.

Lastly, Black dreaded the possibility that the murders had been committed elsewhere, perhaps hundreds of miles away, and the remains dumped in Dumfriesshire. To this day every investigator dreads unidentified bodies or body parts dumped outdoors with no evidence and no local connections. These were, and still are, the most difficult crimes to solve.

Due to Sloan's good work, Black had strong lines of enquiry but no experienced detectives to pursue them. He did, however, have one great advantage – he had friends in the right places. That day he telephoned his old friend Assistant Chief Constable Warnock, right-hand man to the most powerful policeman in Scotland, Glasgow's Chief Constable Percy Sillitoe.

CHAPTER 6

SILLITOE'S MEN

Percy Sillitoe was a Yorkshire man of many parts. As a boy, he was a chorister at St Paul's Cathedral; as a young man a mounted trooper in the South African Police Service. Later, he was a security agent for De Beers diamond mines, and from 1945 as Sir Percy Sillitoe, Director General of MI5, where he was appointed to 'clean the stable' following the penetration of foreign intelligence services by communist agents.

But between 1931 and 1944, he was the Chief Constable of the City of Glasgow Police and arguably Scotland's first modern policeman. He arrived in Glasgow from Sheffield to find the largest force in Scotland unmodernised since the Victorian age. A large man with a presence and forceful personality, he had the reputation of a reformer, and it was justified.

Percy Sillitoe – father of the modern Scottish police service

Immediately he pensioned off half of his older senior officers and appointed younger men with potential to take their place. Using techniques he had first seen in South Africa and developed in Sheffield, he ruthlessly crushed the razor gangs that had been the scourge of Glasgow for a decade. Brutal by today's standards his gang-busting was highly effective and enhanced his reputation as a man of action.

Capitalising on his prestige, he forced the Glasgow Watch Committee, his political watchdogs and paymasters, to close and sell half of the city's numerous decrepit old police stations and, remarkably, managed to retain the capital receipts from the sales. With the money, he introduced the police box and pillar system and brought modern communications to the city in the form of radio cars. He was also credited with the introduction – if not the invention – of the black-and-white hat band. Now worn by police officers throughout the world, this established symbol of police uniform was for many years called 'Sillitoe tartan'.

But it is for his development of forensic services and his enlightened leadership development that he deserves to be best remembered. While in Sheffield, Sillitoe had seen the work of early fingerprint identification. He was convinced that fingerprint examination and other scientific methods were the future of criminal detection and was determined to build the best and most modern system in the British Isles. But he had greater ambition than just Glasgow – he intended to influence the rest of the country's police forces as well.

In 1935 there was a patchwork of police forces covering Scotland, from the big cities of Glasgow, Edinburgh, Dundee, and Aberdeen to the dozens of small, poorly manned, and sparsely resourced county forces. Many, like Dumfriesshire, were tiny with only a handful of men to police huge land areas and no specialist services whatsoever to support them. But while they may have had few men, all these forces, large and small, had immense pride and fierce loyalty. They also had the support of their communities and particularly their local politicians, who then, as now, relished control and influence of their local constabulary.

Sillitoe foresaw a time when many of these small forces would, despite vested interests, be amalgamated to form more viable units, but in the meantime, he had to deal pragmatically with the reality of the time. Using the remainder of his cash windfall from the sale of the old police stations, Sillitoe headhunted established fingerprint experts from his old force and, luring them to Glasgow with a double promotion, tasked them with establishing a modern fingerprints department to rival that of London's Metropolitan Police. But one police force, even as big as the City of Glasgow, could not develop the whole spectrum of scientific methods of detection. So, using his fingerprints department as an example of good practice, he sought to persuade and cajole other large forces to develop new techniques, not to compete with Glasgow but to complement their work by developing strands of what we now know as specialised forensic services.

It took a while but eventually other large forces followed his example and invested in their own specialisations. Edinburgh City Police developed expertise in crime-scene photography and what is now known as crime-scene management. Fifty years later the legacy of these bold innovations and substantial investments could still be seen with hard-won expertise passed down through the generations.

But Sillitoe's ambitions were not confined to police forces. He recognised that enormous untapped expertise existed in the medical and scientific faculties of Scotland's universities. For over a hundred years there had been links between universities, police forces and the Crown and procurators fiscal, but these had been mainly informal and patchy. Using all his considerable powers of persuasion Sillitoe sought to formalise relations between academics in a variety of university departments, particularly forensic medicine. Long before the practice became popular. he recognised and worked to establish a partnership approach to the investigation of serious crime.

And there was more. Sillitoe had a good eye for people; he believed in early and rapid development of men with potential. Over his long tenure as Chief Constable he continuously sought to identify promising officers, promote them early and test them in tough operational posts. He also encouraged them to move from Glasgow to take posts in other forces, to spread his doctrine and to create an informal network of influence far beyond his own city.

Sillitoe's men carried a reputation of professional excellence. They also came with an unspoken but cast-iron guarantee – wherever they served, if they hit trouble or needed help, Sillitoe would back them with all the power and resource he had.

Being underwritten by Sillitoe made his prodigies attractive appointees for senior posts in small forces and gradually Sillitoe's influence and professional ethos spread.

These wider power plays were, however, a long way from Chief Constable Black's mind as he sat in Moffat Police Station on Monday,

30 September 1935, but it must have given him some comfort that he was one of the chosen few – one of Sillitoe's men.

CHAPTER 7

THE MOFFAT RAVINE MYSTERY

MONDAY, 30 SEPTEMBER 1935

The late editions of *The Sundays* of 29 September had carried breaking news of the discoveries, but the Monday morning newspapers had splashed the find at Gardenholme Linn all over their front pages under the headline 'Moffat Ravine Mystery'. The name stuck and the early investigation, like all notorious crimes, had its catchy title. The story had broken too late for anything other than the briefest details the day before, but enough information had leaked to catch the full attention of Monday's papers. All over the UK news editors picked their best hacks and, once they had found the tiny town of Moffat in their gazetteers, dispatched them with all speed by train, coach or car. The story had all the ingredients beloved of the popular press – violent crime, mystery, and a strong touch of the macabre.

The print media was at its zenith in 1935 – immensely powerful press barons battled for circulation and the stakes were high. Fortunes were to be made on the back of big sales, for the rejuvenated advertising industry only backed winners.

It's not as if there wasn't plenty news, but the ongoing shenanigans of the Prince of Wales and his racy divorcee Wallis Simpson couldn't be printed, and while the sinister rise of Herr Hitler in Germany worried many, another war was unthinkable, and the story failed to grip the average reader. Chamberlain put it neatly: it was all happening 'in faraway places of which we know nothing'. In 1935 war was still far away. But bloody murder, chopped-up and disfigured bodies – there was a story with appeal and the potential to run and run. Any newspaper without a strong team covering it was going to lose out, and that would be disastrous.

The coverage of the story that Monday was a mix of truth, half-truth and conjecture, concocted in newsrooms to fill the gaps left by sparse facts and to support the most lurid headlines. Fake news is by no means a phenomenon of the 21st century. But the news editors knew that they would need fresh lines for Tuesday and ongoing. Already the few news staff of the Sundays working that Monday had added it to the top of their list for the coming week. Hopefully the mystery would continue, there would be no arrest and the Sundays could really make a meal of it.

Over the next two days Moffat would become like a Wild West town, full of press men, pseudo press men, opportunists, oddballs, rubberneckers and voyeurs, all seeking and trading information, all speculating wildly and all creating a damned nuisance for the townsfolk. Some were there because it was their job, others drawn by an invisible force, desperate to be in on the act, to be part of it – the flotsam and jetsam that always cluster around dramatic events.

The Moffat Ravine Mystery was a national story and it was journalists from the big national papers who descended on the town. The difference between the national and local press was once described as that between a tiger and a house cat – they are both basically of the same family, but the tiger is larger, angrier, more aggressive, and cynical. It was the tigers that arrived in Moffat that Monday.

For the publicans of the town it was an unexpected bonanza, but for Chief Constable Black and the men of Dumfriesshire Constabulary it was just another problem to add to a long list. Black knew he would have to deal with the press, find some way to satisfy their insatiable appetite. He was very aware that unless he fed the beast, the beast would devour him, damaging and possibly derailing his investigation.

He knew that the nationals could not stay in Moffat long; there weren't enough storylines and they would soon run out of leads. He also knew he had no leaks within the small investigation team he had, so all he had to do was keep feeding the press with what he could and try his best to avoid distractions and red herrings. In one sense it was easy – there were no witnesses for the press to tamper with because no-one in Moffat knew anything. At the same time Black realised how valuable the national press could be if properly managed. Their penetration was immense, by far the best way to reach the public at the time. In the meantime, however, he had to tame the tiger. It sounds simple but many a senior police officer with greater resources and experience has badly mismanaged the national media. In the circumstances Black's managed approach was highly effective.

All that was for later, however, for on the morning of that day, in the middle of the investigation he had other more urgent priorities.

Chief Constable Black's call for support was answered – quickly. Before the day was out, his old boss in Glasgow had pulled out all the stops and sent heavyweight help to assist the tiny Dumfriesshire Constabulary. Recognised systems of mutual aid did not exist then but in effect that is what arrived in Moffat that day.

Leading the party was Assistant Chief Constable Warnock and with him three senior detectives from Glasgow – Superintendent McLaren and his deputies, Lieutenants Ewing and Hammond. It would have been hard to find a more hard-bitten, experienced quartet anywhere in the country. Between them they had seen and investigated just about everything in the criminal code. Chief Constable Black must have been greatly comforted to see them – they were top detectives and his friends, but it also gave him a dilemma. He needed their help, but he had to keep the morale of his own men high. He didn't want them humiliated by the Glasgow detectives. Somehow, he had to blend the enthusiasm of his own inexperienced men with the tough, experienced detectives from the big city.

It is an age-old challenge for leaders of groups of mixed abilities. It's the same in the military, police or any group that faces emergencies, and it's particularly important in murder squads. Any division or discord in a squad is fatal, so it was vital that Black unified the investigation. Fortunately, he knew the Glasgow detectives well enough to speak directly of his concerns and they were wise enough to listen.

The investigation would be directed personally by Chief Constable Black and Dumfriesshire Constabulary, all important decisions would be taken by the Chief Constable himself and the Glasgow men would advise him. In particular, the local men, Inspector Strath and Sergeant Sloan, would continue to play a leading role. This was important for a number of reasons. The local men had personal credibility in Moffat and this had to be preserved. The politics of small county forces was delicately balanced; they could not be seen to be found wanting in the face of serious crime. In days or weeks, the top detectives would return to Glasgow, leaving the local men to pick up the pieces of normal policing. There could be no suggestion that the Dumfriesshire

Constabulary was inadequate. The investigation must leave the local force's reputation enhanced, not only for public reassurance but so that local politicians would consider their money well spent and their support of the local police well placed.

That Monday Chief Constable Black was moving fast. He had already created an incident room in the only large office at the police station. He got the Glasgow men to help establish a basic administration system and then with his top team, a mix of the Glasgow men and his own officers, he sat down to consider their priorities.

His first concern was that all the body parts had perhaps not been recovered. He feared that the Linn Burn in spate had carried major evidence to the River Annan or that foxes or other vermin may have carried off pieces to devour or leave partially eaten some distance from Gardenholme Linn. He knew that even if there were only two bodies, a torso and other parts were missing. He had full confidence in Sloan's initial search but although thorough, it had been limited in scope.

Since there were no reported missing persons in the Moffat area, he feared that the bodies had been brought to there, and the most likely means of transport was a motor car. If that was the case, had other body parts been dumped in roadside ditches or lay-bys? They would all have to be searched thoroughly and systematically. It was a top priority, but it stretched tiny Dumfriesshire Constabulary to breaking point. Again, Black sought outside help, and while his own men checked local farms and scoured the roadsides for ten miles either side of Moffat, a special force of police-firemen came from the neighbouring Lanarkshire Constabulary to complete the search of the Linn and Annan rivers.

Police-firemen were a hybrid body operated by some large county forces of the day. Trained in both disciplines, these officers were clothed, equipped, and schooled in search and recovery. They also came with their own command structures and transport, a blessing for the hard-pressed chief constable. They were tasked and left to do the job. Several small pieces of flesh were recovered in the bed of the Linn over the next few days but nothing significant. Eventually the Annan, a large river, was searched for miles downstream with no further finds.

Later, to be doubly sure that every measure had been taken, a pack of bloodhounds were brought to the area, and though they specialised in tracking the living rather than the dead, the drawing of the Linn and Annan by these natural experts in search reassured Black that the job had been completed.

Black's worst fears were realised when almost a month after the discovery a roadman on the Glasgow–Carlisle road, nine miles from Moffat, found a rain-sodden newspaper package containing the remains of a left foot. Early in November a girl walking on the Edinburgh–Moffat road near the Linn Burn found a package containing a right forearm and hand. Too obvious to have been missed in the early searches, the find confirmed the fears that local foxes had been at work around the Linn before the body parts were discovered.

Later that day, Black received the first important forensic news of the investigation. It closed off one of his potential lines of enquiry, and for the first but not the last time sent the investigation down the wrong track. The local doctors had concluded that the body parts were not medical specimens for they had not been preserved in any way. Anatomical specimens were routinely preserved in formaldehyde, but there was no trace of any preservative and the slim chance of the Moffat Ravine Mystery being an elaborate hoax was gone. The local doctors were also of the opinion that the remains were that of an older man and a young woman who had been dead for a number of weeks and had probably been dissected after death.

It was as Sergeant Sloan's instincts had told him at the bridge and what Chief Constable Black had always really known. This was a case of bloody murder and since there were no reports of any missing persons, let alone an older man and younger woman, it wasn't local.

It was time to go national – with all the information they had and at that time the only method to broadcast details of a crime to police forces nationwide was the *Police Gazette* and, locally, the *Scottish Police Gazette*. These were official weekly publications that circulated details of significant crimes and wanted persons. In special circumstances, a bulletin could be prepared for instant dissemination to all points. These all-points bulletins or APBs were keenly scrutinised by all police forces in the UK.

That Monday, having received the medical men's report, Black authorised the request for a special bulletin giving the details of the find but omitting the suspected age and gender of the victims, until verified. Within days the responses came back. There were similar crimes involving the dismemberment of bodies. In southern England, both the Trunk Murders and the Brentford Canal case were being investigated in a blaze of publicity. Both involved the dismemberment of victims, and these striking similarities demanded close examination.

From early on the Sunday, hours after the discovery at the bridge, Black had been careful to keep the local procurator fiscal fully informed. The fiscal, based in Dumfries, was the local representative of the Crown in whose name all prosecutions in Scotland are brought. The role of the Crown and the fiscal in the investigation of crime is ancient, and while to outsiders it appears sometimes confused and overlapping the police, it is well understood and practised over years. The Crown and fiscal are not routinely involved in the day-to-day investigation of serious crime but are always informed and consulted as the investigation proceeds. This is invaluable and often results in changes in the direction or emphasis of an investigation, to cover particular evidential points. In modern times, fiscals will attend the scene of a serious crime and be involved from the start. In 1935 the fiscal's response was more at arms-length but he was obviously aware enough to realise that this was not a local matter and that his superiors in the Crown Office in Edinburgh should be briefed.

The Crown Office is the headquarters of Scotland's most senior law officer, the Lord Advocate. A political appointment and member of the government, he or she is always a senior legal figure who, together with their deputy, the Solicitor General, take decisions on prosecuting all crime in Scotland 'in the public interest'. All procurators fiscal act in the Lord Advocate's name.

Assisting the senior law officers are a number of advocates depute who make the everyday decisions and do most of the court work. Senior amongst that group was the Home Advocate Depute, the young, up-and-coming John Cameron. Later, as Lord 'Jock' Cameron, he would become one of the most famous and best regarded judges in the High Court of Scotland. The last judge to pass the death sentence, he remained on the bench into old age and is revered to this day for his contribution to Scotland's justice system.

In 1935, as the Home Advocate Depute, in a highly unusual move he recognised the importance of the Moffat Ravine find and quickly opened a direct line with Chief Constable Black to ensure important decisions were quickly made. Both Cameron and Black knew that greater medical expertise was needed quickly. No one doubted the professionalism of the local doctors, but expert assistance was required, and Advocate Depute Cameron was the man to get it.

For many years, the Crown had a relationship with the major universities in Scotland, particularly the departments of forensic medicine. On a case-by-case basis, advice was sought and expert witnesses were called to give evidence. The relationship had been strained by the activities of senior anatomists during the Burke and Hare era, but over time it was repaired and had been enhanced by Percy Sillitoe's drive to encourage the introduction of scientific methods to assist the detection of crime. It was a relationship of mutual benefit. The Crown got access to the best expert evidence and the pathologists got access to research material with which to advance their learning.

As early as Sunday, 29 September the call went out to Edinburgh and Glasgow Universities.

CHAPTER 8

THE FORENSIC DETECTIVES:

PROFESSORS GLAISTER, BRASH AND SMITH

In the police documents of the day they are referred to as, 'the anatomists'. It is a title redolent of both respect and reserve; it was the collective name of the medical men who aided and abetted the bodysnatchers a century before. The notorious anatomist Dr Knox may have escaped legal censure when his part in the scandal of Burke and Hare's activities had rocked Scotland's establishment, but the Edinburgh mob made its own judgement, and the scars on the stonework of Knox's Edinburgh house can still be seen. Folk memories are long. The nomenclature also suggests a degree of ignorance as to the particular discipline these men brought to the investigation. In fact, only James Brash was a professor of anatomy at Edinburgh University; his colleague Sydney Smith was Professor of Forensic Medicine at Edinburgh, while John Glaister was Professor of Forensic Medicine at Glasgow University.

These men were among the most eminent forensic experts of their day. They were public figures, and in a time when celebrity was earned, they were famous in a way academics no longer are. Their books and publications were bestsellers, their public lectures sell-outs, their evidence in court reported verbatim in the broadsheet newspapers – they were big box office. Their fame attracted students from across the world, eager to learn at the feet of these great men, and their reputations were burnished by international case works. Professors Smith and Glaister travelled the length and breadth of the empire giving their expert advice, building an extensive body of expertise as they did, and medical students across the world studied their famous cases as required reading.

They were the professional descendants of the pioneers of Scottish medicine's greatness: Joseph Lister, the champion of antiseptic surgery at Edinburgh Royal Infirmary, and James Young Simpson, the father of anaesthesia, and they were both contemporaries of Alexander Fleming, the discoverer of penicillin.

The legacy of Scottish medicine's supremacy rested easily on their shoulders – they were modest but self-confident men, the experts' experts, and were seen by many as infallible. Even the courts treated them with awed reverence, their evidence invariably accepted as copper-bottomed fact. They themselves, however, never lost sight of the fallibility of their science and this was their greatest strength.

Left to right: John Glaister, James Couper Brash, and Sydney Smith

When the call for assistance came on Sunday, 29 September, Professor Smith was away on one of his many overseas cases, so the call was answered by his senior deputy Dr Gilbert Millar from the Department of Pathology. Early on Monday, he made his way to Moffat to join the police and local doctors who had returned again to the ravine. At the same time Professor John Glaister had been contacted and before the morning was out, he was collected by a Glasgow police car for the fast (three-hour) journey to Gardenholme Linn.

Professor Glaister was as close to forensic aristocracy as it came in Scotland. The son of a professor of forensic medicine – also John Glaister – he had almost literally been born into the profession, and in 1935 he was at the height of his powers. He had followed his father to study medicine at Glasgow University then assisted him in his forensic work before replacing Sydney Smith as Professor of Forensic Medicine at Cairo University in 1928 at just thirty-six years old. There he specialised in the study of hairs, fibres, and pioneered

42

the technique for distinguishing human from other mammalian hairs. In 1931, he returned to Scotland to succeed his father as Professor of Forensic Medicine at Glasgow University and in 1934 received the ultimate accolade of election as a Fellow of The Royal Society. All his eminence, however, was by the way as he cleared his mind and concentrated his thoughts for the all-important inspection of the crime scene.

Glaister described his journey in his memoirs:

As we neared our destination the traffic, normally thin at that lonely spot, began to thicken. For the last mile of distance we were often forced to a crawl, caught up in a procession of vehicles, some of which were press cars but many of which were packed with sightseers, who had travelled down to stand as spectators.

But with the help of a local police escort our car finally got through. At the ravine, a considerable number of uniformed police and detectives drawn from several forces and headed by Chief Constable Black from Dumfriesshire and Assistant Chief Constable Warnock from Glasgow were again at work in a fresh search of the area.

Professor Glaister had arrived in the maelstrom that crashed over Moffat and Dumfriesshire Constabulary that day. Every officer in the force had been recalled to duty and deployed on the numerous tasks thrown up by the rapidly growing investigation.

By the time the professor arrived at Gardenholme Linn, the scene had been trampled by two days of police searching, not to mention the ghoulish sightseers whose lights had been seen by locals in the dead of night.

Nevertheless, he saw there was still work to be done. Glaister was a visionary and an early advocate of the need for a holistic approach to a crime scene. Bitter experience had taught him that the smallest details might be significant, and unless all potential evidence at a scene was secured immediately it would be lost. He ordered that samples of everything possible be gathered from the deposition site – foliage, soil samples and as many of the seething mass of maggots and insects that could be carried.

Once again Sergeant Sloan and his men undertook the grizzly

task – a stinking mass of leaves, bracken, maggots, bluebottles and insects were gathered, filling two stretchers. This putrefied mass was carefully carried back to the police station where the debris was sifted, and samples carefully preserved in specimen jars for future examination.

Seen through the eyes of a modern investigation, it seems remarkable that without formal introduction, an outsider, even an eminent forensic medic, could arrive at a crime scene and immediately impose his will on the senior police officers in charge. But Glaister was no ordinary scientist – his reputation went before him and he spoke the language of the men at Gardenholme Linn. Like many of them, he had seen service in the Great War, as a young officer in the Royal Army Medical Corps. Glaister was one of them, bound by the bond of shared experience. He carried a moral authority every bit as powerful as his reputation as a pathologist.

After a brief visit to the scene, Glaister and Millar made their way to the mortuary, where for the first time the fragments of human remains were examined by expert eyes. What followed was, in his own words, 'an inventory'. The two forensic experts confirmed the number and description of the body parts already noted by the local doctors but immediately made important observations. They quickly agreed that two bodies were present and, noting exactly how the bodies had been disarticulated, they matched one of the heads with the single torso that had been recovered. Then, by using the obvious cut marks on some of the limbs, they began to reassemble the bodies. Sergeant Sloan was dispatched to get the local joiner to make two large coffin-shaped boxes marked Body No. 1 and Body No. 2, and so it was that for the rest of the investigation the remains were labelled with the undignified titles of one and two. But Glaister and Millar made three other important observations that were to affect the course of the investigation.

Firstly, the bodies had been bled, probably after death – there simply wasn't enough blood in the fleshy parts of the remains for it to be otherwise. Secondly, they concluded that the bodies had been dissected by someone who had experience in such tasks, the tools to do the job and a good knowledge of human anatomy.

Lastly, after careful consideration, they agreed with the local doctors that the remains that lay before them were that of a man and a woman.

Glaister noted that elaborate lengths had been taken to mutilate the bodies in such a way as to disguise both their identity and their gender.

Both heads had their ears, eyes, nose, lips and skin removed. Teeth had been extracted. From two of the hands the terminal joints of the fingers had been removed. Sexual features had been extensively obliterated.

The professor had a dilemma:

I had very little doubt about the first body (Body No. 1) which was obviously that of a woman, but the second body (Body No. 2), or those portions of it which had been recovered, posed a much more difficult problem and troubled me to a considerable degree. Like a lot of these other remains, the head had been mutilated. I told CC Black, but the skull had certain male characteristics about it. It's too early to be certain, but the probability is that we are dealing with the bodies of a man and a woman.

Perhaps the redoubtable professor was subconsciously influenced by the views of the local doctors, but whatever the reason the early false identification of the bodies as that of a man and a woman had profound effects, good and bad, on the direction of the early investigation. Uncorrected, it could have been a fatal mistake, throwing the investigation into chaos and down the wrong track. As it was, the early publication of the identification of the bodies as a man and a woman in the next day's extensive news coverage gave Ruxton, who was watching press reports carefully, false confidence that led him to make mistakes – serious mistakes that would cost him dearly.

Glaister's other observations were also of primary importance. His conclusion that the bodies had been bled pointed to an organised and planned disposal. This was no panicked response; a cool head, as well as a degree of knowledge, is required to successfully bleed a human body. And there was the highly competent disarticulation of the bodies. A good degree of anatomical knowledge would certainly be required, as well as the tools, the skill, and the stomach, but did this point to a doctor?

Doctors who kill have always held special fascination as the ultimate betrayal of trust, the ultimate horror. Writers of crime fiction, recognising this morbid attraction, regularly feature homicidal medics, yet the reality is that few doctors kill, and those that do are usually pharmacists who poison their victims. Most doctors are not surgeons, and while they may have the anatomical knowledge, they do not possess the skills or practice required to dismember a body, let alone two. It was as Glaister himself observed, 'grim work.'

In fact, slaughtermen and butchers are much more acquainted with dismembering carcases and have enough anatomical knowledge to do it. Statistics show that slaughtermen and butchers are much more likely to be murderers than surgeons, yet time and again when a dismembered or partially dismembered body is found, the spectre of a demon doctor quickly appears. So, it was in the Moffat Ravine Mystery. Glaister and the senior detectives jumped to the right conclusion for the wrong reasons, but they went further. If it were a medical professional who had committed these foul crimes, he or she could not be in their right mind. The conclusion was obvious – they were not just hunting a doctor but a mad doctor. This despite the obvious fact that at the site of the deposition, the removal of all identifying features and the bleeding of the bodies pointed to a cool-headed and determined plan not normally associated with lunatic behaviour.

Nevertheless, the message went out by special bulletin in the *Police Gazette*. All police forces were to check their local lunatic asylums for escaped doctors with homicidal tendencies. Unsurprisingly, the search was completed with negative results.

Late that Monday evening Chief Constable Black held a press conference at the Moffat police station. The pressure for information from the growing press pack in the town had grown throughout the day. Black wanted to prevent dangerous speculation and harmful storylines while giving as little information as he could.

It is an age-old balancing act as real today as it was then. Reveal too much or too little and it can seriously affect the investigation. Black was brief: the remains of two human bodies had been found, what appeared to be a younger woman and an older man. They had been dead for some time and were not thought to be local. Foul play was suspected.

It wasn't much, and certainly didn't satisfy the ravenous press, but it wasn't far short of all Black and his men knew, and it was at least a gesture.

Photographers snapped pictures of the leading men and places of interest – the bridge at Gardenholme Linn, the mortuary and the very ordinary county police station that served as the command centre for the investigation. It was enough. The press retreated to phone their copy through for Tuesday's dailies giving Black and his senior officers breathing space to hold the first strategy conference since the bodies had been discovered.

Attending the late-night conference were Professor Glaister, Dr Millar and the two local doctors, Jock Cameron the Advocate Depute, Chief Constable Black, the Glasgow detectives and Black's own senior men. No records of the meeting survive – no policy files or action register existed then – but it is clear that the main problem faced by the investigation was the identification of the bodies. Glaister and Millar had done all they could in Moffat; further examination of the body parts would need a fully equipped laboratory and the urgent preservation of the body parts, which were literally decomposing before their eyes, and only the pathology departments at the Glasgow and Edinburgh universities had such facilities.

Glasgow was Glaister's laboratory and although Edinburgh was marginally closer, its head, Professor Sydney Smith, was abroad and would be unable to help for some time. Glasgow was the obvious choice, but instead Glaister and Millar agreed that the Edinburgh lab would be best.

Glaister later said that the decision was based purely on distance but perhaps he was being circumspect. Glaister knew that the major challenge facing them was the reconstruction of the found parts into bodies or as close as possible. That was work for an expert anatomist and there was none better than Professor James Couper Brash, who led the Department of Anatomy at Edinburgh University.

Early the next morning, Wednesday, 2nd October, the contents of the two boxes labelled No. 1 and No. 2 were loaded into the back of a police van and driven to Edinburgh. For years after, rumours persisted that stinking body parts had been transported by bus or train to Edinburgh. The story of a decomposed human head being carried in a paper bag is just one of the enduring legends attached to the Moffat Ravine Mystery. In fact, the contents of boxes one and two were transferred to purpose-built metal tanks in Edinburgh University's old Department of Anatomy in Teviot Place, and a solution of preservative formalin was added to halt the decomposition process.

The scene was set for the best forensic brains of their day to do their meticulous work, the results of which would advance learning in a number of fields of forensic science.

CHAPTER 9

GRIM WORK

2 DALTON SQUARE, LANCASTER
14–19 SEPTEMBER 1935

Hell came to the quiet town of Lancaster on the weekend of 14 September 1935. As reality dawned on Dr Ruxton in the early hours of Sunday, 15 September, the awful consequences of his actions became clear. As he gazed unbelieving at the still bodies of Bella and Mary lying before him on the top landing of their home, he had already decided to do his utmost to cover his tracks and conceal the hideous crime he had no conscious memory of committing.

There was no other course of action. His pride and ambition; his sense of destiny unfulfilled meant that giving in – admitting his guilt – was impossible. It was not in his nature; he had always succeeded against all the barriers and prejudices that faced him. This would be no different – it just required the utmost concentration of effort and all his considerable skill.

But time was short. A plan was forming in his head, but he knew that he had to control his excitable nature, keep calm and think the next steps through. If he got it wrong, he was finished.

His biggest problem was how to dispose of the evidence. Blood was already seeping from Mary's head wounds on to the carpet, something else he would have to clean up. There was no obvious or easy place to dispose of the bodies; there was no place to bury them, no facilities to burn them and he was too far from the sea to dispose of them in the water. In fact, he could hardly move them – Bella was the same size as him and it would be difficult to get her down the stairs, let alone into his car. He only had the few hours left of the night to solve the problem – he had to think quickly.

The answer was blindingly obvious. The few murderers that do decide to cover their tracks by disposing of their victims' bodies naturally tend to favour the methods familiar and available to them. Delivery or lorry drivers tend to dump their victims near roads and lay-bys. Access to land enables burial, etc. Ruxton was a skilled surgeon and thus had the means and the ability to dismember the bodies of his victims and, crucially, to disguise their identity. Above all, he knew that was most vital to his chances of escaping justice.

If his victims had been strangers it would not have been so important, but Ruxton knew that to carry out his plan he would have to report Bella and Mary missing in the next few days. If their bodies were found and identified, it would lead right back to him.

Then the gossip about their rows would surface, the local police would examine their records of domestic disputes and he would become a suspect. Ruxton was self-aware enough to doubt his ability to cope with the pressure of suspicion and interrogation and felt it was best avoided, which it could be if Bella and Mary disappeared and were never found – then he could report them as missing runaways. Eventually the heat would die down, the police would lose interest and he could continue to practice medicine as was his destiny.

In theory, it was simple: Ruxton had dissected many cadavers in his time, and although his recent surgical experience had been limited, he had forgotten nothing of his teaching and had his surgeon's knives, his Syme's amputation knives and his scalpels sharp and ready for use in his consulting rooms on the ground floor. In the 1930s general practitioners often carried out routine surgical procedures and surgery was Ruxton's first love – he was good at it and took every opportunity to practise his craft.

As he began his grisly task Ruxton knew he would have to bleed the bodies before dissection, otherwise the blood would get everywhere and be impossible to clean up. As a police doctor he was sometimes called to assist the local constabulary at scenes of sudden death and crime scenes and was fully aware of their capabilities. They had little in the way of specialist skill, but the Lancashire County Constabulary did have a detective division; they would certainly assist the local force and he couldn't afford to take chances.

He would attend to Bella first, get it over with.

When he looked at her, he saw that the spark of life had already left her. He had seen it many times before. At the moment of death, and for a few minutes afterwards, there remained an intangible essence of life which is difficult to describe but easy to recognise when you see it – the colour of the skin, the tiny movements of breathing and the eyes, they were the giveaway. Dead eyes, the sparkle of life gone, now it was just another cadaver, like the hundreds he had seen and dissected before.

He managed to half-drag, half-carry Bella the few yards to the bathroom then, as quietly as he could, tipped her into the bath. He would have to remove her clothes first, which was more difficult than he thought it would be – he hadn't had to do this in training. After a struggle, he managed to half-cut, half-remove her clothes, which he would destroy later – it would be a giveaway if all her clothes were found in the house.

He was already sweating and realised he was tired, exhausted by the long day of tension, the explosion of violence and the prospect of a long night ahead. He had brought his surgical knives and scalpels upstairs from his consulting room. Everything would be dealt with upstairs; there could be no contamination of the public rooms below.

He took one last look at Bella's body crumpled in the bath, then moved on to his first task.

From the moment the heart stops beating and the blood stops circulating, it starts to congeal, and as the body cools it thickens to a glutinous consistency. Ruxton had to act quickly if he was to bleed Bella before that happened. Running the taps at full pressure to flush the blood away, he hoped all traces of it would disappear down the drain.

As he considered the best way to dissect Bella, he suddenly realised that he was past the point of no return. It was a heart-stopping thought that made him pause. Before he'd made that first incision, he could still have thrown himself on the mercy of the court – perhaps he would have been shown leniency. Now that he had desecrated Bella's body, he could not claim accident – there was no going back.

It galvanised him into action. He had to dismember the bodies into transportable portions, but more than that, he had to remove all identifying marks and physical features. This was vital – if any parts of the remains were found they should give no clue whatsoever as to their origins.

First, he would remove the sexual organs to conceal gender. His knives were sharp and he was not squeamish; he had done this before and he no longer had an emotional attachment to this rapidly cooling cadaver. If he had the choice, he would have left the bodies for twelve hours – cooled flesh was firmer, easier to cut – but it wasn't an option. There wasn't a moment to lose.

He cut out the whole pelvic area from Bella's body, which was awkward and messy in the confines of the bath, and he cursed the fact that he didn't have better lighting or a surgical saw in his equipment. His Syme's knives and scalpels he used regularly, but he'd had no need for a saw since his army days.

Once he was sure the pelvic cavity was empty of all traces of the female reproductive organs, he removed the legs in a clean disarticulation, cutting the muscle and sinew round the joint before separating the head of the femur from the pelvic socket. It was harder work than he remembered, but of course most of the heavy work had always been done by assistants or mortuary attendants. Neither did he have the endless supply of sharpened implements that stocked an operating theatre or mortuary. His knives would soon be blunted. And he was already exhausted, the first adrenalin rush that had carried him on was ebbing and progress was slow. It was already 2 a.m. on the Sunday morning, and although he had been careful his clothes were bloodstained and he still had seven or eight hours of hard work ahead. Sleep was out of the question, so he ate what food was in the kitchen then continued his grim night's work.

Having removed the genitalia, he still had much to do to conceal the gender: He cut off Bella's breasts but realised that the removal was a clue in itself. He would have to skin the torso – it was the only way.

He had skinned body parts before in his student days, but this was different – those medical specimens were preserved and easy to work with on a purpose-built autopsy table. Bella's body was still warm, making the removal of the skin difficult, and her position lying curled in the bath meant it was almost impossible, but eventually he managed to cut it away – not in one piece as he'd intended but in ragged strips attached to lumps of flesh.

As he surveyed the shambles that had been his neat and hygienic bathroom, he was utterly dismayed by the bloody chaos of his work.

Recovering from his daze of self-pity in a jolt, Ruxton sharpened his knives as best he could and started to remove Bella's larynx. It is a little-known fact that male larynges are up to a third bigger than a female's; leaving it in would be a dead giveaway to any pathologist. He was aware that removing it was also a pointer to the knowledge and background of the dissector, but this was less risky than leaving such obvious evidence of gender.

Then came the difficult part – the removal of Bella's head, which was hard both emotionally and physically. Even with limbs removed, a human body retains the resemblance of humanity; without the head, the body loses recognisable structure and becomes merely a pile of flesh and bone.

He struggled to cut through the vertebrae of the neck – it was a difficult job to do with only a small surgeon's knife, but he expected nothing less. Bella was a tough, uncompromising woman in death as well as life.

When eventually the head was removed, the next task was to ensure all distinguishing features were cut off or gouged out. Nose, lips, ears, hair, and scalp were all removed, her cheeks sliced off and her distinctive front teeth pulled out, along with other teeth that had been filled or repaired. When he was finished there was only a bloodied skull, utterly unrecognisable as Bella Ruxton.

But there was more to do. Bella had noticeably thick ankles, meaning the flesh had to be cut from her lower legs, as well as various marks and scars, all of which had to be erased. Then there were the fingerprints.

Ruxton had studied recent developments in fingerprint recognition and knew that bigger police forces had techniques for lifting fingerprints from objects touched by the subject. He couldn't hope to clean all traces of Bella from the house and her car, but he could remove her actual fingerprints. He sharpened his knives again and was pleased with the job he did.

Lastly there were her feet. Bella had a pronounced bunion on her right foot. It had always annoyed Ruxton; it spoiled the symmetry of her feet, but more than that, it was a visible manifestation of her carelessness, her lack of discipline in wearing the wrong shoes. Removing a bunion was a specialist job but he had done it before – indeed, it was one of the routine surgical procedures he regularly carried out.

But as he carefully cut away the swelling on the joint, his knife slipped and cut his hand, a deep and painful wound that stung then ached as his blood joined Bella's in the bath on the top floor at 2 Dalton Square. It was an elementary mistake for a surgeon – careless – and he cursed his failure; his weakness.

As he held the wound tight with his good hand, trying to staunch the flow of blood, he slumped to the tiled floor of the small bathroom. He struggled to get to his feet and, as he did so, he caught sight of himself in the washbasin mirror. The suave, immaculately groomed doctor was gone – staring back at him was a dishevelled wreck of a man, his bloodshot eyes stinging, his skin pallid and sweaty. In a moment of clarity Ruxton recognised the visible symptoms: here was a man in severe shock – a man at the end of his tether, who would be increasingly prone to mistakes.

The self-diagnosis jolted Ruxton back to reality. He knew he had to get back the control that was essential to his survival, and the first thing he needed was to staunch the wound in his hand, retrieving bandages from his consulting room downstairs. As he stepped over Mary's body on the stair landing, he saw she had continued to bleed profusely on the carpet – yet another problem he would have to deal with.

A short while later Ruxton sat slumped behind his desk in his consulting room. It gave him a strange reassurance – this was his comfort zone; in this room, at this desk, he was always in supreme control. He just had to take that confidence and control back upstairs to the slaughterhouse of the top landing.

It was now 4 a.m. on Sunday morning and he knew he could not dismember both Bella and Mary in the time he had left. In two or three hours, he would have to face the new day, meet people, act normally, give the children their breakfast and begin the second phase of his deception.

In the few hours of darkness left to him, he gathered up what old newspapers and clothes he could find and wrapped the bloody pieces of Bella as best he could. His bandaged hand ached, and he cursed his obsessive neatness that meant there were few old newspapers in the house. But there were some old clothes that the children had grown out of – he could use them.

With difficulty, Ruxton dragged Mary's body from the hall landing into one of the main bedrooms then carried the pieces of Bella to the same room, wrapped all the remains in bed sheets and locked the door from the outside. Despite his best efforts, there was blood everywhere – the hall landing carpet was soaked with Mary's blood, the bathroom and his clothes saturated with Bella's. He cleaned up as best he could then tried to eat something and compose himself. He felt dirty and it offended him; he longed for a hot bath, but of course that was out of the question – there was only one bath in the house.

That Sunday morning, Ruxton was beset with problems. He was exhausted and painfully injured. His wound was a serious debility, and his house and clothes were badly contaminated with blood, but he knew he must gather himself to begin the second part of his plan – the deception. He had to get through the day, act normally and, most importantly, keep people away from the upper floor of the house. His story had to be consistent and straightforward. He would say that Bella and Mary had gone away, avoiding any more detail – that could come later. The simpler the story, the less likely there would be difficult questions.

Taking the initiative, Ruxton left the house at 6.30 a.m., while the children were still asleep, and called at the nearby home of the cleaner who was due to work at 2 Dalton Square that morning. Telling her that her services were not required that day and that his wife and maid had gone on holiday to Edinburgh, he began the narrative he intended to carry through, giving information but never detail that might trip him up. The cleaner was the only person due to work at his house that day; dismissing her bought him valuable time and the space to deal with Mary. He scraped together a breakfast for the children then took them to a friend's house, getting back to his grim work as soon as he could.

He dragged Mary's body into the bathroom and toppled her into the bath. Working one-handed made removing her clothes more awkward. The exhaustion had left him, but he knew he was only running on adrenalin and that couldn't last. Bleeding little Mary was only partially successful; her body had lain too long but at least dismembering her was easier. She was smaller, and her flesh was now firmer, but with one hand he knew he wasn't doing as good a job as he had with Bella and he was tiring fast.

At 9 a.m. he was interrupted by a newspaper delivery, the usual Sunday papers, and an hour later by the milkman. By mid-morning he had run out of time and cleaned up as best he could before leaving the house on an important errand. He needed petrol for the next phase of his plan – to burn the clothes and any small body parts he could, but he had to buy it in small quantities so as not to arouse suspicion. He also had to delay the return of his three children to the house, another problem. Mary had always looked after them when Bella was away – now he would have to do it on top of everything else. He collected the children from one friend and took them to another, the local dentist Herbert Anderson, where he left them – explaining that Bella and the maid had gone to Scotland.

One more caller at the house for a pre-arranged minor surgical procedure was successfully diverted, and later that afternoon Ruxton went about his usual business, making sure he was seen acting normally and giving the consistent story that Bella and Mary had gone to Scotland. In order to allay any anxiety from Mary's family, he even called at their home in Morecombe, reassuring them that she would not be visiting them that weekend because she was away with her mistress.

That evening, to maintain the appearance of normality, he brought his children back to the house and, once they were in bed, staggered to continue his ghastly work throughout another sleepless night.

In avoiding detection as well as in investigating serious crime, the first 24 hours are crucial. Most culprits panic or spin out of control as reality bites, leaving a trail of evidence. Few have the nerve to cope with the awful consequences of their crimes as Ruxton did over that weekend. His composure in dealing with the bodies of his victims, one of whom he had strong emotional links to, is remarkable even given his surgical experience. He also established a simple and credible storyline to account for the disappearance of Bella and Mary, and, most importantly, he recognised and managed to control his sometimes-volatile behaviour to give the general impression of life as normal.

Later he would make mistakes, and inconsistencies would creep into his narrative, but for that first, vital 24 hours, given the violent and unpremeditated nature of the crimes, Ruxton's hastily conceived plan to cover his tracks was going well.

CHAPTER 10

RED HERRINGS: THE STRANGE TALE OF 'DR' HOWARD CAMPBELL

1–3 OCTOBER 1935

Every major criminal investigation has red herrings and sometimes they come in shoals. The more publicity surrounding a crime, the more red herrings there are. At best, they are a nuisance and divert resources. At worst, they can disrupt an investigation, lead it on a false trail and even end in miscarriages of justice.

With the huge public and press interest in the Moffat Ravine Mystery finds, it was inevitable that the red herrings would come. Chief Constable Black and the men of the beleaguered Dumfriesshire Constabulary knew it was only a matter of time.

It began almost immediately as ghouls and rubberneckers were drawn to Moffat, eager to be part of the drama. Any event which makes the headlines draws the attention of unbalanced people, and high-profile murders attract hundreds of people who want to get involved – to be witnesses or participants – and they come in various guises: psychics, pretend journalists or pretend detectives. Moffat was within easy reach of the main centres of populations, Glasgow and Edinburgh, and they came in swarms. Family entertainment took on a new complexion as the undergrowth of picnic spots was searched for body parts. And it finally paid off late in October, when a roadman working near the main Glasgow–Carlisle railway line nine miles south of Moffat found a sodden package containing a left foot.

About the same time, a young girl walking along the Moffat – Edinburgh road about half a mile from the Linn, found a newspaper package containing a right forearm and hand lying in plain sight at the side of the road.

But for every genuine find and real lead there were dozens of well-intentioned, timewasting false alarms. Most of them were reports of decomposed body parts or the smell of putrefied flesh. The remains of deer, sheep, hares, badgers and foxes were all found by zealous citizens eager to help. It was discovered that a bog moss common on the moorland in the Border lands gave off a corpse-like smell at the end of the summer growing season, with a dozen picnicking groups reporting the smell. It was a botanical discovery that Dumfriesshire Constabulary could have done without.

In one of the special bulletins of the *Police Gazette*, the likelihood of a car or other vehicle having been used in the disposal of the body parts was mentioned, along with the suggestion that, due to the state of the body parts, such a vehicle may have a smell of decomposition. This naturally caught the attention of the press, who were desperate for content and delighted in such macabre detail. And so quite unintentionally in October 1935 a nationwide hunt began for foul-smelling vehicles of which, according to vigilant members of the public, there were many.

Police forces throughout Britain were inundated with reports of vehicles of all sorts that smelled odd or bad. It may seem farcical, but every report had to be followed up, every foul-smelling car or driver tracked down. This completely unintended line of enquiry threw up some unlikely suspects. One dedicated sportsman was detained by police when his neighbours reported his car as smelling bad. Chief Constable Black tersely described the incident:

He had a fondness for rabbit shooting and, being a careless bachelor with no wife to look after him, he often left his kill rather longer in the back of his car than was wise. On this occasion, the dead rabbits were beginning to proclaim their presence to any fastidious person and so the 'clue' was furnished to us.

A comic incident it may have been but there were dozens like it, all taking valuable time and resource from a fully committed and rapidly tiring police force. By this time, the long shifts spent searching and responding to the numerous pieces of information were taking their toll. The many outlying farms and cottages were still being meticulously checked, and the tiny Dumfriesshire Constabulary, even with the generous assistance of neighbouring forces, was at full stretch. As a last resort, the full complement of the force's Special Constabulary was mobilised to assist the regular force. As unpaid volunteers, the Special Constabulary have always been – and still are – a vital assistance to regular police forces. In the cities and larger county forces, the Special Constabulary was important, but in small forces like Dumfriesshire they were essential to the viability of policing, and in the early days of October 1935, the Specials of Dumfriesshire once again proved their worth.

In the week after the find at Gardenholme Linn, Dumfriesshire Constabulary was swamped by thousands of pieces of information which they had to carefully sift through to make sure nothing important was overlooked. It was a period of great risk, a time when costly mistakes could be made. Fortunately, the Glasgow detectives had brought the skills to establish a rudimentary card index system. It wasn't fool-proof, but it was state of the art – and better than nothing. Carefully, whilst working long hours, they sorted through the deluge of information, avoiding distractions and blind alleys. Among the mass of information that came in over the first few days of the investigation, there were a few nuggets, strong lines of enquiry that looked promising, and none more so than the case of 'Dr' Howard Campbell.

The initial information came from the most credible of sources, none other than Dr Gilbert Millar, Professor Sydney Smith's deputy, who had attended the scene at Gardenholme Linn on the day following the discovery. On Monday 30th September he had been making his way to Moffat Police Station through the throng of journalists and rubberneckers when a man in the crowd that he knew very well spoke to him.

For Millar, it was a shock – for the same man had been at the centre of a scandal that had rocked the rarefied academic atmosphere of Edinburgh University's esteemed Department of Forensic Medicine. It had been a severe embarrassment to Professor Sydney Smith himself, but in the manner of the day it had been dealt with confidentially and internally within the university – not a word had leaked that could besmirch the gilded reputation of the great man or the college. But when Millar recognised the man, he knew immediately that the secret must come out. There would be no opportunity to consult Sydney

Smith, no opportunity for a cover-up – this time the police must be informed immediately, for the man in question fitted all the criteria for a suspect in these murders.

Robert Howard Campbell was a man of precocious talents – smooth, sophisticated and urbane, though still in his early thirties – and he had befriended the legendary Professor Smith while working in obscurity at Edinburgh Royal Infirmary.

Campbell was a self-styled medicolegal specialist and so impressed Smith with his knowledge and verve that he adopted him as his protégé, taking him to Edinburgh University as one of his assistants on appointment to the Chair of Forensic Medicine. There, Campbell – along with other bright young medics like Gilbert Millar – not only assisted the great professor but often acted on his behalf, proving himself to be an able surgeon and knowledgeable anatomist. So close was Campbell to Smith that the professor even married Campbell's cousin. All seemed set fair for the bright young man – Smith's reputation was growing and his protégés rose with him.

By this time, Campbell was ready to move on, a teaching post at Edinburgh University was vacant and with his connections he was a strong candidate. It came spectacularly unstuck when the University carried out routine background checks which revealed that Dr Campbell had no medical qualifications whatsoever. He was a fraud, a fake doctor. Professor Smith and his colleagues had assumed he was a qualified doctor, but he was not. It could have been a scandal that rocked the world of medical academia if the University had not acted quickly to expel the embarrassing fake.

Thankfully, during his time at the university he had not been exposed to living patients, and since the dead made no complaints, the unpleasantness was quickly smoothed over and forgotten. Until, that is, Campbell introduced himself in a familiar way to Dr Millar in Moffat.

By the time the sighting was reported, Campbell had disappeared, so an urgent message was passed to his home city and Edinburgh City Police to T.I.E. (trace, interview and eliminate). To the beleaguered investigators at Moffat, Campbell looked like a good suspect. He had the knowledge to dismember the bodies, and from the briefest description of his past deeds he certainly had the nerve; his presence in Moffat was also seen as suspicious. It was well known that offenders were sometimes drawn back to the scene of the crime to monitor progress; to exert some control or for some gratuitous satisfaction.

The letter to T.I.E. Howard Campbell was dispatched to Edinburgh and to the desk of Detective Superintendent Berry of the Edinburgh CID.

Francis Horace Berry was a formidable man with a tough reputation, and he ran the CID with an iron grip. A stranger to any notion of political correctness, he had his men ruthlessly harass any criminal that dared operate in his city. Among his many specialties was the daily 'prisoners' parade' in the cavernous underground cell complex at the old Central Police Station in Parliament Square. The practice had started as early as 1840 but Berry took it to a new level. At 8 a.m. sharp every day except Sundays, all prisoners in overnight custody were paraded along the long central cell corridor before the assembled group of all CID officers on duty that day. The officer in charge ensured that the terrified prisoners not only paraded themselves but spoke and answered questions about their offences.

It was a calculated exercise in humiliation, but it also served to ensure detective officers got to see close up the active criminals of the city. No excuses for absence from the prisoners' parade were accepted.

Another of Berry's innovations was the CID 'special fund', a slush fund he used to pay informants and operate a repatriation scheme. Active criminals from outwith the city were met on the court steps or the release gate of Saughton Prison and escorted to a railway station, where a one-way ticket home would be purchased for them. They would then be put on the train with a message straight from Berry: 'You are not welcome in Edinburgh. If you return the consequences will be dire.' Such was Berry's reputation that the message was usually heeded.

Appalling to today's liberal sensitivities, these and other practices kept Edinburgh's crime in check and prevented the migration of the gang culture so prevalent in Glasgow before Percy Sillitoe's time.

In the Edinburgh CID, all detective officers were personally selected by Berry from the best and most active thief-takers in the uniform branch. And there was no room for complacency – weekly returns of arrests were kept for all detectives. If you performed badly you were out and returned to uniform – the ultimate fall from grace for a detective.

Berry operated an elite group and he exercised his considerable power through a handful of trusted lieutenants, foremost among them Detective Inspector John Sheed. If Berry was known to be tough, then DI Sheed was his strong right arm, his enforcer, and he held his boss's absolute trust.

Sheed was 49 years old and had not only the organisational power of Berry's authority but the personal prestige of being a decorated war hero, having been awarded the Distinguished Conduct Medal on the Western Front. Recognised as second only in prestige to the Victoria Cross, the DCM gave the veteran detective a status unmatched in Edinburgh City Police.

Sheed had been awarded the DCM in 1918 when, as a sergeant in the First Battalion of the Scots Guards, all the officers in the battalion had been killed or injured. He had led his platoon against enemy machine guns, killing several of the crew himself, and capturing the gun. On a subsequent occasion, though wounded at the assembly point, he continued to lead his men in the attack.Many believed he should have been awarded the VC.

Although ambitious young men like the great self-publicist Willie Merrilees grabbed the headlines, the police and criminal communities alike knew where the real power lay and that Sheed was not a man to be trifled with. Critical to his grip on the criminals of Edinburgh was Sheed's network of informants woven through the city's underworld. Key amongst them were the streetwise 'ladies' who plied their trade in the old Port of Leith and the long avenue of Leith Walk that led from the docks to the City Centre. Street prostitutes have often, over the ages, acted as the eyes and ears of trusted detectives. It was no different in 1930s Edinburgh.

When the Howard Campbell enquiry arrived at the HQ of Edinburgh City Police, Sheed was the obvious man to take it on. Not only was he Berry's trusted enforcer, but his professional reputation meant any urgent or sensitive enquiries were routinely allocated to him.

As he scanned the brief report sent from Dumfriesshire, Sheed realised that he already knew of Campbell. Just a few weeks earlier his name had been mentioned in connection with the minor theft of walking sticks from a hotel outside the city. About the same time, Sheed had started to hear reports from some of the street ladies about a well-to-do young man who variously described himself as an advocate or doctor or both, who drove an expensive car and who had peculiar sexual tastes. These little pieces of information amounted to very little on their own but were filed away for future scrutiny and developments that might add to the picture. Howard Campbell was certainly not a priority to the The Edinburgh CID before the letter from Dumfriesshire, but he was very much on the radar of Sheed, for, as he put it, 'moving on the edge of criminality'. The receipt of Dumfriesshire's request changed everything. Campbell became a suspect of prime interest to Sheed and his trusted partner, Detective Sergeant Sutherland.

On the same day, a seemingly unrelated call came to the Central Police Station. A local garage had just repossessed a Morris Cowley car for default in hire-purchase payments. On the way back to the garage, the driver had noticed a foul smell coming from the back seat and boot. A search revealed several items of blood-soaked underwear, women's pants and stockings and two ladies' handbags. The clothing had been so soiled that the garage foreman had ordered them burnt immediately, then, thinking better of it, had kept the handbags. The news of the find at Gardenholme Linn was prominent in the local newspapers by this time so the foreman notified the police that the car had been repossessed from none other than one Dr Howard Campbell.

Campbell could not have known it but the chance encounter with his erstwhile colleague Dr Millar in Moffat and the coincidence of the repossession of his car had placed him firmly as a strong suspect in a fast-moving murder investigation and into the sights of one of the most determined and experienced detectives of his day.

Sheed soon had an address for Campbell, a remote rented lodge house at Eskbank, just outside Edinburgh. A secret visit established that no one was in residence at the semi-derelict lodge and arrangements were made with the local Midlothian Constabulary that the building would be entered and searched by detectives from Edinburgh that night.

Meanwhile, Sheed contacted the Lord Advocate personally and, using the pretext of the suspected theft of walking sticks, obtained a warrant to arrest Campbell. The investigation was moving quickly.

It was discovered that Campbell often stayed with his wife at his mother-in-law's house in a wealthy suburb of Edinburgh. The address was soon traced, and Campbell's doting mother-in-law told Sheed her story, explaining that her son-in-law – who she believed was both a barrister and a doctor – was presently assisting the Crown Office in the investigation of murders at Moffat. She went on to say that she was the widow of a wealthy timber merchant in Hartlepool and that, following his marriage to her daughter, she had been so charmed by Campbell that she had sold up and moved her entire family to Edinburgh. She knew that Campbell had left his previous post at Edinburgh University but was unsure of the details and was happy to support him financially until he found a position suitable for his specialist skills. She kept no record of the financial support she gave Campbell and simply gave him whatever he asked for whenever he asked for it. In addition, she happily loaned him the use of her Talbot limousine, with or without her chauffeur.

Campbell's young wife was also interviewed. She added little, but her vagueness gave Sheed and Sutherland the firm impression that she knew a lot more about her husband's activities than she cared to admit. A picture of Campbell was starting to emerge as a fraud and a fantasist but that did not mean he wasn't a murderer.

A thorough search of the lodge house at Eskbank revealed nothing of importance, and while the evidence of the blood-soaked women's clothing found in the car had been destroyed, they still had the handbags and the description of the other items.

The pressure was growing; the new chief constable of Edinburgh was pressing for progress. Campbell fitted the bill in so many ways, a fantasist with a double life, with surgical experience, who had peculiar sexual tastes and reliable motor transport.

It was all adding up. He had the motive; a sexual motive, and the means; his medical background and the opportunity; on top of his lifestyle and transport. All Sheed needed now was to get his hands on the fake doctor. Few criminals could withstand the force of Sheed's interrogation and Campbell would be no different. The mystery could be solved, and the victims identified just a few days after their discovery.

Wary of newspaper coverage, Sheed did not broadcast the search for Campbell by *Police Gazette* or by telex. Instead, by confidential routes he alerted his contacts through the lowlands of Scotland to be on the lookout for Campbell, who may be on the run under a false identity.

It didn't take long – on Thursday 3rd October, Campbell was spotted back among the press pack still gathered in Moffat and without fuss he was arrested and quickly transported to Edinburgh. Chief Constable Black and the Glasgow detectives were desperate to interview him in Moffat, but good sense prevailed. They knew Sheed's reputation, and although they were investigating Dumfriesshire crimes, the arrest warrant for the theft of walking sticks and the evidence recovered from the car were all in Edinburgh.

Later that evening, Howard Campbell was taken to the subterranean cell complex beneath the old Central Police Station in Edinburgh and ushered into the presence of Sheed and Sutherland.

At that critical time Campbell faced the choice of all guilty men facing police interrogation – to lie, bluster or tell the truth. As far as he knew, he had been arrested for the theft of walking sticks, but he was not a stupid man and as he was ushered into the presence of two obviously senior detectives, it must have occurred to him that his past had caught up with him.

Over the course of the next hours, Campbell's life of fantasy and deceit was revealed. He had been born into a middle-class family in the north of England and went to a good school. He was destined for medical school, but while the practical side of his studies came easily, the academic part did not, and he quickly dropped out. He drifted north and got a job as a medical assistant, little more than a porter, at Edinburgh Royal Infirmary, where he met rising star Sydney Smith. Like all confident con-artists, Campbell had an affable manner and he quickly befriended Smith, introducing him to his family and to his cousin, with whom Smith became romantically involved. So able and willing was Campbell at the practical aspects of medicine that he was quickly accepted at the Royal Infirmary – everyone assuming he was a qualified doctor. When Smith returned from a sojourn at Cairo University to take the Chair at Edinburgh, it was logical that Campbell be appointed his assistant.

All was well until a lecturer vacancy occurred in the university and Campbell was encouraged to apply. Like many seasoned imposters, he had begun to believe his own falsehoods, or at least forgotten some of them. Such was his self-confidence that he was shocked when the university actually checked on his medical qualifications.

His decline was fast; the revelation that he had no qualifications so embarrassed Smith that Campbell was dismissed immediately. A man like Campbell could not confront the truth himself, let alone admit it. So, while his wife and mother-in-law still believed he was an eminent doctor, he took odd jobs. He sold vacuum cleaners before talking himself into the position of political agent to the famous writer Eric Linklater, when in 1933 he stood unsuccessfully for the emerging National Party of Scotland in a Parliamentary by-election in Fife.

His career in politics didn't last long – Campbell's views were too extreme even for the new nationalists and he quickly moved on to try his hand at freelance journalism. All this time he was being supported by his doting mother-in-law and enjoying the Edinburgh nightlife, but it couldn't last – eventually his lack of basic salary led to increasing financial pressures. He would soon be evicted from his bolthole, his rented house at Eskbank and his own car, the Cowley he had bought on hire purchase, would soon be seized for missed payments. His mother-in-law was generous, but it wasn't enough to support the lifestyle he aspired to.

Salvation came with the discovery at Gardenholme Linn; Campbell immediately offered his services to a number of national newspapers, presenting himself as a medicolegal expert.

Desperate for copy on what was emerging as the story of the year, several newspapers hired him as an expenses-only freelance. Campbell was back in his element, holding court in the bars of Moffat, blinding attentive journalists with his brilliance and getting paid for it. He began to believe it was the start of a prosperous new chapter in his life, a breakthrough in his journalistic ambitions. And it could have been, if his vanity had not overridden his common sense.

When he saw Dr Millar entering the Moffat police station that night on 30 September, he should have shrunk from view – after all, Millar was one of the few people who knew the truth about Campbell's duplicity. But he couldn't help himself. Desperate to prove to his new press friends that he knew the men at the heart of the investigation and therefore had the inside track, he approached Millar in the crowd, chatting to him as if they were still professional colleagues. Such hubris was to backfire badly, leading to Campbell's ignominious arrest and delivery into the hands of the formidable Inspector Sheed.

Sheed suspected Campbell was a fantasist from the intelligence he had already picked up, and he doubted he was a murderer, but one key question remained, and it was a trap set by the detective inspector. Where had the bloodstained women's underwear found in Campbell's Cowley come from?

Sheed already knew the answer – it was a test of truth. And Campbell made the right decision, admitting that he had a fondness for having sex with street ladies who were menstruating. It was exactly what had been reported to Sheed weeks before. For once in his life, Campbell had told the unvarnished truth and it saved him.

Sheed made sure he was alibied as far as he could be without an identified victim and time or date of death, but he also had to eliminate Campbell from other crimes. Just because he apparently had no connections with the bodies at Gardenholme Linn did not mean he was in the clear.

Perhaps the bloody garments still had significance; perhaps one of the street ladies had also fallen victim. Like the true professional he was, Sheed left no loose ends and covered it with a neat paragraph at the end of his report:

> The presence of the knickers and ladies' handbags he frankly confessed was due to his association with women of doubtful morals. The names of his lady companions were already known to several officers of Edinburgh City Police who found that none of them had made any mysterious disappearance.

It was masterly in its understatement. The truth was that it had been Sheed's network of informants who had reported Campbell's activities weeks before the fake doctor's unfortunate appearance at Moffat. For Sheed it was just another sensitive investigation dealt with quickly and thoroughly. Later he would undertake other enquiries in the case but for now, in just three days, he had closed down a dangerous red herring and prevented it from distracting and misleading the investigation.

As for Howard Campbell, despite his bruising encounter with Sheed, he had been very lucky. He had come out in the clear, the dubious charges relating to the theft of walking sticks were soon dropped. His nocturnal activities were never revealed and, in deference to the reputation of Professor Sydney Smith, neither was his chicanery at

Edinburgh University.

It seems remarkable now in an age of leaks that such a scandalous and newsworthy affair should remain entirely secret. Yet it did. This is the first time the strange tale of 'Dr' Howard Campbell has been revealed.

CHAPTER 11

DECEPTION

15–25 SEPTEMBER 1935

The first 24 hours after the catastrophe at 2 Dalton Square had gone as well as could be expected, with Ruxton going through the usual spectrum of emotions that followed severe trauma. First came the shock, almost paralysing in its effect, then the fatigue – the adrenalin that fuelled the natural 'fight or flight' response first flooded then ebbed away. Then the depression – the normally strong, confident doctor weeping uncontrollably, not from grief but from self-pity. How had the fates conspired to put him in this situation?

Last came the cold reality that dawns only after the passage of the other emotions. For Ruxton it was time to review his plan. The first few hours had been a panicked response to an emergency situation, and he had survived that first dangerous 24 hours by a supreme effort of will, but now was the time for cool reflection.

It was like surgery. There was the crisis response to emergency situations, then there was the meticulously planned approach to complex elective surgical procedures. The clinical planning process was his strength, every contingency must be foreseen and catered for, with fallback plans if things went wrong.

He had coped well over those first 24 hours and had now regained his composure. He was still tired, and he knew from the sideways glances of his neighbours that he looked scruffy and dishevelled. He could take comfort from the fact that this could be expected from a man whose wife had just run off. For that was the simple cover story he had decided upon. It was the obvious choice, for there was a credibility to it. Friends and neighbours knew of Bella's frequent trips and her independent spirit. He hoped they would sympathise with him, their hard-working doctor.

He had the problem of Bella's car, which was still parked outside their house – just where she'd left it that awful night of 14 September. It was Bella's pride and joy, a symbol of her independence and freedom. She always took the car when she went on her trips, and their friends and neighbours knew it. Now it stood almost accusingly outside the house for all to see. He had thought of ways to get rid of it, but that would be more suspicious than leaving it, so in the end he decided to ignore it and carry on as normal, hoping no one attached significance to it.

But he knew he had to do more, to take the initiative and convincingly act out the role of the worried, abandoned husband. He would plan that out as well, make sure his behaviour was above suspicion. But first he had to find a way to dispose of the body parts still lying wrapped in the bedrooms on the top floor of the house.

It had taken him the best part of 24 hours to dismember and disfigure both bodies and remove as many identifying features as possible. Working without his injured right hand and with blunted instruments he was no longer able to sharpen, it had been exhausting and messy work. He had tried to clean up as best he could, but every time he thought he'd finished the job, he'd noticed something else – another bloodstain.

Around this time a simple truth must have occurred to him. Committing a murder is easy – getting away with it is much harder. He knew he hadn't made as good a job of dissecting Mary as he had Bella, but one-handed, he had done the best he could.

The next challenge was how to dispose of the pile of body parts, some large, many small, and some he knew could be identified as belonging to Bella or Mary. Burying them was out of the question – he didn't know where and he wasn't fit enough to do it. He could throw them in the River Lune, which ran through Lancaster, but he had no knowledge of the river, and if any bits and pieces were found washed up on the banks it would lead straight back to him.

He would have to go further afield, but before that he could burn the smaller body parts and the numerous blood-soaked cloths and carpets that seemed to fill the top floor of the house. He had bought enough petrol to do the job and had an old barrel in the backyard, where he could discreetly incinerate a good quantity of incriminating evidence.

As soon as it was dark and the children were in bed, he started to burn the smaller soft tissues as well as carpets, rugs and towels. Lips, ears, noses, scalps, fingertips and other strips of flesh all went into the fire. But it was harder to burn these small fleshy parts than Ruxton had imagined and almost impossible to burn the carpets completely. Over several nights he burned the bloody evidence in the backyard at 2 Dalton Square, but cleaning up entirely was impossible – he had to think of other ways to get rid of the evidence.

By this time the surgery at 2 Dalton Square was open for business after the weekend and various people were coming and going around the house. The rooms on the top floor were securely locked, and while the absence of Bella and Mary was nothing out of the ordinary, Ruxton's obsession with cleaning the house and renewing carpets and fabrics did attract attention.

Ruxton was fighting on all fronts now with no respite. His busy surgery was carrying on as usual, the three young Ruxton children were back home and had to be cared for, and there remained the little matter of the dismembered bodies lying in the upstairs bedrooms and the remnants of the blood-soaked carpeting still awaiting disposal. It would have been enough to break most men, but Ruxton was composed – he knew what he had to do, and he had planned how to do it.

He was also aware of his weaknesses; his excitable nature had landed him in this trouble in the first place. He had concocted a credible storyline and he now had to strictly stick to it. But there were a number of obstacles and one of these was the man who worked just across Dalton Square in the municipal building that housed Lancaster Council and the offices of Lancaster Borough Constabulary.

The man in question was Captain Henry Vann, the Chief Constable. Lancaster was a tiny police force and Captain Vann, another seasoned veteran of the Great War, was not the kind of man you would expect to command such a small outfit. Ruxton had, of course, met Vann several times on the small but select social scene that was Lancaster's county set. He judged him to be intelligent, shrewd and ambitious, not a man you would wish to be investigating you as a suspect in a serious crime. Ruxton assessed that, once he got his teeth into you, Captain Vann would be a dangerous and tenacious adversary, and he was right.

All aspects of the crime – all potential evidence – had to be taken as far from Lancaster as possible, not only into another police-force area and out of Vann's reach, but into another jurisdiction altogether. Ruxton had worked and studied in Scotland; he knew that the legal system was completely different from England's and doubted that there would be any effective cross-border cooperation between police forces or the legal authorities. It was a reasonable assumption but, in any case, it was the best option in the circumstances Ruxton faced.

He would take the body parts as far north as he could travel without attracting suspicion, then dispose of them in small packages across as wide an area as he could. The dismembered bodies had already started to decompose and while that would soon cause a problem in the house, it was to his advantage when he disposed of them. Wild animals, even the small ones found in Britain, would soon be attracted by the smell and devour the rotting flesh. The jackals and wild dogs of his homeland would have done the job in hours, but even the foxes he knew roamed the British countryside would surely complete the task that he had so ably started. Even if they didn't, Ruxton calculated that the body parts would be so widely scattered, so thoroughly mutilated and so decomposed that if any were found they would be beyond recognition or identification as human.

But despite his composure that Monday morning of 16 September, Ruxton was starting to make small mistakes, individually insignificant, but in a desperate endeavour like this, mistakes that would count eventually.

Working in the big house at Dalton Square were a number of local people, mostly women, who cooked, cleaned and acted as receptionists. Mary had been the only full-time live-in servant, but there were others, usually patients who helped out as and when needed. Among these casual helpers were Agnes Oxley, Mary Hampshire and Elizabeth Curwen. They were all capable, hard-working women who were friends of Bella and Mary. They were also shrewd observers and judges of character.

Late on Sunday, Mrs Hampshire had been called in by Ruxton with urgent instructions for the next day. She was to clear the house, ready for extensive redecoration, and she was surprised to see that the doctor had already started the work. It was raining heavily that afternoon, and Ruxton had spread the hall and stair carpets out in the yard in an attempt to clean them. He told Mrs Hampshire that he had sprinkled them with Lux detergent to aid the cleaning process. She noticed that the stair carpet had been taken up and in the bathroom there was a dark yellow stain round the bathtub. Two of the upstairs rooms were locked with the keys removed, and Mrs Hampshire saw what looked like straw sticking out from the bottom of the doors. It was odd – Mrs Hampshire had never seen doors locked in the house before.

In the waiting room, she saw another pile of carpets and lying on top was a heavily stained blue suit which she recognised as the doctor's. Mrs Hampshire took it away to have it professionally laundered but when she got it home, she saw that the waistcoat was so heavily stained that it was uncleanable. Thinking the staining was blood, she burnt it on her stove that night.

Early the next morning – Monday 16th September – Mrs Oxley called at the doctor's house to cook the meals for the day and help with the children. She did not receive a reply so left and returned at 9.30 a.m. to be greeted by the usually immaculate doctor, dishevelled and unshaven. The house lights were on but no one else was in, and Ruxton told her that Bella and Mary had gone to Edinburgh.

Having put off Mrs Oxley, Ruxton left the house at 10 a.m. to get a shave at the local barber's. On the way, he called at Mrs Hampshire's house and, realising that he had let incriminating evidence out of his control, demanded his stained suit be returned to him. She told him that the cleaning was in hand, which seemed to reassure him, but Mrs Hampshire knew Ruxton well and was concerned by his appearance and demeanour. He wasn't the confident and smart Dr Ruxton of old.

As they discussed the suit, Ruxton became more agitated, eventually taking the jacket and tearing the identifying name tag from it, throwing it in her fire. Following this outburst, he became melancholy and confided in Mrs Hampshire that his wife had run off with a man, a lover she had been seeing for some time. This disturbed Mrs Hampshire because he had previously told her that Bella and Mary had gone to Edinburgh then Blackpool or Birmingham and, knowing Bella well, she did not believe she had a lover.

Ruxton's behaviour had been unsettling, but before he left her house, he said something which positively alarmed Mrs Hampshire, blurting out, 'You will stand by me, won't you?'

The strain was showing, the small mistakes of a man under extreme pressure, the compunction to speak to someone, to offload the burden of anxiety was normal if dangerous. But the inconsistencies creeping into the storyline were more important. After only 48 hours the simple narrative was unravelling.

He had already decided to take the body parts north by car, but his own car was too obvious for the job. His Hillman Minx had been picked to stick out, to declare to the world his style and status. Now it was too identifiable; he would have to get more anonymous transport. He hired an Austin 12 from a local garage. It was a very ordinary car, but it had a powerful engine and a big boot.

Early in the afternoon, Mrs Hampshire was back at Dalton Square, her suspicions now aroused. Once again Ruxton spoke of Bella leaving, this time for London. The exasperated woman was so concerned that she challenged her employer – she had now been given several contradictory accounts of Bella's whereabouts. It wasn't good, but such was the respect Ruxton had in the community that still Mrs Hampshire put her suspicions aside. It was probably the behaviour of a man worried sick by his runaway wife.

This belief in Ruxton's account was partly explained by his position of trust and respect but also because all who knew the couple knew Bella was an independent spirit, who frequently took off on her own. It was unusual behaviour for a married woman in 1930s Lancaster, but she always returned, her usual bubbly self, and things settled down.

The next three days, 17 to 19 September, were crucial to Ruxton's plans. The remains of Bella and Mary had already started to decompose. The doctor did all he could to mask the unmistakable stench, but nothing really could. He kept several surgical samples, preserved in formalin, in his surgery and tried sprinkling the preserving fluid on the bloody bundles, but it wasn't enough – he had to move faster.

Early on Tuesday 17 September, Ruxton set out to drive north in his hire car. With him was his two-year-old son Billie and a boot containing part of the mortal remains of the boy's mother and beloved nursemaid. It is 100 miles from Lancaster to Moffat, and the Austin 12 obviously made good time – at 12.25 p.m. a cyclist in Kendal, Westmoreland, just south of the Border, was knocked from his bike by a speeding car travelling south. With great presence of mind, the shaken man noted the registration number of the car and immediately reported the matter to the town's police station. There was only one road south, so it was a simple job to phone the next police station on the route.

The constable on duty at Milnthorpe, the next village south, stepped on to the main road and within a few minutes saw the same car approaching at high speed. The Austin 12 was stopped and the driver, a very excitable Dr Buck Ruxton was detained for questioning. In a highly agitated state, Ruxton jabbered that he had been on urgent business in Carlisle and was now on his way back to Lancaster, where he had patients to see at 3.30 p.m.

The incident in Kendal had been minor; no injury or damage had been sustained and since the doctor was accompanied by his two-year-old son, he was quickly allowed to go. In his report, the constable noted that the car had not been examined and the boot not searched, there being no reason for doing so. It didn't matter – the boot would have been empty, given that he was on the return journey from Moffat.

For the police in Westmoreland it was a minor incident even for a quiet county force, but in the manner of the day it was fastidiously recorded in the day's incident log. For Ruxton it was a disaster. He had been identified in a strange place acting in a suspicious manner. The story about a meeting in Carlisle would not hold up if checked, and the cover of his hire car, so crucial to his deception plan, was blown – the police now had it on record.

Worst of all, his carefully choreographed plan was coming apart and it was his own fault. He knew he had been driving the hire car too fast, desperate to distance himself from Moffat and the bridge at Gardenholme Linn. He had intended to scatter the body parts over a wide area but had lost his nerve. The more stops and the more deposition sites, the more risk, and when he stopped where the road crossed over the Linn, he thought he'd found an ideal spot.

First, the road was quiet and there was a clear line of sight in both directions. There were no houses or buildings nearby, no one to observe him. Looking over the parapet of the bridge he saw a raging torrent rushing beneath the bridge and down the hill. The water would do the distribution of the body parts for him, sweeping them downstream for miles, so he quickly unloaded his gruesome luggage and tossed the stinking packages over the parapet.

His young son Billie had fallen asleep in the front seat of the car but woke as Ruxton turned the car back south towards home. He had disposed of half the evidence – now he had to get back to carry on life as normal and plan his next moves.

After he had been stopped by the police, the plan had to change; he would have to get rid of the hire car and use his own. That carried risks of its own. More importantly, he had now come to the attention of the police, his name was on police files.

Wednesday, 18 September was a bizarre interlude in Ruxton's desperate endeavour. Many weeks before he had agreed to go on a family outing to the nearby seaside resort of Morecambe, where the annual end-of-season carnival was to be held. His oldest daughter, six-year-old Elizabeth, was due to take part in the formal procession that was the centrepiece of the event. In the circumstances, with rapidly decomposing body parts still locked in the top-floor rooms of the house, a day at the seaside was the last thing Ruxton needed or wanted, but to call off would have looked suspicious and disappointed the children.

Used to their mother taking short trips, the three young children had taken their mother and nursemaid's sudden disappearance without upset, but part of this was due to their excitement at the prospect of the carnival. Ruxton loved his children and did not want to disappoint them. More crucially, he could not afford to unsettle them. They were living in the house at Dalton Square for at least part of the time, and while the two younger children were oblivious to their surroundings Elizabeth was not. At an inquisitive age, her father had to distract her until the house was cleaned up thoroughly.

Throughout the day, Ruxton seethed at the waste of valuable time but tried his best to force some semblance of gaiety, not only for the children but for appearances. The carnival at Morecambe was one of the social gatherings of the county – many of the Ruxton's family friends were there, and Ruxton was desperate to cast himself as a victim to win their sympathy and support. As he had revealed to Mrs Hampshire, he craved the acceptance of Lancaster's society, partly because of his innate insecurity, his need to fit in and be accepted, and partly because he knew that eventually he would face questions about Bella and Mary's disappearance, and he would need all the friends he could get.

Returning from Morecambe, Ruxton dropped the children at a friend's house to spend the night, explaining that he had an urgent job to do the next day. He then returned his hire car, picked up his own, filled it with petrol and returned to the house at Dalton Square. It was late in the evening by this time, and the house had lain empty most of the day. As soon as he opened the door, he could smell it – the unmistakable stench of putrefaction. He had kept the house cool to minimise it, but it was now obvious, and he knew he had to act quickly. That night a large fire was seen burning in the backyard of the house as Ruxton tried to destroy more of the smaller, identifiable body parts.

Early the next morning – Thursday 19th September – Mrs Oxley was cleaning the ground-floor surgery at Dalton Square when she heard Ruxton make several journeys from the top floor through the back passageway and to the backyard, where his car was parked. The boot of his own car was small, and it was a struggle to fit the last of his stinking packages in, but eventually the job was done, and he drove off north, telling Mrs Oxley that he would be back late.

His original intention was to scatter the body parts over a wide area north of the border, but the incident with the police two days before had unsettled him. He stopped several times on the road but couldn't find many spots remote enough. He managed to dispose of one or two packages, but driving such an obvious car registered to him made him nervous, so he still had the majority of his load when he reached Moffat. Once again, he stopped at the bridge over the Linn and, seeing the coast was clear, quickly tipped the remaining packages over the parapet before heading south again.

The disposal had gone smoothly at the end but had he taken a few seconds to look over the parapet before dropping the last of the packages, he would have seen that some of the parcels he had dumped two days before had not been swept downstream but were stranded high and dry on the banks of the Linn.

Ruxton drove the 100 miles back to Lancaster carefully, without stopping or drawing attention to himself or his car.

That night the fire burned again in the rear yard, and by the next morning Mrs Oxley noticed that the previously locked doors on the top floor were open. Dr Ruxton was in a good mood that day, but both Mrs Oxley and Mrs Hampshire noticed a foul smell throughout the house. It had stopped raining, so all the windows and doors were opened to air the house, but the smell lingered, as if it impregnated the very stone of the old building.

Ruxton had now completed the first phase of his deception plan – he had dismembered the bodies of his two victims and disposed of them in what he believed were unidentifiable pieces. While undertaking this gruesome and difficult task, he had carried on his life as normally as he could, cared for his young children and carried on his practice as a busy doctor.

Having survived the first three days after the murders, he could be satisfied, as most murderers do not make it through the first 24 hours, but still he had made mistakes. The inconsistencies in his account of where Bella and Mary had gone aroused some suspicion. Likewise, his behaviour in the house – the cut hand, the locked rooms, the awful smells, the bloodied suit, the carpets and the fires – would eventually be problems for Ruxton. Some of these slips were unavoidable in the panicked circumstances, but the incident in Kendal that led him to be stopped by the police was not.

The first phase of his plan having been completed, Ruxton now moved straight to the second. He had to act out the natural reactions of an innocent man, a man cruelly abandoned, left with three young children by a wayward wife. He had thought it through and calculated what a wholly innocent man would do, and how he would act.

The first problem was when to report Bella and Mary missing. It was common knowledge that Bella often went away for two or three days so to report her missing too early would seem odd, though leaving it too late would look suspicious. His natural inclination was to leave it as long as possible, avoid police visits to the house, questions and scrutiny, but he knew this was the wrong move. For if he did not raise the alarm and report the two women missing, who would? If someone else contacted the police before him it would look suspicious.

It was a fine balance. He wanted to buy as much time as possible to clean and re-clean the house, to allow his hand to heal and, most of all, to regain his composure and his confidence.

He thought that Bella's family in Edinburgh would be the first to show concern. Bella had sisters there and they were close – in constant contact – and Bella had told them all about their domestic arguments. At first, he'd thought their antipathy towards him was because of his race, but later he came to realise it was because of the tales Bella had told them. He had tried a charm offensive with no discernible results; Bella's sisters were still decidedly lukewarm towards him, which was even more reason to demonstrate his care and concern. He needed to appear to be desperately looking for her and worried for her safety.

Without telephones the only way to communicate was by letter and Ruxton went to it with a will, writing to any family member he could, pleading for help or information that could lead him to find his beloved Bella. Every letter was carefully typed, with copies retained by him in case he needed them in his defence. The theme was worried and outraged innocence. Typical was a letter he wrote to Bella's sister early in October:

My Dear Sister,
I am heart broken and half mad. Isobel has again left me. She has done this trick again after about ten months. Do you remember she left me bag and baggage last November when I came to your house. She told me she was going to Eden to take the sole agency for a Mr Wm Murphy, for his football pools. I have found that she had been trying to hire rooms in Preston to provide football pools on her own. Then again, I was informed that she actually has taken rooms in Blackburn and furnished them, but is not using them. The rent is mounting up.

I am sorry to have to tell you a tale, but ever since she has left there is no end of bills that I am getting. She has bought clothes and other things to the tune of £100 from various shops in Lancaster. She has been evidently backing horses and a prominent bookie in Lancaster is demanding £21.15 from her.

The most important thing is this, that she is trying to help our maid who is in a certain condition. I hope she does not involve herself in any trouble with the law because she will be liable for helping her for such affairs.

The children are asking for her daily and I really cannot sleep without her. Mine is only a temper but in my heart of hearts she is my all in all. She has taken my £30 and two gold coins.

According to the latest information she is somewhere in Birmingham, but I cannot keep on running after her. Have you any relations in Canada? I know you have relatives in Queensland but I did not know that you had relatives in Canada. Sometime ago she got into her head to go to Canada. I really don't know one minute what next she is going to do. My life is impossible without her presence in my house. I admit I have a temper but your sister gives me strong cause for provocation now and again. In spite of all that I am terribly fond of my Bella. How could she be so heartless to leave me like this?

Could you do me a favour? Can you supply me with the addresses of any friends of hers where you think she may have gone.

Has she been at your place or not? I want you to tell me the honest truth. Please do not intentionally help Isobel to keep away from me. I want you to help me keep my home together. I am simply distracted. I cannot even keep my mind on the practice. You must ask her on your own to come back to me. I am surely coming to see you soon.

Till then, yours affectionately,
Bommie

Bearing in mind that these letters were written days after he had killed, dismembered and disposed of Bella and Mary, they show a cool and deliberate attempt to deceive and distract Bella's family, who he saw as a major threat.

He wrote dozens of similar letters, cleverly designed to demonstrate his worry and concern, play down his own shortcomings, which the family already knew of, and to sow as many doubts, slurs and false trails as he could. He suggests Bella's dishonesty, unreliability, deceit and wilfulness, and implies that the pair had run off to procure an abortion for Mary. He also introduces the prospect that the two women might even have fled the country.

The letters served their purpose. Bella's Edinburgh family were worried and confused. They knew Bella was an independent, high-spirited woman, and while they were convinced that she had not been involved in any serious trouble, she had left home before. The doubts and uncertainties paralysed them into inaction. She would turn up soon enough, as she always did. There was no need to raise the alarm, no need to get involved in her domestic squabbles.

In the end, Ruxton did not have to report Bella and Mary missing either. When trouble came, it came from an unexpected quarter.

* * *

Mary Rogerson had worked for and lived with the Ruxtons for three years, yet apart from her devotion to Bella, Ruxton knew little of her or her family. It was as if she had become part of the wallpaper – seen but never heard. She was described patronisingly as plain or simple, and known by the Ruxtons as 'little Mary', even though she was of average height for the time. In fact, she was not only a devoted and much-loved nursemaid and friend to Bella, she was also very close to her family. She spent all her infrequent days off in the family home in nearby Morecambe and, if she was away, wrote daily letters to her father and stepmother.

Ruxton had called at the Rogerson's home on the weekend of the murders and believed he had allayed any concerns they may have had, but he was wrong. For a day or so the Rogersons accepted the story of Bella and Mary having gone to Edinburgh or elsewhere, but when, after a few days, no letters had arrived from Mary, they began to worry. The Rogersons were a simple family – their statements given later to investigators demonstrate this – but they weren't stupid. From a few days after the women disappeared, they took the initiative to try to trace their daughter.

On 25 September, Mary's brother called on Ruxton at Dalton Square and questioned him about his sister's disappearance. It was the first time Ruxton had been confronted and he made a mistake. Instead of sticking to the simple narrative of his wife and Mary running off to destinations unknown, he elaborated. Judging himself more than a match for Mary's brother and losing his composure, he babbled out various and sometimes conflicting theories, including his line that Mary had a boyfriend, a local lad, and was in 'a certain condition' as a result.

This was incredible to the Rogersons – they trusted their daughter, and they knew she had a childlike innocence. They were sure that they would have known if she had a boyfriend. Now angry and very alarmed, the deeply suspicious accounts given by Ruxton, together with the lack of any communication from Mary, convinced them that harm had come to her and they were determined to take action.

The Rogersons reported their daughter missing, in the company of Bella Ruxton, to the police at Lancaster, who promptly called on Dr Ruxton to establish the circumstances.

The call was expected and had been prepared for and rehearsed. Ruxton stuck to his vague and impassioned line about being deserted by his wife, left with three young children, heartbroken and desperately worried. The Lancaster Police knew of the domestic squabbles of the Ruxtons – Bella had run across Dalton Square to the police station on several occasions, fearful of her husband's temper – but they also knew that she had left home on a number of occasions and had always returned. The strong inclination of the police at that time was not to get involved in domestic disputes, particularly where a much-respected middle-class family was involved. Subconsciously they weighed the credibility of the Rogersons versus Ruxton, which naturally came down in favour of the doctor.

The missing person report was noted and filed but nothing much was done and no proactive investigation was launched. Lancaster Police believed that Bella and Mary would eventually turn up safe and sound, as they always had. But the Rogerson family were not to be fobbed off. If the Lancaster Police wouldn't take action, then they would.

As September came to a close, Ruxton began to relax. As each day passed, he scanned the national newspapers and, seeing no stories about found body parts, he became more confident that the remains of Bella and Mary had been carried away by the river at Gardenholme Linn or devoured by the local foxes.

But just as he was regaining his composure, a shock came from an unexpected source. By a strange coincidence, another major police investigation was launched in Morecambe, just a few miles away. The body of Florence Smalley, the 56-year-old wife of a prominent Lancaster businessman, was found lying in a stable yard. Her injuries were so severe she was at first unrecognisable, and it was assumed that the body was that of Bella or Mary – after all, in a quiet, law-abiding county like Lancashire where crime was rare, what were the chances that it wasn't one of the two missing local women?

Ruxton was caught completely off balance. He was the only person who knew for certain that whoever the woman in Morecambe was, she was not Bella or Mary, but he had to feign concern and shock until Mrs Smalley was identified. But now there was cause for real concern, as one of his house servants Elizabeth Curwen was called in for police questioning. It was a routine interview about the Florence Smalley case, but Ruxton panicked and once again lost control. Mrs Curwen knew of the disparities in the accounts of Bella and Mary's disappearance, knew of the carpets and the blood-soaked suit, and he was desperate to know what questions the police had been asking. Thus the poor charwoman was subjected to close questioning by the doctor. She was already bemused and wary of her employer, but now her suspicions were well and truly aroused.

Not satisfied with Mrs Curwen's responses, Ruxton stormed across the square to police headquarters, protesting his innocence, volunteering that he had cut his hand while opening a tin – he had previously told friends he had cut it on his car – and repeating time and again the slur that Mary was pregnant. This was suspicious behaviour by any standard and should have raised the alarm, but still the Lancaster Police did not recognise what was staring them in the face just a few yards from their front door. In a bizarre sequel, the death of Florence Smalley was improbably written off as a hit-and-run vehicular accident, although how her body ended up in a stable was never explained, nor was the 'vehicle' that killed her ever traced. Not all police forces were imbued with professional excellence in 1935!

When the morning papers of 30 September carried the news of the find at Gardenholme Linn, Ruxton was shocked. How could the remains of Bella and Mary still be there? It was impossible.

But two days later his mood changed to glee. The news-papers were reporting that the bodies were that of an older man and a younger woman. Despite his injured right hand and the unfavourable circumstances of the dissection, he had successfully obliterated and disguised the gender of the bodies. He could not help but celebrate, cheerfully referring to the story and telling several of his friends, 'Ha ha – it can't be our two.'

CHAPTER 12

THE PIECES COME TOGETHER

3–11 OCTOBER 1935

By Thursday, 3rd October the main focus of the investigation had moved from Moffat to the Department of Forensic Medicine at Edinburgh University. It had been four hectic days for Dumfriesshire Constabulary, but they had coped well. Chief Constable Black had kept control, and the senior Glasgow detectives Ewing and Hammond had added their experience to the tireless and dedicated local men. Inspector Strath and Sergeant Sloan had been on duty constantly throughout, snatching a few hours' sleep when they could.

It reminded many of the intensity and camaraderie of the front line, the forward trenches they had experienced as younger men. There were no bullets or whiz-bangs but the bone-weary tiredness was the same – the inability to sleep, the snatched morsels of food – the only comfort the focus on the task and the sense of comradeship from working in a small team in adversity.

The team – including the police-firemen, Special Constabulary and the anatomists – had melded together exceptionally well; Black had recognised the threat of discord and worked hard to avoid it, successfully keeping control, while feeding the ravenous, unruly beast of the press corps that had descended upon Moffat and camped there, baying for information.

But now the circus was leaving town – the press, the sightseers and the voyeurs. Not that the work at Moffat was finished – far from it; there were dozens of enquiries to follow up – but as the days passed without reports of any local missing persons, they were getting nowhere, and it was clear that the mutilated body parts found the previous Sunday did not belong locally. Black's worst fears had been realised: a hideous crime had been committed elsewhere and the putrefied, mangled and disfigured remains of two victims had been dumped on his patch in Dumfriesshire.

Sergeant Sloan had felt this from the start. Intuitively he'd known these bodies were not from his patch; if something had gone that badly wrong in Moffat, he or his network of contacts would have got wind of it. The body parts had now been taken to Edinburgh, but he had retained other vital material evidence from Gardenholme Linn and his enquiries still had a distance to run.

But if the heat was dying down in Moffat, the temperature was rising in Edinburgh. In one of the large laboratories and dissecting rooms at the university's Department of Forensic Medicine, special arrangements had been made for a task unprecedented even in the institution's long and glorious history. The long north-facing laboratory had been locked to ensure no press intrusion; only senior staff had access as confidentiality was imperative. Professor Smith was still abroad so his deputy Dr Millar took daily charge while Professor Glaister and his deputy Dr Martin travelled daily from Glasgow to supervise and help in the investigation. The anatomist Professor Brash completed the team of investigators, along with a small hand-picked number of technicians and laboratory assistants.

James Couper Brash – at fifty years of age, the most senior of the medics involved in the case – was the only true anatomist. He was already famous as an embryologist, and, like so many others in the case, he had served with distinction in the Great War, winning a Military Cross as a major in the Royal Army Medical Corps. He had been Professor of Anatomy at Edinburgh University since 1931, the successor to a long line of famous anatomists stretching back to Dr Knox, of Burke and Hare infamy. Like Glaister and Smith, he was at the height of his powers, and like them he was keen to apply his knowledge and expertise to the practical investigation of crime. No rarefied ivory towers for these men. They had been in the trenches – they were practical and had no compunction over getting their hands dirty.

The two bespoke metal tanks had been put in place and filled with a concentration of 2.5% formalin. After being washed with ether to kill the maggots, the contents of each box were carefully placed in the tanks. This would halt the rapid decomposition of the body parts and preserve them for the painstaking examination that was to follow. After a day or so of immersion, the flesh and bones found at Gardenholme

Linn took on a rubbery grey consistency, unrecognisable as human flesh to all but an expert eye.

As the medical men got to work, a highly unusual meeting took place in the office of the Lord Advocate in Parliament House, Edinburgh. Held between 8.15 p.m. and 11.15 p.m., to avoid undue attention, the attendees were the Lord Advocate, his deputy the Solicitor General, three advocate deputes, including Home Advocate Depute Jock Cameron, the procurators fiscal for Dumfries and Edinburgh, Chief Constable Black, the Glasgow detectives, Detective Inspector Sheed from Edinburgh and the anatomists.

It was a meeting unprecedented and never repeated. A full summary of the case so far was discussed and lines for future investigation were agreed. Recognising the unique nature of the enquiry, a strict protocol for the passing and updating of information was established. The key now lay with the pathologists, so it was agreed that at the end of each day, they would prepare a bulletin with updated information, which Sheed would then cascade by secure means to the other members of the group. Any developments in Dumfriesshire or elsewhere would likewise be communicated from their end. Decades before policy files and other sophisticated systems evolved, this simple system ensured that all elements of the investigation remained accurately and confidentially informed. Cameron would act as ringmaster and Sheed as the conduit to ensure the system worked. It was a novel approach to criminal investigation, but it strongly resembled the military system of command and control in the front line. As such, it was a system everyone round that top table knew well and trusted.

By 4 October the pathologists had organised themselves, but all were aware that they were academic medics usually slightly removed from the operational hurly-burly. They were determined to cover all eventualities so began their investigations by seeking the views of a noted Edinburgh police surgeon Mr D.P.D. Wilkie FRCS. Wilkie's initial report of 6 October made several highly relevant points:

I beg to certify that at 5 p.m. on 4 October 1935 in the presence of Dr W. Gilbert Millar and two representatives of the police (DI Sheed and DS Sutherland, Edinburgh City Police), I examined the portions of two bodies lately recovered from the ravine near Moffat.

From the elaborate and systematic manner in which the bodies had been cut up, it appeared to me that certain conditions must have been present.

1. Time of at least eight hours for the work of dismemberment.
2. A table with good light and large sharp knives.
3. Someone either with a knowledge of human anatomy or with experience of cutting up animals.

I base these conclusions on the following observations: The great majority of the incisions were clean cut and purposive, not hacked or ragged, and suggested that they were made by someone who was accustomed to cutting flesh.

The elbow joints were clearly disarticulated, without injury to the cartilaginous surfaces – a difficult piece of work for the uninitiated.

The most striking example was the lumbar spine of the female subject; here the vertebral column had been divided through the intervertebral disc and the joints between the articular processes divided without any injury to the bone – a procedure requiring some skill.

The disjointing at the hips had also been carried out in a workmanlike manner, without injury to the joint surfaces.

The procedures which had been carried out to remove all possible marks for identification were very thorough, and betokened considerable knowledge, thus the removal of the hairy scalp, both eyes, the tip of the nose, the skin of the hips and chin of the male, the incisor teeth, the fingertips of the male.

In the female subject [Mary Rogerson], the nipple and areola of one breast were removed and the nipple on the other side cut and disformed.

In the portions of the male body [Bella's body] available, there was nothing to indicate how death had occurred.

In the skull of the female subject there was evidence of a bruise and a slight depression on the vertex of the skull slightly towards its posterior aspect. Removal of the skull cap revealed a small depressed fracture and a projecting fragment of the inner table. There was no haemorrhage or gross injury to the underlying brain.

The nature and seat of this fracture strongly suggested a blow with some blunt instrument.

The injury did not appear of sufficient severity to have – by itself – caused death but would almost certainly have resulted in concussion and unconsciousness.

The remarkable absence of blood in all the tissue examined suggests that either the parts must have been washed before being disposed of, or possibly that the subject after being stunned was bled to death.

Finally, in a calculated reproof to the mad doctor theorists he concluded:

I submit that the dismemberment and mutilation of the two subjects was not the work either of a maniac or ignorant individual but must have been carried out by someone with previous knowledge of cutting up a body and familiar with the medicolegal value of parts used in identification.

Wilkie had summarised the case with remarkable prescience, and had unintentionally paid a compliment, for Ruxton did not have a table or a good view for his dismemberment. He had a tiny bathroom with poor lighting, limited time and a severely injured hand.

But for all of Wilkie's insight, he, like all the other medics, still saw the body parts as that of a man and a woman. They were all still deceived by Ruxton's determined attempt to disguise the identity of his victims.

The previous day, 5 October, the first report from the Department of Forensic Medicine was forwarded under secret cover to the senior police and law officers. After long debate, Professor Glaister and his team had decided to prioritise examination of the two skulls and the one recovered thorax. Likewise, they noted the proficiency with which the nose, lips and eyes had been removed but then, for the first time, studied the teeth remaining in the two skulls, paying particular attention to those that had obviously been removed post-mortem. Fortunately, there were forensic odontologists within the university and they were called upon to join the team and give their expertise. It was an important move; across the country dental records, albeit held on card index systems in local surgeries, were often better than medical records. Odontology would not trace the origins of the bodies but could well confirm identity if suspected victims were traced.

–Their report concluded that:

> Our examination today had endorsed the view which we originally expressed on 1 October 1935 after our preliminary examination of the remains at Moffat, which was to the effect that the mutilation had been carried out with skill and dexterity by one who not only appreciated anatomical relationship, but who seems to have displayed an intimate medical knowledge.

Bizarrely the report ended:

> Although rather apart from the scope of our investigation, we take the liberty of suggesting that it might be expedient to trace the relatively recent liberation of any medical man, medical student or of others with medical knowledge who might have been recently discharged from local asylums.

It was a view that utterly conflicted with the evidence of the cool-headed, professional dismemberment that faced them on the examination tables.

We will never know the logic behind the theory but perhaps it was simply because the luminaries of forensic medicine could not bear to think of a sane member of their proud profession being responsible for such butchery. Whatever the reason, Professor Glaister, Dr Millar and Dr Martin formally threw their professional weight behind the mad doctor theory.

Back in Moffat, the Dumfriesshire men continued their end of the investigation. All hoped that the anatomists would work their magic and that science would provide the answer. Chief Constable Black, however, was not counting on it. It was still his investigation, and he would not allow his force to take a back seat.

Sergeant Sloan had also continued his efforts to preserve the rotten, stinking garments and newspapers that had wrapped some of the body parts. He had already identified the dates and titles of some of the newspapers and had sent urgent messages to the two great newspaper printing centres, Manchester and London, where the local police forces were doing their best to speed up enquiries.

Sloan had been sure from the start that answers lay in the wrappings and he intended to pursue his hunch. What were the circulation areas of these papers and could that give a clue to the origin of the bodies?

While he waited impatiently for results from the newspapers, he turned his attention to the pieces of garment that had wrapped a head and parts of the body – the same fabric that his wife had gently hand-washed again and again before pressing them with a warm flat iron so as to preserve their fragility. Many of the wrappings were simple rags or so rotten that they were beyond recovery. Two complete garments had, however, survived and cleaned up well. They became the focus of Sergeant Sloan's attention: a woman's blouse of cheap manufacture, made of georgette but with a distinctive hand-sewn repair on the collar and the left armpit, and a child's knitted romper suit, canary yellow in colour and of cheap machine manufacture. It had shrunk considerably during the repeated washing, but it was estimated to fit a child of three or four years. It too had been hand repaired, its elastic obviously replaced. They were mass-produced garments and cheap to buy, a few shillings each, and there would be thousands like them, but the repairs made them distinctive.

Sloan knew that they were vital pieces of evidence – identifying them or, more importantly, the hands that had repaired them could, in turn, lead to the identification of the bodies. The press, now suffering a dearth of new information, were summoned and the next day every front page in the land carried pictures of the garments along with pleas for information.

As the first week of the investigation passed, frustration crept into the Dumfriesshire Constabulary men. They had to wait for developments from the anatomists at Edinburgh, but progress was gradual. The daily reports from Professor Glaister described the painstakingly slow process that the pathologists were following.

Not included in the daily report from Edinburgh University was a development which was puzzling even the great Professors Glaister and Brash. Once the dozens of body parts had been stabilised in the tanks of formalin, a careful examination began first to try to identify the various parts of the anatomy, then if possible to fit them to one of the two bodies. Many of the lumps of rubbery grey flesh were hard to identify as human, let alone anything more specific, but Professor Brash and his assistants did their utmost and made good progress by building the bodies from the components in the two tanks. One mass of tissue, however, had them stumped. A relatively small, round lump of resistant tissue roughly three inches in diameter, it had a different texture to the other remains and it seemed in better condition, almost as if it had been previously preserved. At first it was thought to be a deformed or monstrous foetus at an early stage of development but on further examination the view changed. All agreed it was an eye – a huge eye. As Professor Glaister later explained:

> The cyclops eye of Greek mythology is the complete fusion of both eyes into one. This specimen, however, was, strictly speaking, not a true cyclops eye but two eyes set close together without any intervening bone, and detailed examination confirmed our first impression that it was not of human origin. Where it came from, how it came to be found among the remains at the ravine, will always be regarded as a minor mystery.

Both the professors had seen such cyclops eyes before, usually from sheep or pigs, in anatomical collections and it made them pause for thought. One of the early theories had been that the find at Gardenholme Linn was a hoax, a medical student's prank; if that was the case, this cyclops eye was exactly what they would expect to find. Except that the other body parts had not been preserved, and while the dismemberment of the bodies had been well done, it was not quite the standard you would expect in anatomical samples. The pathologists set the 'cyclops eye' aside for further consideration; there was no point in causing confusion at this stage. Besides, there were still plenty of other body parts in the boxes to be identified and reconstructed in bodies one and two.

All of this was unknown to the police, who were desperate for any developments that would take the investigation forward, but there was nothing of real significance. There was, however, work to do: the avalanche of information that followed the early nationwide press coverage all had to be bottomed out. But, nothing looked promising until Sergeant Sloan started to get replies to the enquiries he had made about the newspapers the body parts had been wrapped in. Following his careful removal and drying of the newspaper fragments, Sloan had mounted them on celluloid, scrounged from the local hospital's X-Ray department. He then sent a selection showing dates and the names of the newspapers to Manchester and London, where most national newspapers were printed. After a few days elapsed, Sloan again took the initiative, telephoning the other forces to emphasise the importance of his enquiry.

Eventually on the morning of 9 October he got a response and described it in his report to Black:

I telephoned twice to Manchester City Police and asked if they could now give me the result of their enquiry. In answer to my second message I was informed that the papers I had forwarded to them were portions of newspapers circulating throughout practically the whole of the North of England and part of North Wales. I also put through calls to Scotland Yard and learned in answer to my second call it had been ascertained that the portions of the *Sunday Graphic and Sunday News* newspapers of 15 September which I had sent to London was part of a 'slip' edition numbering 3,700 copies which had been prepared in connection with a carnival held at Morecambe on 4 September and had been issued to a few distributing agents in a very small area round about Morecambe.

It was the breakthrough they had been waiting for; what Sloan had always suspected – the sodden newspaper wrappings held a vital clue. The newspaper could only have come from a very small geographical area – the net was closing.

Black immediately telephoned Lancashire Constabulary and demanded to speak to the most senior officer on duty. Referring to the special notices in the *Police Gazette* describing the find at Gardenholme Linn, he explained the significance of the limited circulation of the newspaper wrappings and asked Lancashire to make a very special enquiry. The urgency of his message obviously got through – Lancashire County Constabulary, a large modern force, promised urgent action but added that no man and woman were reported missing in suspicious circumstances as far as they knew.

Following that conversation, Black called an urgent conference with his senior officers and the Glasgow detectives. As Black described the developments and the connection with Morecambe, it struck a chord with one of the Glasgow men, Lieutenant Ewing. That very morning, 9 October, he had read a strange story in his local paper, the *Daily Record*. It was a side column on an inside page, headed 'Lost Nurse

Mystery' followed by an account of the disappearance of 20-year-old Mary Rogerson, who had vanished three weeks previously from the house of her employer, a Mohammedan doctor named Buck Ruxton, in a practice in Lancaster.

Mary's family, for all their simplicity, had taken the initiative and written to anyone they could think of to try to trace their daughter. They had also written to all local and national newspapers with the story of her disappearance. Most papers had not carried the story, but by good fortune, on 9 October the *Daily Record* had a space to fill.

Black and his team re-read the story several times then stared at each other in amazement. After all the special notices in the *Police Gazette*, the messages to Lancashire Constabulary, they had learned of Mary Rogerson's disappearance only because of the tenacity of her family and the fortunate contents of a Scottish newspaper.

In its long history the *Daily Record*, one of Scotland's most popular newspapers, has often claimed credit for solved crimes and societal change. In this case such a claim was entirely justified.

Black was like a man possessed – he immediately telephoned Lancashire Police again and demanded to speak to the officer in charge at Scorton, the divisional HQ covering Morecambe. The hapless superintendent explained that while the missing girl's parents lived in Morecambe, she had actually gone missing from her place of employment in the borough of Lancaster. He went on to explain that Lancaster Borough Police were dealing with the case and that Lancashire County had not even been officially notified that the girl was missing.

It was incomprehensible – after all the publicity, the special notices in the *Police Gazette*, the massive press coverage, how could Lancaster Police not have noticed?

Black composed himself then telephoned Lancaster Borough Police headquarters, a stone's throw from Dr Ruxton's house in Dalton Square. The duty superintendent took the call and Black, containing his temper, patiently referred him to the special notices in the *Police Gazette* and sought information about the missing nursemaid.

It was explained that while the Rogerson family had reported Mary missing, the police in Lancaster had not officially recorded it. It was known that the girl had worked for the French-Indian doctor who had his surgery close to the police station, he was married to a

Scottish woman and it was common knowledge that they had a fiery relationship. The doctor's wife had left him before but always returned, and it was believed she had stormed out about three weeks previously, taking the nursemaid with her. As in the past she was expected to return once tempers had cooled. Lancaster Police had seen the special bulletins from Dumfriesshire, but since the body parts recovered at Gardenholme Linn belonged to a man and a woman, there was apparently no connection to Lancaster or to the two runaway women.

Black was not so certain; the connection between the fragments of newspaper and the area around Morecambe and Lancaster could not be a coincidence. He asked that they contact the Lancashire Police at Morecambe urgently and call him back immediately with a full description of the missing Mary Rogerson and Mrs Ruxton. Chastened by Black's urgency, the superintendent promised he would act with all speed and also inform his own chief, Captain Vann.

Back in Dumfriesshire, Black shared the information from Lancaster with his top team, but how could their bodies – a man and a woman – be the missing women from Lancaster? That very day they had released to the press an updated description from the pathologists in Edinburgh. The male body was of medium height and build, approximately fifty years old with a pronounced lantern jaw; the woman was young, in her twenties and small in stature.

Yet how could their body parts not be those of the Lancaster women? The time of their disappearance was about right for the state of decomposition, and parts of the bodies had been wrapped in newspapers only distributed in the Morecambe/Lancaster area. Added to that, there were no other missing persons anywhere in the UK that matched the descriptions of the older man and young woman that they had found and that now lay in those metal tanks in Edinburgh University.

Black and his men looked at each other around the table where they sat analysing the new information, each coming to the same conclusion. The only explanation was that the medical men, the most illustrious of their generation, had got it wrong, had mistakenly identified the gender of one of the bodies. It was a difficult moment, awkward for medically untrained policemen to challenge experts like Professors Glaister and Brash.

But it had to be done and, as so often was the case in his long career, the sensitive task fell to Detective Inspector John Sheed of

Edinburgh City Police.

Advocate Depute Jock Cameron had asked to be kept fully briefed on any developments, and since it was the Crown, not the police, who were employing the pathologists, Sheed contacted Cameron and asked him to accompany him to meet the anatomists.

At the university's secure examination lab, the medical men, pathologists and anatomists had proceeded systematically with their work. First, they had stabilised and preserved the body parts in the tanks, a process that took several days, then, as agreed, they had started by examining the two skulls. It was logical: the two heads were most likely to provide evidence of identification – teeth, hair colour, physical features – as well as potential cause of death. At the same time, junior members of staff were tasked with completing a thorough audit of the body parts and, under Professor Brash's supervision, trying to match them to the two bodies, literally reassembling them. They had already discovered the cyclops eye and, after momentary pause, had continued their gruesome jigsaw.

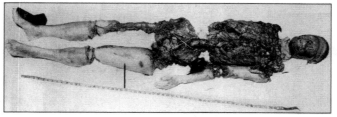

Brash's jigsaw - the reassembled Body No. 2

Early on 10 October, Cameron and Sheed called at the university for an update and to discuss the ticklish issue of the gender of the bodies.

The professors knew Sheed as their police liaison officer, though Dr Millar had worked with him before and Cameron as a rising star of the legal profession, so there was a mutual respect and easy rapport between the men.

Sheed was direct – he explained the significance of the newspaper wrappings and the two women missing from Lancaster then asked if there was any possibility that the body parts they were examining could both be female.

As a lengthy discussion ensued, the meeting was interrupted by a junior member of the forensic staff, one of those carrying out the audit of the body parts. To the stunned ensemble of doctors and detectives, the young man apologised for interrupting his seniors but thought they would like to know that among the body parts, they had now positively identified three female breasts. There could be no doubt: the nipple had been cut off one and disfigured on another but there were definitely three female breasts.

It was almost a comedic moment as the group of distinguished men looked at each other, the significance of the find sinking in.

After a momentary pause, Professor Glaister, as chair, cleared his throat and politely thanked the young man, dismissing him to carry on with his work.

Professors Glaister and Brash and Dr Millar were all wise men, and they knew that while many outside their profession thought them infallible, there were limits to their science. They knew the difference between professional opinion and fact, and when the facts changed, so did their professional opinions. No one, no matter how senior, was infallible, and they were secure enough in their profession not to feel obliged to stand on their dignity. The cast-iron fact of three female breasts among the parts of what were certainly two bodies pointed to only one thing. Their professional opinion as to the gender of the bodies had been wrong; for the first crucial twelve days of this most intense investigation they had been barking up the wrong tree. Yes, there was the slight chance of an outlier, a foreign object introduced to deceive – they had already found a cyclops eye, after all – but now they had to look at the body parts through new eyes, without the assumptions made on that first medical examination by the local doctors at the primitive mortuary in Moffat on 30 September.

Back in Dumfriesshire, there were some wry smiles when they heard the news; some of the police who had dealt with the body parts had suspected that they were female, mainly because all the skin that remained on the limbs was hairless. Of course, they would never have considered challenging the anatomists, but there was a quiet satisfaction that they had probably been right after all.

Immediately on hearing the news, Chief Constable Black telephoned Lancaster Borough Police and demanded to speak urgently to his counterpart, Captain Vann, in person. Vann was an able and ambitious man who commanded a tiny police force of only forty-five men, half the size of Dumfriesshire. His force was only responsible for the town of Lancaster itself and then only for minor crimes and incidents. Like Dumfriesshire, Lancaster Borough had no specialist detectives or forensic capability and depended on its larger neighbour Lancashire County Constabulary, one of the largest county forces in England. Despite its size, however, Lancashire Constabulary had little in the way of specialist or scientific equipment or training. Lancashire had proficient detectives but little else to equip it for a major criminal investigation. In part, this was a legacy of the tradition of calling in 'the Yard' – Scotland Yard – to investigate any serious crime. The fact was that in the quiet, law-abiding county of Lancashire there was very little serious crime – certainly not enough to justify a well-equipped and expensive criminal investigation department.

Vann had been aware of the ongoing situation at 2 Dalton Square; he knew Ruxton socially, professionally, and, like the other officers in Lancaster, held the able doctor in high regard. He was also aware of the strained relationship of the Ruxtons but accepted their volatile romance as a reality of life and not one that Lancaster Borough Police should become involved in. Black's urgent telephone call changed all that, as for the first time he became aware of the possible seriousness of what had been going on literally under his nose.

Black briefed Vann in detail, leaving the Lancaster chief stunned. He knew he was behind the game and had to catch up fast. His own reputation, and that of his force, depended on it. He requested that, as a priority, the most detailed description of the two missing women be obtained and sent to Dumfriesshire. It was 10 October; twelve crucial days had been lost. Despite this, Black was pleased with their progress, and for only the second time since the discovery at Gardenholme Linn felt they were following a positive line of enquiry. He was also confident of Lancaster's support. He judged that Vann was a man he could do business with.

That night he sent a message to Detective Superintendent Berry in Edinburgh:

Lancaster are only now stirring themselves, but I believe we will see some action soon.

Later that night an emergency meeting of the top team of investigators was convened in Edinburgh to discuss developments, Black laying out the facts known so far:

- It was believed the two people whose bodies had been found at Gardenholme Linn had been deposited there prior to 19 September and had therefore died before that date.
- While the gender was still uncertain the bodies could be those of two women.
- Newspapers that had wrapped some of the body parts were distributed only in the Morecambe/Lancaster area.
- The pathologists believed a degree of medical knowledge and skill had to be employed in the dissection of the bodies.
- Two women of roughly the same physical description as the bodies were missing from Lancaster.
- The husband and employer of the two women was an experienced doctor and surgeon, possessing all the necessary skills and knowledge to dissect the bodies.

The group paused to reflect on Black's summary of their knowledge after almost two weeks of supreme effort before Advocate Depute Jock Cameron, chairing the meeting, broke the silence:

All well and good, gentlemen. It looks as if this could be our breakthrough. Now we need evidence – best evidence.

CHAPTER 13

BEST EVIDENCE

The investigating team at Moffat, the pathologists in Edinburgh, and now even the police in Lancaster were agreed. It looked as if the body parts found at Gardenholme Linn on 29 September could well belong to the women missing from Lancaster since 14 September. It all seemed to add up. The state of decomposition of the body parts suggested a time of death which coincided with the disappearance of Bella Ruxton and Mary Rogerson. The reassembled skeletal remains indicated one taller, older person – one smaller and younger, again matching Bella and Mary. Then there were the newspaper wrappings dated 14 September, from a newspaper local only to Morecambe and Lancaster. This was the direct evidence, such as it was, though there was also the indirect evidence of the apparently professional dissection of the bodies and Dr Ruxton's expertise. But even to the most optimistic eye it wasn't nearly enough, and no one was more painfully aware of that than Advocate Depute Jock Cameron.

Cameron had the responsibility for assembling the evidence that the police had gathered then begin building a case for prosecution. His role, on behalf of his boss the Lord Advocate, was to prosecute in the name of the Crown and always to act in 'the public interest'. But he could only proceed if there was sufficient evidence. It was the well-established convention that the right to prosecute rested with the prosecutor 'where the body lay' – in other words, where the bodies were found – but Cameron knew that if evidence was uncovered to suggest the crimes had been committed elsewhere, then the jurisdiction may change. Eventually the case could be handed over to Lancaster, and in itself this could cause problems.

Of course, there had been cross-border cases before, but Cameron was acutely aware of the potential difficulties. The Scottish and English legal systems were quite different. From very different origins, gathering of evidence was different, as were police procedures. The pitfalls were obvious, and Advocate Depute Cameron was determined to avoid them. He was intensely proud of the Scottish legal system and would make sure that any case being prepared in Scotland was of the highest standard – and able to stand up in any court either side of the border. But this was a long way in the future; for now they had to build a case. Positively identifying the body parts as belonging to Bella and Mary was the first and by far the highest priority; without that they had nothing. Then there was the cause and time of death, also vital to a viable case. And it all had to make sense to a jury.

Cameron was aware that he was surrounded by some of the finest medical and scientific minds of their age, but their meetings were laden with complex medical phrases and scientific language. Like all good advocates, Cameron knew he had to translate this, and condense it to a strong, compelling narrative that a jury of ordinary folk would understand and believe. But as Advocate Cameron and the medical men pondered how they could positively identify the body parts and establish a time and cause of death, things were moving fast in Edinburgh, Dumfriesshire and Lancaster.

The same day it emerged that the bodies might be those of Bella Ruxton and Mary Rogerson, 9 October, Detective Inspector Sheed had learned that Bella had two sisters living in Edinburgh. Mrs Nelson, Bella's older sister, had readily recounted the long and troubled story of Bella's relationship with the glamorous and passionate Dr Buck Ruxton – the rows, the separations, the reconciliations – but neither she nor any of the family in Scotland knew where Bella was, only that she had apparently left home in the company of her nursemaid, Mary Rogerson, in mid-September.

Mrs Nelson had received a letter from Mary's father, worried about his daughter, and Bella's Lancaster friends had also been in touch, anxious for news of her. Finally, a few days earlier she had received the letter from Ruxton himself, implying that the two women had absconded to cover Mary Rogerson's pregnancy and requesting an urgent meeting in Edinburgh, late on 9 October. Mrs Nelson had been wary of meeting Ruxton on her own and did not want him to visit her home. She could not explain why, just an uneasy feeling, so knowing he would not be put off, had arranged to meet him with her other sister in her home at Heriot Mount.

Ruxton had travelled by train to Edinburgh and did not arrive until the evening. The meeting had been short and dominated by Ruxton, who, in a highly agitated state, frequently repeated the account of Bella's disappearance he had already set out in his letter. As he left to catch the last train back to Lancaster, the dumbstruck sisters, far from being reassured by the doctor's protestations, were becoming ever more suspicious and worried. Ruxton's dash to Edinburgh had misfired, but Bella's sisters did nothing. They did not want to get involved in her dramatic personal life and besides, what could they do?

The answer came in the form of Inspector Sheed. The two sisters told him all they knew and also gave him a detailed physical description of Bella. It was the first accurate description of Bella that the police in Scotland had.

On hearing Sheed's account of his interview with Bella's sisters, Chief Constable Black again telephoned Lancaster, urgently requesting a detailed physical description of Mary Rogerson. It was now clear to Black that the 'male' body could well be that of Bella, her sisters having described her as physically strong and raw-boned, with prominent facial features and teeth – characteristics more usually associated with males. This new information was quickly passed to Professor Glaister and his team, still pondering how to positively identify the body parts.

The next day, 10th October, was pivotal to the investigation. Things were at last starting to move in Lancaster, and Black and his team spent much of the day telephoning Scotland Yard and Lancashire County Constabulary, who had now moved in to assist the tiny Lancaster Borough Police. The head of Lancashire CID, the highly experienced Detective Chief Superintendent Gregson, was personally involved. They were behind the game and desperate to catch up.

Early in the afternoon Black received another important piece of news. During the previous few days, Sergeant Sloan, still working non-stop on pursuing his hunch about the Lancashire connection, had contacted all the police forces between Dumfriesshire and Lancaster seeking any information about suspicious incidents or vehicle movements. In the very quiet rural areas this was not as big a shot in the dark as it now sounds. Black later described the news:

Shortly after 1 p.m. a special messenger of the Cumberland and Westmoreland Constabulary delivered to me a communication from the Chief Constable of these counties covering reports by officers to the effect that at 12.45 p.m. on 17 September Dr Buck Ruxton had been involved in a very slight traffic accident in Kendal. The police had taken the number of his car and telephoned to the constable at Milnthorpe to stop him and take the usual particulars. The constable at Milnthorpe stopped Dr Ruxton at Milnthorpe crossroads at 1 p.m. and proceeded to take the usual particulars and examine the driving licence and insurance certificate. Ruxton had been wildly excited and it was noticed that his hand was bandaged.

Ruxton's worst fears had been realised – his momentary lapse of concentration and his aggressive driving of the hire car had come back to haunt him. If only he had stopped in Kendal and apologised to the cyclist, but once again his compulsive nature had got the better of him. Now the police investigating the find at Gardenholme Linn had a record of him in a suspicious location at a highly relevant time. Later that afternoon Black telephoned Advocate Depute Cameron, who was still in consultation with Professor Glaister and his team.

The pathologists needed recent photographs of the two women, shoes they had worn and their gloves to gauge the size of their hands. All distinguishing features had been removed from the bodies but perhaps there were other ways to identify them. Even the renowned Professor Glaister was in new territory, but it was a challenge that he and his team relished. They discussed the new information and decided that the time was right for a visit to Lancaster.

Black had been keen to travel south ever since the information about the newspapers had been revealed, but Cameron had resisted, thinking it was too early and hoping for more certainty about the identity of the bodies. Now he agreed that Black and his team should travel to Lancaster. The response from the English force had improved day on day, especially since Lancashire CID had become involved, but telephone calls and telex messages could only go so far – a face to face was now urgently required as more pieces of the puzzle fell into place.

Late that night Black telephoned his counterpart in Lancaster, Captain Vann, to arrange an urgent meeting. Vann told him that Dr Ruxton had called at his office that day in a state of great excitement, complaining about police attention, although there had been very little

– again vociferously declaring his innocence. Wisely, Vann made no mention of the Moffat investigation but patiently listened to Ruxton's rantings, making careful notes of his complaints. Unlike Black, Vann was not an experienced investigator, but he was an intelligent and determined man, and he knew how important all communication with Ruxton may turn out to be.

Black had updated him on the information about Ruxton's hire car having been stopped in Milnthorpe and, as subtly as he could, suggested that the car be traced and examined. Once again, he pressed Vann for a detailed description of Mary Rogerson and any photographs of Bella and Mary in the hands of the police. Stung into action, Vann immediately instructed that a full description of Mary Rogerson be sent by the overnight train to arrive in Dumfries at dawn the next day. Before the two chief constables hung up, it was arranged that Black and senior members of his team would travel to Lancaster the next day in order to fully discuss the case.

On 11 October, Black set out for Lancaster in the company of Inspector Strath and the Glasgow detectives, Lieutenants Ewing and Hammond, who were taking the role of senior investigators in the case. Among the numerous documents and photographs they carried with them as they drove the 100 miles south were the blouse and child's romper suit so carefully recovered from the body parts by Sergeant Sloan and so delicately cleaned and pressed by his wife Annie. They took the same road they believed the killer had taken through Kendal where the cyclist had been knocked from his bike, then Milnthorpe, where Ruxton had been stopped three weeks earlier.

As they drove down the quiet A roads through the beautiful autumn colours of rural Cumbria they could not help but wonder what vital clues to their case still lay decomposing on the roadside verges.

The party arrived in Lancaster late in the evening and were immediately ushered into the presence of Captain Vann, who was accompanied by Detective Chief Superintendent Gregson and Detective Inspector Green of Lancashire Constabulary.

It was the first time that Black and Vann had met, and they were both wary. Black needed Vann's active cooperation if he was to progress the case. He was very aware that he had absolutely no police powers in England. Advocate Depute Cameron had briefed him carefully the night before; there were significant jurisdictional differences, so the active assistance of the Lancaster Police was essential. At the same time, Black was less than impressed by Lancaster's efforts so far. He had made his frustrations clear in several telephone conversations but now that he was on their turf, he was at his diplomatic best.

Captain Vann was also nervous. He realised that his force had been slow to realise the significance of the disappearance of Bella Ruxton and Mary Rogerson. There were various mitigating circumstances but even so, as the chief of a small borough force always wary of being swallowed up in an amalgamation, the last thing he wanted was for his force, or himself, to be seen as inadequate. At the same time, he appreciated how much work had been done in Scotland. If he and his force were to make up lost ground, he needed Black's help.

Neither men need have worried though; after the formal introductions the meeting went smoothly. Black and Vann liked each other instantly. They were very similar: competent, professional and ambitious, and necessity brought the men together – they needed each other, and they both knew it. The long meeting took place in Vann's office at the front of the municipal building overlooking Dalton Square and Ruxton's house less than a hundred yards away, and over copious quantities of tea and sandwiches, the two parts of the investigation came together.

Black began by carefully rehearsing all the information known to date, sharing the numerous crime-scene photographs and laying out the two garments they had brought from Dumfriesshire. Vann and his force may have been slow to start but in the short time they had been truly investigating the local women's disappearance they had already made progress. Later, recounting the meeting, Black recalled that:

The Lancaster Police told us of statements made by charwomen and others regarding Ruxton having removed carpets heavily bloodstained from the staircase in his house and given to one of the women a suit of clothes, the waistcoat of which was so badly bloodstained that it had to be burned.

By this time, it was 1 a.m., but due to the urgency of the situation and to keep momentum, Black suggested that Mary Rogerson's parents be woken from their beds in Morecambe and immediately brought to Lancaster Police HQ. Black described the meeting:

We had Mr and Mrs Rogerson brought to the office and I then learned why we had so much difficulty in getting a proper description of the girl. The parents were very simple people and Mrs Rogerson was Mary's stepmother. Mrs Rogerson was shown the blouse and rather hesitatingly identified it as one she had bought at a church bazaar, made a repair in the left armpit and given to Mary. Her identification could not be called a good one.

We were told by the Rogersons that Mary had taken the Ruxton children on holiday in the month of June of that year to Grange-over-Sands where they lived with a Mrs Holme.

Mary had received from Mrs Holme a number of garments for her small brothers and sisters. These garments Mary had taken to Ruxton's house and she told her stepmother that she had received them. Mary's sister called one night at Ruxton's house and took some of the garments home; others she rejected and left at the doctor's house as rags.

Black's assessment of the Rogersons was unduly harsh. They were simple people, but it is worth remembering that they had been woken from their sleep in the dead of night and taken to a police station where they were questioned by a group of senior police officers about their beloved and long-missing daughter. Little wonder they were stressed and not at their most convincing as witnesses. Uncharacteristically for such a balanced and thoughtful man, Black also failed to reflect on the vital contribution already made by the Rogersons, for without their perseverance and the *Daily Record* story about the missing nursemaid, the investigation may still have been stalled in Scotland.

By the time the bewildered Rogersons were returned to their home it was the middle of the night, so it was decided everyone should get some rest and regroup in the morning to double-check all the information before planning a way forward.

In the early hours of the morning, as he struggled to sleep in the makeshift accommodation at Lancaster Police HQ, Black had a flash of inspiration and next morning, after a few hours' rest, he shared his thoughts with Captain Vann.

Black was in a difficult position – having driven the investigation since the discovery of the body parts, he had now lost control. He had no power in Lancaster other than the power of persuasion, but he still firmly believed that the two garments of children's clothing he had brought from Scotland held the key.

The Rogersons had failed to convincingly identify the blouse and romper suit, but that didn't mean they couldn't be identified. The meticulous home repairs to both garments made them distinctive; they would certainly be recognised by the person who had carried out the repairs. Black suggested that the child's garment – the romper suit – be shown urgently to Mrs Holme, the lady who Mary Rogerson had holidayed with that summer, and who had given Mary the bundle of old children's clothing for her younger siblings. Perhaps the romper suit found in the shambles of Gardenholme Linn had been among that bundle of old clothes taken to the Ruxton's house, rejected as suitable for further use and left there as rags.

It was a long shot, but Vann readily agreed, and, without delay, the Glasgow detective Lieutenant Ewing was dispatched to drive the 30 miles to the seaside resort of Grange-over-Sands, just across the border in Cumbria. There was no time to abide by the usual protocols and seek permission from Cumbria Police – this was urgent, and Black was desperate to know if his hunch was right. Waiting in Lancaster Police HQ, Black expected to hear back from Ewing by mid-morning, but as the hours passed he began to worry about the Glasgow detective. As Black put it:

He was absent so long that I became uneasy and began to conjure up visions of him lying by the roadside in the wreckage of my car and a bill for compensation to the Glasgow Police Authority for damage sustained by one of their leading investigators that I feared I might not be able to shoulder on to the Lancaster Police.

He needn't have worried – Ewing was delayed because he was doing a thorough job, and at last Black got news:

However, in the late afternoon he called me on the telephone and I could gather at once from his tone that his mission had been successful. He told me that Mrs Holme was a most intelligent person and that after a long interview in which she mentioned giving Mary Rogerson garments to take home to her small brothers and sisters, he had uncovered the romper suit and placed it before her when she immediately exclaimed, 'My Benny's knickers.'

Her identification, Mr Ewing said, was definite and without the slightest reservation – not at all like Mrs Rogerson's identification of the blouse the previous evening.

She said she had put the garment on her child's body times without number and washed it repeatedly and had threaded a fresh piece of elastic through the top and tied it in a very badly made knot. She identified the elastic then in the romper suit, also the knot securing it, saying she always made knots in that way and demonstrated the fact; she produced three kinds of elastic which she had in the house and selected one which she said was part of the piece in the garment.

Expressing my satisfaction at receiving this highly important evidence I asked Mr Ewing to hasten back to Lancaster. I informed Mr Vann of the successful issue of the visit to Mrs Holme and gave it as my opinion that there was now sufficient information in our possession to warrant our calling upon Ruxton to account for his movements from the date of the disappearance of his wife and maid and to hear from him in detail as to the manner of her going.

Black was right – the children's romper, or knickers as Mrs Holme described them, was the first piece of direct evidence connecting Ruxton's house at 2 Dalton Square to the recovered body parts at Gardenholme Linn. Mrs Holme's identification of the garment and, particularly her repairs to it being unequivocal, the circumstances of the recovery of the romper suit by Sergeant Sloan well documented and corroborated in Scotland.

For all Black's strength of view though, it was Vann's decision. He had to consider the evidence and weigh in the balance whether to wait for more or question Ruxton now. He knew that if he acted too early he could damage the case, but on the other hand he was being pressed by the senior detectives to urgently get access to the house, where they believed there may be vital forensic evidence.

Captain Vann quickly decided that the time was right; they now had hard evidence and enough time had been wasted. His force had been slow to react to the missing women and now he was determined to redress the balance and act dynamically.

Once the plans about the next steps had been agreed, Black made a private telephone call back to Sergeant Sloan at Moffat Police Station. Swearing him to secrecy, Black told Sloan that the romper suit so carefully retrieved and preserved by the sergeant's wife had been positively identified as being connected to the home and possession of Dr Buck Ruxton. That night, for the first time in the two weeks since the horrific discovery at Gardenholme Linn, Sloan would sleep peacefully, knowing his efforts had not been in vain.

Directly across the square, Ruxton had been watching the greatly increased activity at the police station. It was now almost a month since the horror of that weekend in mid-September. From the desperate panic of those first few days and the nightmare of the journeys north, life had settled down. The children still asked for their mother and nursemaid, of course, but seemed to accept his explanation that they had gone on holiday. The neighbours and friends also seemed to accept the story of the two women running off for whatever reason. The surgery was busy, and many patients and neighbours obviously felt sorry for the hard-working doctor, left to bring up three young children alone. Ruxton sensed their sympathy and it reassured him; he knew he had a lot of public support and it gave him confidence.

The local police had called a couple of times, but they didn't seem overly suspicious. Only the Rogersons were a cause for concern. He knew they hadn't believed the story of Mary's alleged pregnancy and were alarmed at her lack of contact. But they were a poor, simple family; he was sure the authorities would always believe him, an eminent, professional man, over them.

It had all been going so well, but in the last few days he had noticed a marked increase in people coming and going at the police station – he could see the front door from his consulting room. Men he didn't recognise, who all looked senior, in plain clothes. He knew all the local policemen and they definitely weren't local.

Strange cars stood outside the police station as well, and the lights of Chief Constable Vann's office burned late into the night. Ruxton had cause to worry, he had made some elementary mistakes - some could be explained as the natural reactions of a distraught husband, but the incident with the cyclist in Kendal could not.

Still, he was self-aware enough to realise his shortcomings – his high-strung nature, inability to remain cool under pressure – so over the last few nights he had carefully prepared a written statement, a comprehensive account of his version of the circumstances of Bella and Mary's disappearance. If and when questioned by the police, he would simply refer to the statement and elaborate no further. It reassured his highly organised personality to know he had this document to fall back on.

He had also felt compelled to approach his charladies, Mrs Oxley and Mrs Hampshire, repeatedly reminding them of the sequence of events that weekend of 14 September. Instinctively he knew this was a mistake, but his compulsion drove him to school them, badger them into agreeing with his version of that fateful weekend.

The call came shortly after 9 p.m. on Saturday, 12 October – almost two weeks to the day from the time Sergeant Sloan had been struggling up the banking of Gardenholme Linn carrying the putrefied body parts. Vann had decided he could delay no further, but still respecting the doctor's status, he telephoned Ruxton and casually asked him to step across to the police station as he would like to have a further talk with him about Mrs Ruxton's disappearance.

Black later described the scene that followed:

> At 9.25 p.m. Ruxton arrived in Mr Vann's room where there were assembled besides Mr Vann two of his officers, Mr Ewing, Inspector Strath and myself. Ruxton, a typical Eurasian, looked worried, and in the interview which followed he frequently lost all control of himself; he had a typewritten statement with him which he often consulted, and he talked faster than I ever heard anyone talk, his voice sometimes rising to a scream.

From Black's account this most important interview was obviously both unplanned and unstructured. No doubt Vann felt pressurised. All the progress on the investigation so far had been made north of the border, and he would have been desperate to seize back the initiative in what was almost certainly becoming his case.

Black's observation of Ruxton's behaviour is also interesting. The casual racism of his description of Ruxton as 'a typical Eurasian' can be placed in the context of the day, but his observation of Ruxton's 'loss of control' was more important. Despite his mental rehearsals and his written 'script' the fiery nature that had dogged his life and led him to the catastrophe of 14 September was still beyond his control.

Black, now in the role of observer, made careful notes of the proceedings to feed back to Advocate Depute Cameron. At that moment, the bulk of the investigation and the evidence lay in Scotland. Jurisdictional issues would be dealt with by the senior law officers of Scotland and England, but in the meantime, while no longer in the driving seat, Black was a very interested observer.

Black's detailed notes, taken at the time, described what followed:

Mr Vann, according to the English method of procedure, committed to writing in longhand every question put to Ruxton and the answers received – or at least what was extracted from the terrific torrent of words which fell from Ruxton's lips and which he agreed should be taken as the answers to the questions.

This took a very long time indeed and Ruxton begged to be allowed to go and to come back about 9 in the morning after he had had a rest.

This request was not granted and twice during the long sitting refreshments in the shape of tea or coffee and sandwiches were provided. It was a good thing that Ruxton was not a man who took drink – he was a teetotaller and non-smoker – for during the first part of the interview, that is before he was cautioned, had he asked for alcoholic refreshment instead of coffee, and had he got it, what capital might his counsel not have made of it? Overcoming the man's resistance by plying him with strong drink and thereafter extracting a statement from him would have been seen to be improper.

The questions and answers were being typed page by page by clerks in another room and, when finished, the document was handed to Ruxton with the request that he go over it, make any alterations he desired and sign it. It took him 20 minutes to check the statement and frequently he lay back in his chair and audibly pondered over the value of a word or phrase, making changes to suit him.

He was then cautioned, and further questions were put to him bearing more directly on matters which ultimately figured in evidence – the bloodstained carpets, suit of clothes, etc. – and these were also laboriously committed to writing, with the answers.

Finally, at 7.25 a.m. on Sunday, 13 October, he was charged with the murder of Mary Rogerson only – the romper mainly decided this – and he was locked up.

Looking at this description of the interview process even eighty years on is highly instructive. Unplanned and unstructured, it would not have passed a modern test of fairness. Ruxton had been coaxed to the police station and into a suspect interview with no less than six interrogators. The interview lasted through the night without rest, a caution only being given towards the end. Intriguingly, while Black makes mention of the potential legal pitfalls of giving Ruxton alcohol, there is no mention of the offer of legal representation whatsoever. Even by the standards of the day this was a very unprofessional episode. It speaks to the enthusiasm, determination and lack of experience of Captain Vann; the experienced detectives present must have been uncomfortable to have been part of it.

It was fortunate that in the end, the interview played no significant part in the subsequent trial. On the positive side, the interview and arrest of Ruxton broke the deadlock and, most importantly, gave unrestricted access to Ruxton's house at 2 Dalton Square, which the detectives were confident had secrets to reveal.

It was time for Black and the Dumfriesshire Constabulary to step back into a supporting role. There was much work still to be done in Scotland but Captain Vann and the police in Lancashire were now in control. The transition was, however, far from simple. Lancashire did not have the forensic capability of the Glasgow detectives or the specialist photographic skill of the Edinburgh Police, and Vann knew that to complete the investigation he would need to keep the services of these specialists. Black described the process thus:

I telephoned Mr Cameron (Advocate Depute) whom I had previously advised of my visit to Lancaster and who was eagerly awaiting the result and informed him that we in Dumfriesshire had reached the end of our enquiry and that Dr Ruxton was in custody on a capital charge.

Mr Vann, having got in touch with the Director of Public Prosecutions, obtained permission to engage the Glasgow fingerprint and Edinburgh photographic experts who were already on the case.

This entirely logical move broke with a long-established convention, in the scientific investigation of crime in England and Wales. Up to that time only Scotland Yard had provided forensic expertise, and the science of fingerprints in particular was seen as Scotland Yard's alone. The Ruxton case was to break many old conventions, however, which were to have profound effects as the case developed.

Before leaving Lancaster the next afternoon, Black and his party visited Ruxton's home, where Lieutenant Hammond, the Glasgow fingerprint specialist, had already set to work, starting with Mary Rogerson's bedroom. With his fingerprint powder, he was trying to bring up Mary's fingerprints from the furniture and her sparse possessions. He had a theory that he wanted to test and which he hoped would help identify the young woman.

As he was driven home, Black carried with him the best photographs of Bella and Mary that could be found, together with shoes and gloves belonging to the two women. Few photographs existed of Mary. Poor servant girls did not get photographed, and all they had was a small, smudged image, cropped from a family snap, which showed a pleasant, round-faced girl with bobbed brown hair. In contrast, there were numerous photographs of Bella, and Black had chosen the most striking – a three-quarter head and shoulders profile showing her strong features, her firm jawline, and her prominent nose and teeth. It was a high-quality portrait photograph taken earlier in 1935 and Bella was dressed in her finest, including a tiara.

The photographs, shoes and gloves and ongoing information from the examination of the house at 2 Dalton Square were quickly passed to Professor Glaister and his team at Edinburgh University. The next episode of the investigation would be played out there.

CHAPTER 14

NEW SCIENCE

Telephone calls followed by formal letters between Jock Cameron at the Scottish Crown Office and the Director of Public Prosecutions in England established the protocol for transferring the case from the jurisdiction of Scotland to England. It had already been agreed that the detectives from Glasgow and Edinburgh would stay on the investigation and also quickly agreed that the forensic work would remain in Edinburgh, under the supervision of Professors Glaister and Brash. This made good sense – the initial work had been done in Edinburgh and the practical difficulties of transferring the special tanks and their contents to another location would have been immense. Despite this, it must have been a difficult decision, not least because of the enormous influence of the most famous pathologist of his day in England, Sir Bernard Spilsbury.

Spilsbury was the dominant figure in English pathology during the 1920s and 1930s. He had led the forensic investigations in the notorious case of Dr Crippen and numerous other famous murders. He was seen as infallible by the British public, many juries and probably himself, but this reputation was not shared by all in his profession. Sydney Smith, his contemporary, once described him as, 'very brilliant and very famous but fallible and very obstinate.'

This perfectly sums up his character – Spilsbury was brilliant but feigned omnipotence. Professors Glaister, Brash and especially Smith were also eminent men but humble enough to recognise their own fallibilities. Spilsbury had no such humility. He also had an eye for the headlines, famous cases with which to further burnish his public reputation. He would certainly have tried his utmost to get his hands on the Ruxton case, though the surviving papers do not reveal how this was avoided, and the memoirs of Glaister and Smith are silent on the subject. Perhaps it was simply expediency and the fact that the reputation of Scottish forensic science, coupled with the names of

Glaister, Brash and Smith, also enjoyed a worldwide reputation.

And as far as the investigation was concerned it was still all to do. For despite Ruxton's near-hysterical interview and rambling statement, he had admitted nothing, nor had he revealed any special knowledge that might incriminate him. Later, detectives would wonder if he really had lost as much control as it seemed. Was there method in his madness? Considering Ruxton's character it seems unlikely; he had lost control of his emotions too often for it to be faked. More likely is that, despite his loss of control, he had managed to roughly stick to the script that he had prepared for himself or even that, after the passage of two weeks, he had simply convinced himself of his innocence, blanked out the nightmare of that weekend in September and begun to believe his own cover story. Either way it meant that the successful prosecution of the case rested on whatever evidence Professors Glaister and Brash could discover. For the first time, the success of a major case in England depended on forensic experts from Scotland.

Professors Glaister and Brash, together with Dr Millar and their team, were only too aware of the unique position they were in and the weight of responsibility they carried. In response, over the next three months they were to achieve a number of remarkable developments in forensic science, landmark advances greater than in any criminal investigation before or since. The developments would come in fingerprints, entomology and superimposition, each representing a breakthrough in learning and forensic science that would benefit generations of investigators that followed.

The positive identification of the bodies was still the major problem. The evidence of the romper suit was key to the arrest and detention of Ruxton, but without unequivocal identification of the bodies, murder would never be proved. In the present day, DNA analysis would have made it simple, but in 1935 with the limitations of blood typing, fingerprints were the obvious choice.

The technique of identification by fingerprint comparison emerged in the late nineteenth century as a development of the theory of anthropometry, the belief that human beings are unique in their dimensions, height, foot and hand size, etc., and therefore by comparing and analysing these dimensions, identity could be established. While the general theory of anthropometry was impractical and always peripheral to criminal investigation, the technique of fingerprint analysis spread quickly and developed as a distinct specialisation. The classification of fingerprint patterns – the friction ridges found on the skin on the palm side of the fingers, thumbs and palms of the hands and the toes of the feet – were, however, only accepted as unique in the early years of the 20th century, a relatively short time before the Ruxton case, and even then, courts and juries were sometimes sceptical. The success of fingerprint evidence always depended on the ability of the expert witness to convince, to paint a picture of the loops, whorls and arches and interpret their findings so that judge and jury accepted the expert's conclusion.

Expert testimony was often theatrical and keenly followed by the popular press, hungry for details of this 'new science'. As with most developments in policing in the UK, fingerprint analysis was championed first by the London Metropolitan Police at Scotland Yard, who established one of the world's first fingerprint bureaux, which trained and retained specialist fingerprint officers as well as an archive of the fingerprints of criminals and unidentified marks found at the scenes of crime.

So specialised was the technique and so fragile was the evidential credibility of fingerprints that for the first decades of the 20th century only Scotland Yard were thought capable of practising the art. Many police forces, even large ones, still had no specialist criminal investigation departments and with low levels of serious crime could not justify them. This meant that when a serious crime was committed they had to call in the Yard. For decades in the first half of the 20th century, Scotland Yard sent small teams of specialist detectives to help their non-Metropolitan colleagues and blind them with their brilliance. Thus was borne the worldwide reputation of the Scotland Yard detective. It was a reputation that was jealously guarded by the Met, as was the science of fingerprints.

But by the 1930s things were changing – larger city forces had the crime to justify specialist detective and fingerprint bureaux, they could not depend on the Met and so fingerprint bureaux began to spring up across the country. Even so, the credibility of the Met was still considered vital, and well into the 1930s only Met fingerprint officers had given evidence in court to support fingerprint evidence.

In Scotland, Edinburgh and the City of Glasgow Police had operated a rudimentary fingerprint examination system since the 1890s, but it was only on the arrival of Chief Constable Percy Sillitoe in 1931 that the first real fingerprint bureau came to Scotland. Leading that effort was Detective Lieutenant Bertie Hammond, the man Sillitoe had headhunted for the job.

Hammond was a complete professional who, over only four years, had built the Glasgow Fingerprint Bureau to a position where it was second only to the Met. His system of record-keeping and the skill he brought in the examination of scenes of crime for fingerprints, together with his system of matching by crime type and characteristics, led to a rapid improvement in the solution of crimes like housebreaking, the menace of big urban areas like Glasgow. It was exactly as Sillitoe had planned and further enhanced his reputation as a crime-busting chief constable. Sillitoe placed his absolute trust in Hammond and used his success as justification to continue investment in Hammond's expansion of scientific methods of detecting crime.

When Glasgow got the call to help tiny Dumfriesshire following the find at Gardenholme Linn, Sillitoe had sent his best men, among them Lieutenants Ewing and Hammond, the best investigator and fingerprints officer in Glasgow.

It wasn't quite the selfless act that it first seemed. Sillitoe wanted to encourage the practice of professional investigation and scientific methods, and what better way to spread the message than to let his best men work their magic in notable cases. It was obvious from the start that the find at Gardenholme Linn was just such a case.

Inspector Hammond had attended the makeshift mortuary at Moffat the day after the discoveries and saw straight away that the fingertips of one of the bodies had been cut off, removing the fingerprints.

Ruxton was of course forensically aware; he was a keen student of scientific methods, and as a police doctor he knew the basics of fingerprinting. He had deliberately sliced off Bella's fingertips and the palms of her hands as part of his efforts to disguise her. But he hadn't done the same to Mary's. In the interim he had badly cut his working hand and lacked the dexterity to carry out the delicate work. Like the other remains, he had hoped Mary's severed hands would be carried away by vermin. Instead, severed from the arms and tied together with string, they had been taken to the makeshift mortuary at Moffat.

Hammond observed that they appeared to come from the smaller body, first identified as the young woman. The fingers on these hands were complete but the inspector was dismayed to see that the decomposition process had already led the outer layer of skin, the epidermis, to peel off the fingers. Up to that time all fingerprints had been identified from the ridges on the epidermis, but Hammond was not to be deterred; he believed that the underlying skin, the dermis, could also show the loops, whorls and arches sufficiently to identify the sixteen points of comparison needed for a positive identification, and once the body parts were back at Edinburgh University, he asked one of the local fingerprint men to take impressions from the decomposing fingers. It wasn't easy – the fingers had to be soaked in warm water to remove the wrinkles, but eventually prints were taken.

The results were not ideal, but Hammond felt that they were good enough; if he found a good fingerprint for comparison, he thought he could achieve a positive identification. When the investigation began to point to Lancaster, Hammond was eager to join the travelling party; above all he wanted to get access to any house or possessions of the suspected victims, thinking he might be able to find good quality prints – good enough to compare and identify.

Immediately following Ruxton's arrest, Hammond, taking a local officer as corroboration, got access to the house at 2 Dalton Square. It was the early hours of the morning, not the time to begin a forensic examination, but the lieutenant didn't want to start his examination yet. First, he wanted to sketch a plan of the house.

The forensic examination of the house at 2 Dalton Square would be thorough and systematic. In time, Professor Glaister and his team from Edinburgh would join them and the house would be taken apart, the main staircase dismantled and removed to reveal bloodstains of a type and quantity that would later impress the jury. Once an accurate sketch had been made and numerous photographs of the interior taken, Hammond would start his search for fingerprints to match the specimens that had been taken from the severed hands found at Gardenholme Linn. From the rough descriptions of the two women, Hammond thought his best chance was in the maid's bedroom on the top floor of the house.

Mary's room lay just as she had left it that fateful night of 14 September; her few possessions – comb, hairbrush and hand mirror – lay on a small dresser, and her few clothes hung in a small wardrobe.

Hammond got to work immediately on the articles and furniture he thought most likely to carry Mary's fingerprints – the mirrors and brass bedstead. Then as now fingerprints were detected by using a small, soft brush to spread fine powder, mercury or graphite across the surface of an article, hoping it would adhere to the fingerprints left by the sweat attached to the ridges on the skin.

After eleven days of fastidious work, Hammond had identified numerous full and partial prints that he carefully photographed and enlarged, making comparisons with the impressions he had taken from the dismembered hands. He would take them back to his laboratory in Glasgow for detailed examination to try to identify the sixteen points of comparison he needed for a positive identification. He was hopeful, and when the full examination was completed he was proved right.

He identified thirty finger impressions from plates, a glass decanter and other items that Mary would have handled. Some had only ten points of comparison, but others had as many as twenty, well above the sixteen points required for a positive identification. It was proof positive – the prints found at 2 Dalton Square matched the finger impressions taken from the partially decomposed severed hands at Moffat.

The comparison had been difficult; dermal impressions were not as well defined as epidermal ridges, but using all his skill and experience, Hammond did it. It was important that the identification be verified independently, and in another unprecedented move, the prints were sent to the FBI Fingerprint Bureau in Washington DC for verification – not Scotland Yard.

As Glaister later explained:

As this was the first time identification had been attempted on a dermal print in the British Isles, enlarged copies were forwarded to the Director of the FBI with the request that these prints be examined by three experts and a decision given.

The American experts concurred. Their unanimous verdict was that the prints matched.

The fact that the distant FBI were used to verify the prints rather than Scotland Yard is surprising. Perhaps it was a deliberate snub to the all-powerful Met. More likely it reflected the long relationship between J. Edgar Hoover, Director of the FBI, and Sillitoe – or perhaps it was because it added an international lustre to what was always going to be controversial evidence.

It was, however, a breakthrough.

It was the first time dermal prints had been used to positively identify fingerprints and it proved beyond doubt that one of the bodies found at Gardenholme Linn was little Mary Rogerson. The fingerprints matched the hands and the hands matched the arms of the smaller female body that Professor Brash was painstakingly reassembling in Edinburgh. It was a huge step forward in the investigation, proof beyond doubt that they were on the right track and a personal triumph for Lieutenant Hammond, who had pursued his theory and in so doing advanced the science and practice of fingerprinting.

Hammond's identification was a huge boost for the team of pathologists at Edinburgh University, but they still had major problems concerning the identification of Bella Ruxton and the determination of a time and cause of death.

The cause of death was fairly easily discovered – evidence of blunt-force injury was found on both skulls and signs of strangulation detected on the one neck recovered (Bella's). Time of death was more difficult yet vitally important. It had to be proved that the two women had died close to the time they had gone missing from Lancaster. Dr Ruxton's cover story was always that the women had run off that weekend. Proving they had been dead from about the time of their disappearance would throw doubt on that story and point directly at him.

Even today with all the brilliance of 21st century science, establishing a time of death is inexact – there are simply too many variables. This is true of all bodies where death is not actually witnessed, and more so if the bodies or body parts have lain outside, exposed to weather, or insect or animal life. A child's body left in a warm environment can decompose to skeletal remains in days, while an older person left in a cool or cold location can remain virtually intact for weeks or even months.

The time elapsed between death and the discovery of the body is known as the post-mortem interval, and in the Ruxton case it was vitally important that it be established.

Ruxton had planned for this as well. He knew that dissecting the bodies would aid decomposition; disfiguring the body parts and keeping them in the relative warmth of the house at Dalton Square, even for forty-eight hours, also assisted the process. Ruxton hoped that the body parts would not be found, but he was confident that if they were it would appear that the bodies were not theirs as the post-mortem interval was far greater than the last public sightings of Bella and Mary. But as in so many calculations, he had reckoned without the expertise of the Scottish forensic scientists. As a postgraduate student in Scotland, he had attended the lectures of Professor Glaister and had marvelled at his brilliance, but now he had underestimated him.

Glaister had long been interested in the study of forensic entomology – the study of insect life, and particularly the life cycle of the fly, in relation to a criminal investigation. He believed that the full understanding of this specialist field could unlock the mystery of the post-mortem interval.

In theory, it was very simple. After the human body expires it begins to decompose, the natural process in which the components of the body break down. Almost immediately, flies begin to infest the body. Like decomposition, this of course depends on a number of variables – temperature, exposure to the air, etc., but generally very soon after death flies and insects will find a corpse and the females will begin to lay eggs in protected areas such as the orifices of the body – the eyes, ears and genitals. In a strict time cycle, the eggs hatch into maggots or fly larvae that feast on the body and grow rapidly.

As early as the nineteenth century, the French entomologist, Mengin, had described the life cycle of different insects and how they could be used to approximate the post-mortem interval even after several months.

As a junior pathologist, Glaister had studied Mengin's research, and while on his many sojourns abroad, he had experimented with the process to prove the technique. After trial and error, he had become convinced that the study of the life cycle of the common fly was a valuable tool in criminal investigation. Thereafter, at crime scenes he always insisted on gathering samples of the flora and fauna from the surrounding area, but maggots were his specialty – maggots that he searched for and carefully gathered and preserved until they could give up their secrets.

Glaister had no difficulty finding maggots at Gardenholme Linn –

the body parts had been seething with them, and a good number of prime samples had been preserved and taken with the body parts to the Department of Pathology at Edinburgh University. While Glaister was convinced of the potential value of the maggots, he was not a specialist in their life cycle. He did, however, know a man who was. Dr Alexander Mearns of the Institute of Hygiene at Glasgow University was called in to help. With Glaister, Brash and Smith, Dr Mearns was one of a remarkable cohort of medics and scientists working in Scotland during the 1930s. By coincidence it was a time when cutting-edge work was being done in a number of branches of forensic and public health science and Dr Mearns was at the forefront.

His position at the Institute of Hygiene gave him rich opportunities to study at close quarters the many public health and hygiene challenges posed by the crowded slums of the East End, where the unsanitary conditions endured by many of its population still led to outbreaks of typhoid fever and the old killer diseases of children – diphtheria and scarlet fever – still claimed too many victims. Dr Mearns spent his life battling these diseases of poverty and squalor, and it shaped him as a highly regarded original thinker, so it was no surprise that Glaister, pursuing his interest in forensic entomology, called on him for help.

It was a chance for Mearns to do pioneering work and use a new entomological technique. He would determine the age of the samples recovered by Glaister at Gardenholme Linn once he had first identified the exact species of fly that had infested the body parts.

He was fortunate that he had plenty of samples to choose from and quickly established that the maggots gathered were those of one of the commonest blowflies in Britain – the horse fly, bluebottle or greenbottle. He then dissected samples and, after microscopic examination, identified them positively as bluebottle larvae. This was good news – the bluebottle had highly specialised sense organs which allowed them to locate dead organic matter far quicker than other insects and flies.

Another characteristic of the bluebottle is that they do not return to re-lay eggs in the same place. This meant that ageing the maggots could determine fairly accurately how long the body parts had lain in the ravine at Gardenholme Linn. Each larval type has its own life cycle, which differs from a few hours to several days depending on the species, but by dissection and comparison with samples he had grown for just such comparability studies, Mearns established exactly where the samples were in their life cycle. He concluded that the total life cycle of the largest, most developed larvae taken from the remains could not have exceeded twelve days. Allowing for 24 to thirty-six hours at most for the bluebottles to find the body parts meant that the remains had been dumped in the ravine at Gardenholme Linn twelve to fourteen days before they were discovered. That calculated the date of deposition as 16 or 17 September, two days after Bella and Mary were last seen.

Dr Mearns' work was ground-breaking, the first use of forensic entomology in the UK, and it vindicated Glaister's belief that the study of insects and flies had an important place in the scientific methods that aided criminal investigation. Later, techniques would be refined and forensic entomology would become mainstream, but that distinct branch of forensic science had its first application due to the skill of Dr Mearns, the vision of Professor Glaister and the accidental participation of the humble and utterly predictable bluebottle.

Now the forensic team at Edinburgh and Lieutenant Hammond at Lancaster had answered two of the three questions asked of them. Mary Rogerson's identity had been confirmed by the first identification of dermal fingerprints, and the post-mortem interval had been established by Dr Mearns and Professor Glaister. But there was one important outstanding issue – the identification of Bella Ruxton. Chastened by his initial misidentification of the remains as a male and a female, Professor Brash had been putting his anatomical expertise to good use and by the time of Ruxton's arrest had reassembled what parts he could into two bodies.

It had been an exacting job; many lumps of flesh had been undistinguishable, and even after the most detailed examination 43 out of the total of 86 pieces of soft tissue could not be identified as coming from one body or another. To add to the confusion, limbs wrapped together in the same cloth or paper were from different bodies. It was as if a careful and calculated attempt had been made to deceive and mislead throughout. But despite the extraordinary lengths gone to, the flesh and severed limbs were still giving up some important secrets. It was noted that a long strip of flesh had been cut off one of the legs where Mary had a prominent birthmark, and one of the feet had been badly disfigured where Bella had a noticeable bunion, the same one Ruxton had cut his hand removing.

The smaller body now identified as that of Mary Rogerson was as complete as it could be, although missing its torso and spine, and Brash was content that the pieces he had matched. The risk was still that body parts had been mixed up, but the cut marks on the wrists, alongside the identified fingerprints, matched the arms, and rubber casts of the feet and hands fitted the shoes and gloves recovered from Mary's room. Crucially, the head that had first been identified as having male characteristics had part of the neck attached and this stump matched exactly the stump on the one torso recovered – a torso that was obviously female. It was proof positive that the two bodies were female. Brash checked and double-checked for there could be no room for error. Now they could concentrate on identifying Bella.

This was much more difficult than identifying Mary. In one sense it was simple – the two women had disappeared together so who else could it be. But all knew it was vital for any forthcoming trial, where unequivocal identification of the bodies would be key. That was the difference between presumptive and positive identification. Presuming that the second body was Bella was plain common sense, but positive identification required so much more – it had to be science-based and unimpeachable.

The problem then was that the body thought to be Bella's was incomplete; missing important parts, the fingerprints removed. From the start, Brash and Glaister had realised that they had to concentrate on the two heads. Now they knew that one was definitely Mary's, they could concentrate on the other, to somehow prove it was Bella's.

The head was in very poor condition, little more than a skull with strands of scalp and flesh attached but no distinguishing features – the nose, eyes, ears and chin were missing, the lips had been cut off and most of the teeth had been removed. In a way, Brash and his team admired the work; whoever was responsible had done a thorough job in completely anonymising the skull. But Brash was not to be defeated. Like Glaister he considered this case a supreme professional challenge, and the knowledge that he was now working on a job in the jurisdiction and under the critical eye of the famous Sir Bernard Spilsbury only stiffened his resolve.

Professor Brash had long been interested in the then obscure field of forensic anthropology, defined as the identification of human remains and the analysis of unrecognisable remains with a view to identifying them. Brash believed that using the skull believed to belong to Bella and the good-quality photographs of her, he might achieve a positive identification by superimposing a photographic negative of the skull over a photographic negative of the photograph of Bella. It was an exacting process that would require pioneering work, the technique never having been used as evidence in a criminal trial, but the idea was an old one.

As early as 1883, attempts had been made to compare a skull with a portrait of its owner, then in 1909, an Austrian anatomist using this method succeeded in identifying the skull of Austrian Composer, Joseph Haydn, 100 years after his death. But this was a step further – the first skull-to-photograph superimposition ever attempted in a forensic setting.

Although the photographs of Mary in life were of very poor quality compared with the professional portraits of Bella, Professor Brash was determined to attempt superimposition with both skulls.

The first stage was to clean the skulls thoroughly so as to identify and match the different anatomical landmarks of each one. It was another gruesome job for the lab technicians at the Department of Anatomy. Using the finest of scalpels, the grey and blackened flesh that remained was stripped from the skulls and what remained was removed in a mild acid bath. Maggots were routinely used for such clean-up jobs, but with the bodies having been preserved in formalin, even they would have found the remaining flesh on the skulls unpalatable.

Once thoroughly cleaned it was seen that the skulls were very different, quite distinct from each other in terms of both general features and proportions. Bella's long, thin face and pointed features were evident, as was Mary's smaller, rounder face. It was a good start – whatever else; the two skulls were clearly identifiable as belonging to their individual owners.

But this was not nearly enough; the skulls had then to be orientated to match the existing photographs of Bella and Mary. It wasn't sufficient that an expert eye could see the similarities. A jury of ordinary folk had to be convinced, and this was completely new evidential territory, certain to be robustly contested by any defence barrister. To aid the precise orientation, both skulls were mounted on swivels so that they could be moved into different positions to match the life photographs of the women. Then painstakingly, so as to eliminate all risk of error, Professor Brash and his team set to work establishing basic characteristics before moving on to identify skeletal peculiarities and unique characteristics which could be matched to similar features in the life photographs.

The theory was that in the same way that people have unique fingerprints, no two people's identical, so faces and the skulls beneath them are also unique, giving everyone, even seemingly identical twins, slightly different features. Bella's long, thin face and the large teeth that made her upper jaw protrude slightly were already highly distinctive. Brash felt that with this advantage, he and his team had a good chance of a convincing superimposition.

After the skulls had been mounted, the first step was to get expert help from a forensic odontologist, to try to recreate the missing teeth from the socket sizes and angles. Detailed examination quickly revealed that the teeth had been forced from their sockets sometime after death, a troublesome task no one would have undertaken unless necessary to disguise the identity of the skull.

With the odontologist's work done, the next step was to get highly specialised photographic assistance.

By the 1930s, photography had been commonplace for eighty years, yet high-quality specialist photography was still a rare technical skill. Fortunately for Brash, such expert help was near at hand.

For some years Edinburgh City Police had invested in training specialist officers in crime-scene photography. It was part of Edinburgh's contribution to Percy Sillitoe's drive to improve scientific methods of detection in Scotland. Foremost among Edinburgh's expert photographers was Detective Constable Kenneth Stobie. He was typical of the new breed of specialists in the police, thoroughly trained in house, with a complete devotion to his speciality that had made him a true expert in his field. Hand-picked by DI Sheed, he quickly joined the team with firm ideas about how to get the best result.

Brash and Stobie knew that they would have to produce as many superimposed skull-to-photograph examples as they could in order to convince a court, but equally they knew that one striking image could go a long way to swaying a jury. All the photographs of Mary Rogerson were poor, but there were far better images of Bella, and by far the best was the recent portrait photograph that Chief Constable Black had brought from Lancaster. The minute Detective Stobie saw it he knew it was his best chance.

The portrait photograph was a very high-quality, formal, black-and-white, head-and-shoulder shot of Bella, dressed in her finery, including a diamond tiara. It showed clearly her strong jawline, prominent nose and cheekbones, her large teeth and distinctive brows. The photograph was a three-quarter shot, which is to say she is looking just to the right of the camera. But the main reason Stobie chose this particular photograph was because of its superb quality. He knew he would have to reproduce it several times and that he could do it without great loss of quality. Fortunately, the original negative still existed and the photographic studio in Lancaster that had taken the photograph was happy to hand it over to the police.

But first the skull had to be prepared - the eye sockets, nose holes and tooth sockets filled with clay so as not to cause shadowing on subsequent images. Then Brash and Stobie carefully orientated the skull on its swivel mount so that it was angled in exactly the same way as the portrait photograph. Stobie had set up a temporary photographic studio in the anatomy lab and he now carefully re-photographed the mounted skull. The original negative was then magnified to life size to match the photograph of the skull. The images both in negative form were then overlaid using the eye sockets, nose holes and mouth to align them.

As Brash and Stobie stood back to examine the result, they were both stunned by the striking picture before them. It was astonishing, an ethereal image showing the negative of the skull matching perfectly the portrait of Bella on which it was superimposed. The two men were delighted. Brash's vision and Stobie's technical skill had combined to produce a piece of visual evidence that no jury could ignore.

The threshold of proof in a criminal trial is beyond reasonable doubt, and in the opinion of Brash and his team, that standard had been met. It was beyond all reasonable doubt that one of the heads found at Gardenholme Linn, a head that matched a body, was that of Bella Ruxton.

The process was repeated with the other skull, believed to be

Mary Rogerson's, but the result was nowhere near as good. The only photographs of Mary were of such poor quality, blurred holiday snaps, that no clear superimposition could be made. Some scale was achieved by measuring a garden gate in the background of one of the snaps, but it wasn't convincing.

Brash was disappointed; he had hoped to identify both women by superimposition, but the priority had always been Bella. Mary had already been identified by fingerprint, so both women had now been positively identified, and a cause of death and post-mortem interval – a time of death – established.

The pathologists and anatomists at Edinburgh University could be well satisfied – with the help of police specialists in fingerprints and photography, they had done all that was asked of them. Professor Glaister, however, was far from finished.

As he lay on remand in Strangeways Prison, Manchester, Ruxton was in the worst of worlds. A naturally controlling man, he had now lost all authority; isolated and incommunicado, he veered between moods of near hysteria and desperation to sullen morosity.

Remand prisoners had privileges convicted men did not, including some freedom of movement within the prison, and Ruxton knew from the stares of the other prisoners that he was a celebrity. Outside, the investigation was still heading the news, an international story now, and although police were keeping tight-lipped, that only made the press speculation wilder and more sensational.

Ruxton had no contact with the outside world, other than a local solicitor who had volunteered to represent him and to whom he continued to strenuously deny guilt, but alone in his cell, he was less confident. He worried about what was being said about him in Lancaster. Had his friends turned against him? Had his house servants shared the gossip about Bella, and what were the police doing? During the long night of interrogation before his arrest he had been unsettled by the Scottish detectives, their accents so familiar from his time in Edinburgh.

He knew Captain Vann was a capable man, but the three Scotsmen who had sat in on the interview had looked a hard lot. They hadn't said much but sat throughout making notes – grim-looking men, professional, determined, relentless. He hoped he had done a goodenough job cleaning up at the house; he was a fastidious man and had tried his utmost, but he was concerned he may have missed something, a tiny clue that might count against him.

Ruxton had very good cause to be concerned for in the weeks following his arrest, his home at Dalton Square came under the most minute examination.

As the task of reconstructing the bodies had begun, Professor Glaister had left the work in Edinburgh to Brash, the anatomist, wanting to concentrate on Ruxton's house in Lancaster. He knew that unless Ruxton confessed, this would be a case based on circumstantial evidence. This was Glaister's speciality, and he knew identification would be:

> The whole pivot of the case, the building up of a circumstantial web of fact, fact so close, so stringent, so coherent in its texture, that no effort on the part of the accused could break through.

He also knew that despite their progress in identifying the two bodies, there was still work to do, and the house at 2 Dalton Square was the key. As soon as Chief Constable Vann had formally requested the Scottish team of scientists and police to stay on the case, Glaister made his way to Lancaster to take control of the scene. He feared contamination and loss of valuable evidence by untrained policemen trampling about the house, though he need not have worried – Detective Lieutenant Hammond had been there from immediately after Ruxton's arrest and had everything completely locked down. From then on Glaister and Dr Millar travelled regularly by train and car to Lancaster, but it was the train journeys that Glaister enjoyed most, as he later described:

> The train journeys were often interesting in their way as we sat listening to a crowded compartment exchanging views on the case and where lines of investigation were 'slipping up'.

Press interest in the investigation was still at fever pitch, which was clear from Glaister's descriptions of his visits to Ruxton's house:

> At Dalton Square the house blinds had to be kept drawn so that we could work in privacy. Each visit to the house quickly gathered a

crowd of spectators, though what they hoped to see we couldn't fathom.

The first time I went there, walking round the large, now cold and unheated rooms with their oriental décor highlighted by blue ceilings scattered with golden stars, I soon found many traces of bloodstains. Some were large; some like a petal-shaped peppering found on the stair bannisters were small. As darkness fell, the local fire brigade rigged flares indoors to give us increased illumination as we continued our work.

The work at the house continued for weeks. Between them, Glaister with his forensic eye and Hammond with his technical skill supervised the piece-by-piece examination of the old house, and gradually it gave up the secrets of that bloody night of 14 September. The yellow stains on the bath were found to be consistent with marks left by blood, and numerous bloodstains were found throughout the house. Bloodstains were not unusual in a surgeon's house, but not in the quantity or locations found at Dalton Square.

And then there were the drains.

As many criminals seeking the disposal of incriminating evidence by way of the public sewage system have discovered, while it may be difficult to thoroughly clean a bloody crime scene, it is impossible to clean drains. Once Glaister got to work on the traps and bends of the drains at Dalton Square, the evidence was in abundance; blood was found throughout, along with scraps of rotten flesh and other tissues. It was a painstaking process, but once complete Glaister had another request – he was nothing if not thorough.

When we'd finished a complete survey of the house it was arranged that scale cut-away 'dolls house' models of the building should be made. But I felt this wasn't enough.

There's a lot of detailed examination work to be done, I told the Lancaster men. It's the type of work that can really only be completed in a laboratory.

They blinked. You mean…

I'd like to move parts of the house en bloc to Glasgow if that's possible.

No one would argue with the great professor; his air of authority was total, and so in another unprecedented move, major parts of the staircase, doors, the complete bathroom and even sections of wall were carefully dismantled and transported north to Glaister's laboratory at Glasgow University. There the parts of the house were reassembled, including portions of some of the rooms and the entire bathroom.

All the trouble proved worthwhile; the minute examination that followed revealed more incriminating evidence, but there was another advantage. As Glaister put it:

> The length of time we spent working in and around these reconstructed rooms not only allowed us to complete our tests and checks with accuracy, finding highly incriminating bloodstains, but resulted in a developing familiarity with the minutest detail of layout, a familiarity which we were to require in full under cross examination at the trial ahead.

But the partial demolition of the house had unforeseen and sometimes comedic consequences. The removal of the main staircase meant the upper floors of the house were only accessible by long, almost vertical ladders. Full forensic examination of the house was not complete by the time the staircase was removed, so for weeks Glaister and his senior colleagues had the hazardous and undignified experience of scaling and descending the steep ladders to get to their work. Once, to the quiet amusement of the detectives working in the house, the eminent professor and Dr Millar were trapped on the upper floors until they were guided to safety by detectives returning from a longer-than-usual lunch break.

But in his quest to weave the 'web' of circumstantial evidence as thoroughly as he could, Glaister had another strand to pursue. Much impressed by the work done by Sergeant Sloan on the newspaper wrappings, he was eager to pursue forensic investigation of the scraps of cloth wrapping some of the body parts. The children's romper suit and the blouse had already been identified, but he still felt there was evidential value in the other scraps.

As soon as the house at Dalton Square became available to him, Glaister had all bed linen and other cloth material removed for examination. Microscopic comparison of the single bed sheet retrieved from Bella's bed and some of the rags used to wrap body parts showed them to be identical, and this find was enhanced by an expert in textiles, who made a further startling discovery. The cotton in question had a flaw in its weaving – the selvedges or edges of the cloth had a border of only twenty-three threads instead of the usual twenty-six. It was the result of one faulty warp on one faulty loom. A peculiarity so rare as to make it highly improbable that the sheet from Bella's bed and the strips of cloth used to wrap the bodies came from separate sources. The implication was clear: there had been the usual pair of matching sheets on Bella's bed and one had been torn into pieces on the bloody weekend of 14–15 September.

As Glaister put it: 'The missing threads took their places in the web of fact.'

Professors Glaister and Brash, and Dr Millar were prototypes and role models for the expert witness we are now so familiar with in both fact and fiction. By any standard and in any time, they were remarkable men, and it was just as well, for their expertise and knowledge would soon be severely tested by the finest legal minds of their day in what was to be justifiably called the trial of the century.

CHAPTER 15

THE TRIAL OF THE CENTURY

Professor Sydney Smith arrived back in Edinburgh on 7 November and immediately made his way to his laboratory at Edinburgh University, where for over a month his colleagues Professors John Glaister and James Brash had been leading the forensic investigation into the body parts found at Gardenholme Linn. It could have been awkward – Smith, Scotland's most eminent pathologist, was senior to Glaister, and it was his laboratory that had been hosting the forensic work, but the two men knew each other well, and there was a deep mutual respect borne of numerous collaborations over the years. Glaister had followed Smith as Professor of Forensic Medicine at Cairo University, on Smith's recommendation. Later, as Professors of Forensic Medicine at Edinburgh and Glasgow respectively, Smith and Glaister had shared experience and learning without the toxic rivalry so often found in public figures. Smith had, of course, been kept informed about the course of the investigation, but in the days before electronic communications this amounted to cryptic telegrams, heavily censored for reasons of security.

The same evening he arrived home, Smith was fully briefed by Glaister, Brash and his own deputy Dr Millar. Glaister put it in a nutshell:

> Probabilities, possibilities and facts all woven together formed the web of circumstantial evidence that pointed to Dr Buck Ruxton, and only to him, as responsible for the murders of the two women.

Smith listened attentively and, making comprehensive notes, questioned his three colleagues on points of detail.

One area of contention was 'the Cyclops Eye'. All agreed it was not human but its presence could not be explained. They knew that Ruxton had been a keen ophthalmologist, so the most likely explanation was that 'the eye' had been a sample preserved in formalin and kept by Ruxton for research. As the body parts had started to decompose the formalin and the eye had been sprinkled on the rotting flesh to subdue the smell. But that was speculation, it was sure to be an issue at the trial.

At the end of the long interrogation, all four men were content. Smith was completely satisfied with the work done and knew he would not have the difficulty of having to intervene or redirect the forensic investigation. Glaister, Brash and Millar were also relieved – they had rehearsed their techniques and evidence-gathering before one of the sharpest minds in their profession. If Smith was satisfied, they hadn't missed much.

It was an important reassurance. Glaister had heard rumours that down south, Sir Bernard Spilsbury was making discreet enquiries, apparently with the prospect of offering his services to the defence. It made sense – if Spilsbury couldn't get in on the act as the Crown's expert, he would try to grab the limelight by appearing for the defence. It may seem bizarre that the foremost pathologist for the Home Office should appear for the defence, but then as now the strength of expert witnesses was that they were completely independent, and that meant they could appear for whoever consulted them, defence or prosecution.

The prospect of being challenged and, worse still, bested by their old English rival gave an extra edge to the Scots pathologists' work. Their techniques, their conclusions and the science on which they were based had to be flawless.

Immediately upon leaving his professional colleagues, Smith made his way to meet the two senior policemen now running the case. Since responsibility for the investigation had been passed to Lancaster, Chief Constable Black and Dumfriesshire had taken a step back; Captain Vann, the Lancaster chief, was now driving the case, with William Morren, the newly appointed Chief of Edinburgh City Police, coordinating the forensic work at Edinburgh.

Morren was new to the detail of the case, although he had been regularly briefed by his CID Chief and Inspector Sheed on the Edinburgh end of the investigation. He was, however, well equipped as one of the new breed of professional chiefs. After distinguished war service that saw him commissioned from the ranks on the Western Front, he had rejoined the police and worked his way through the ranks to be appointed a young chief constable earlier in 1935. Like his colleague William Black in Dumfries, Morren was experienced in criminal investigation and realised how important the forensic work being done in his city was to his force's reputation and the success of the case. Morren was a disciple of Percy Sillitoe in Glasgow. He knew that a triumph for new scientific methods in this case would strengthen his arm when he sought funding to improve Edinburgh City Police's specialist services. This was an important case for a number of reasons.

After listening to Smith's views on the forensic evidence gathered so far, Vann and Morren quickly agreed that the eminent professor should take an overview of all the forensic work being done on the case. He would act as a 'critical friend' to both challenge and support the team working on the forensic case. Hopefully this fail-safe would ensure no errors or weaknesses were there to be found by Spilsbury or the sharpest defence King's Counsels.

Smith, Glaister and Brash were all highly experienced expert witnesses but they were not overconfident. They knew from bitter experience the pitfalls of overstatement. To be credible they always stuck tightly to the facts, for it was in speculation that they exposed themselves to skilful cross-examination. And skilful cross-examination there would be, for as the Crown case was being put together the word came through that Dr Ruxton's defence would be conducted by Norman Birkett, KC, assisted by Philip Kershaw, KC.

Birkett had a formidable reputation as one of the finest minds at the English Bar. He was known for his unfailing courtesy and complete mastery of his brief, no matter how technical or specialised. Smith, Glaister and Brash had often been cross-examined by Scotland's best defence advocates, but they had no experience of England's finest and little experience of English courts. The publicity that surrounded the case and the notoriety of the crime had attracted the finest defence barristers of the day, but in response the Crown also wheeled out its big guns. The management of the Crown case rested with the Director of Public Prosecutions and he quickly appointed a powerful team to act as counsel for the Crown: J.C. Jackson, KC, Maxwell Fyfe, KC and Hartley Shawcross.

Seldom, if ever, was such an eminent group of legal luminaries deployed on one case. As Glaister later put it: 'Thus were gathered together two future Chancellors and a future Law Lord.'

As the legal teams were being appointed, the police investigation and the forensic examination were coming together, and files of evidence were being passed to the Director of Public Prosecutions and the senior counsel for the Crown, who would direct the tactics of the prosecution. But as the evidence-gathering came to an end, a last piece of incriminating evidence came to light. During the detailed examination and dismantling of the house at Dalton Square, a number of Ruxton's diaries came to light. Not so much hidden as concealed, they revealed a full and candid account of his daily life, including his sometimes-volatile relationship with Bella.

His 1931 diary revealed an entry for 5 August:

Bella came to my consulting room when I was quietly doing my work and told me that she had wired her sister, Jean Nelson, to come and stay with us to keep her safe because she felt she was not safe with me in the house. I told her, if you feel unsafe you may go wherever you like, but none of your relations or friends can come to my house without my permission and pleasure.

Other entries described journeys to Edinburgh and Moffat, showing familiarity with the road passing Gardenholme Linn.

Though the Ruxtons' fiery relationship was well known and many of his diary entries are open to interpretation, it remains a puzzle as to why with the weeks he had to clean up, Ruxton did not destroy these damaging diaries. It could not have been an oversight. The diaries obviously meant a lot to the complex psyche of Dr Ruxton.

The investigation was nearly complete, the evidence handed over and now it was out of police hands.

This was and still is a tense time when the investigators hand over to the Crown prosecutors; while they may still influence, they ultimately lose control of the case from thereon. It is always a time for reflection for investigators and scientists alike. Have all the angles been covered, all the details included, and what will the prosecutors do with the product so laboriously gathered? Will they treat the evidence and the case as seriously as the investigation team? Will they see it as a case of the best of legal arguments or as a case of justice with real victims, real families?

No records of the feelings of the investigators in Lancaster, Edinburgh and Moffat survive, and the pathologists are predictably sanguine in their biographies, but it's certain that when the last files of evidence were delivered to the Director of Public Prosecutions at Lancaster, there would have been feelings of satisfaction, relief and some apprehension. For everyone on the investigation team knew this was far from a straightforward case.

It was, as Professor Glaister correctly described, a 'circumstantial' case based on probabilities, possibilities and facts and therefore vulnerable to attack, especially from such a skilled interrogator as Norman Birkett. All knew that the identification of the bodies of Bella and Mary was key, and the fact that they had only been identified by new, novel and untested techniques did nothing to settle nerves. There wasn't a single eye witness, no murder weapon found and no confession. On the contrary, Dr Ruxton was continuing his vehement denials from remand in Strangeways Prison.

Ultimately, as is always the case, the success or failure of thousands of hours of superhuman efforts, from the sodden ravine at Gardenholme Linn to the pathology lab at Edinburgh University, rested on the shoulders of Crown Counsel – J.C. Jackson, KC, Maxwell Fyfe, KC and the young and upcoming Hartley Shawcross. They were a formidable combination of experience and precocious talent, and in November 1935 they got to work on a case they knew could make or break their reputations.

For the first three weeks of his remand, Ruxton had only been charged with the murder of Mary Rogerson, identified by fingerprint and the romper suit, but on 5 November, when he appeared at Lancaster Assizes for a routine remand hearing, he got a nasty shock – there was a second charge.

A contemporary account described the scene:

It came as a shock to Ruxton, who by now was showing signs of the strain of protracted remands. He was pale and haggard, walked with a stoop and made a thoroughly dejected figure. He lapsed into broken English when under duress and reacted in a frenzied fashion when he heard the second charge. The court was hushed as the clerk read it out: 'You are further charged, Buck Ruxton, that between September 14 and 29 you feloniously, wilfully and of malice aforethought did kill and murder one Isabella Ruxton.'

Ruxton shrieked a torrent of abuse and broken English, mixed in with cries and sobs.

'It is impossible! It is a damned lie, it is. It is damned rotten. My religion would not permit it! It is one damned thing after another... Is this court crazy? I can't bear this damned thing! It is racial prejudice. Who is at the bottom of the damned thing? I condemn the whole damned thing... Is there no justice in this world? That damned man has wrecked my happy life! I have got three children to support... that damned rascal. Damn blast the man... My blood is boiling now.'

So violent was this outburst that the magistrates retired for five minutes. The day had started badly anyway. By now the public had learned when the Ruxton hearings were to take place, and on this morning a big crowd had gathered outside the courthouse and, in their enthusiasm to get in, broke one of the doors.

This description of Ruxton's remand hearing is highly instructive. First it is obvious from his physical description that in less than a month from his arrest, and only seven weeks since the murders, he had deteriorated badly – he was only 36 years old. Second, one of the main thrusts of his defence was emerging: he intended to impeach a young man, Robert Edmondson, whose family had been friendly with Bella and who Ruxton suspected of being her lover.

In a strictly logical sense it didn't add up. Even if he and Bella had been lovers – and there was no evidence to support it – he lacked any motive to murder Bella, let alone Mary.

This outburst also reveals Ruxton's intention to play the race card. This is the first time in any of the case papers where his racial origin is mentioned.

But lastly, perhaps the most devastating blow delivered to Ruxton during that remand hearing is that, throughout the process, he was never given his title of doctor. He must have known then that the net was closing, that he was being treated as a common criminal.

But things were not all going the Crown's way. The local Lancaster solicitors, Messrs Gardner and Slinger, who had volunteered to represent Ruxton, were taking their jobs seriously and there were problems. Ruxton was remanded several times before eventually being committed for trial, and the solicitors regularly complained about the confused and inadequate nature of the procedure. Because of the intense media interest, the remand hearings were frequently held in private. This denial of public access was excusable and, in the circumstances, a minor point; more important was the fact that the defence had been given no access to the house at Dalton Square in the first weeks after Ruxton's arrest.

The reason for this was simple. Professor Glaister, Lieutenant Hammond and their teams had taken possession of the house, and in the weeks following the arrest were examining minutely and, in some cases dismantling, the structure in their desperate search for evidence. Glaister would not have tolerated anyone contaminating his crime scene, especially not defence solicitors. But Edwin Slinger, the solicitor leading the defence, had a more important complaint – the lack of any hard evidence to identify the bodies. Initially the only charge was the murder of Mary Rogerson, but how could Dr Ruxton be charged with killing Mary when no hard evidence had been produced to identify her?

Slinger was also frustrated by a lack of access to the list of Crown witnesses. How could he begin to gather his own witnesses if he didn't know who was on the Crown's list?

In hindsight, these irregularities are easily explained. In most criminal cases a substantial amount of the evidence is gathered before the arrest, but in Ruxton's case there was a huge amount to do after the arrest. It was a desperate race against time. The defence was not denied access to the list of Crown witnesses for any reason other than it was still being compiled well into the remand process. Even so, it was dangerous. Crown Counsel knew that such procedural irregularities were not to be taken lightly. Many an important case had fallen for just such legal details.

But finally, all the available pieces had been drawn together and passed to the Director of Public Prosecutions and on to Crown Counsel. It was for him and his team alone to decide the tactics of the Crown case, to play on the strengths and downplay the weaknesses. The principles were straightforward: keep the Crown case simple and strong; the standard of proof was 'beyond all reasonable doubt' so any doubts had to be eliminated where possible.

Jackson and the Crown team now examined the evidence carefully. The fact that so many new, untested scientific techniques underpinned the identification of the two women worried them. Both legal teams, Crown and defence, had long experience working in the north of England. They knew local juries and that trying to bamboozle them or blind them with science wasn't a good idea; all possible doubts had to be excluded, and the evidence had to appeal to the sound common sense of the ordinary jury members. The case had already had enormous publicity, and there were strong and divergent public opinions. Jackson and his Crown team knew they could easily lose what was, despite its high profile, a very circumstantial case.

The first big question for the Crown was the sufficiency of evidence in the identification of the two women. The identification of Mary Rogerson rested on the new technique of dermal fingerprints, supported by the romper suit linked to Mary and found wrapping a human head. At first sight, it was more than sufficient, but it depended on the credibility of the new variation of fingerprint evidence, the pioneering work of Bertie Hammond, supported by the FBI.

It was natural for the Crown team to take their own expert advice and who could they turn to except Scotland Yard, the world leaders in fingerprints? The Yard's experts were unequivocal – they strongly recommended that the fingerprint evidence from dermal impressions was unreliable and should not be produced in evidence.

Hammond and Glaister should have foreseen this but didn't. After all, Scotland Yard's experts had been excluded or at least not included in the groundbreaking work; they were bound to be suspicious, wary that the hard-won reputation of fingerprint evidence they had worked fifty years to build would be jeopardised by an ill-conceived gamble with untested evidence in a high-profile case.

There were less benign interpretations – jealousy or spite – but whatever the reasons, Jackson and the Crown Counsel, having asked the question, had little choice but to heed the answer and secretly decided to drop the charge of murdering Mary Rogerson from the indictment. Without that identification, there was no evidence to substantiate the charge that Ruxton had murdered Mary.

It was a straightforward though difficult decision. The dermal fingerprint evidence identifying Mary would still be led but only as another strand of circumstantial evidence to support the charge of murdering Bella Ruxton. Bertie Hammond was devastated; his vision, all his pioneering work to identify Mary, had been in vain. Professor Glaister was also hugely disappointed, but in the manner of the day nothing was said. Everyone knew the rules – it was the prerogative of Crown Counsel to decide on the indictment and what evidence was led.

Back in Edinburgh, Glaister and his team were worried. If Crown Counsel had shied away from the fingerprint evidence, what about the other forensic evidence they had painstakingly assembled? The fingerprint evidence was new and ground-breaking, but so was a lot of the other evidence. If it had been a Scottish case, Glaister could have approached the Crown Office to thoroughly explain the evidence, the science, the relevance. As it was, the Scottish scientists had no relationship with the English Crown Counsel – there was no opportunity to explain or argue for the science behind the evidence.

Glaister and his team were concerned that the lack of confidence in their science and their evidence might jeopardise the whole case. They need not have worried however; Jackson and his team were simply being careful. They realised how important the case was; it would make or break their reputations, and they knew first-hand the formidable abilities of the defence team, particularly Norman Birkett. They also knew Lancashire juries, and they couldn't afford to take chances.

The evidence supporting the charge of murdering Bella Ruxton was stronger, though still circumstantial. The prosecution had now traced many witnesses speaking to previous rows between Ruxton and Bella, threats of violence and the times Bella had run back to Edinburgh to get away from Ruxton. Then there were the bloodied cloths, the rugs, the differing accounts Ruxton had given and the police stop at Kendal. It all added up. But at the heart of the Crown case was a weakness, and everyone on the Crown and defence teams knew it – the identification of Bella and the evidence to support that was new and circumstantial. It would depend on expert witnesses, their explanation and interpretation of facial superimposition, the reassembled body parts and all the other forensic evidence that identified the decomposed body parts as belonging to Bella Ruxton.

While Crown Counsel was building its case and the defence team was scrambling to find expert witnesses that could cast doubt on the identification of Bella, the town of Lancaster had become a febrile hotbed of argument and debate, its usually cold and conservative citizens polarised by the case of Dr Ruxton and the alleged murders of Bella and Mary.

Both women had been well known and popular – Bella with her charm and personality, Mary with her quiet devotion to the Ruxton children – and the town had huge sympathy for them. But there was also great support for Dr Ruxton. He was, all agreed, an excellent doctor, but more, he had brought an empathy to his medical practice, often waiving fees for his poorer patients. He was also a first-class obstetrician; during his time in Lancaster he had delivered over two hundred babies without loss of mother or child. In a period when post-natal death was still common, this was a record that was deeply impressive and much appreciated in Lancaster.

As the time for fixing the trial date approached, the authorities faced a dilemma. By rights the trial should have been held in the old court in Lancaster Castle; it was a large court as befitted the county town and appropriate since the crime was alleged to have been committed in Lancaster. But there were misgivings. Feelings were running high in Lancaster on both sides – could an impartial jury be empanelled from the local population? The defence might reasonably object to the fairness of the trial, especially given the enormous publicity that had filled the local and national newspapers since the arrest.

Then there was security. The scenes of disorder at the remand hearings had unnerved the court authorities in Lancaster. Captain Vann, his tiny police force already stretched by the investigation, could not guarantee security at the court for a long trial, nor could Lancaster likely cope with the huge influx of press and spectators expected to flood the town.

In the 1930s, high-profile criminal trials were important public spectacles, none more so than the trial of Dr Buck Ruxton, which was already being trailed as the trial of the century. Finally, it was decided to hold proceedings at the Assize Court in Manchester, one of the largest criminal courts in the country and immediately adjacent to Strangeways Prison, where Ruxton was being held. There would be no transportation issues, as the court and prison had connecting doors, but the decision was controversial, not least because the huge costs and disruption of the trial would fall on the City of Manchester – not

Lancaster where it belonged.

But the decision had been made and preparations began. Large as it was, the Assize Court was nowhere near big enough for the trial and the hundreds of visitors expected. Over a hundred journalists from all parts of the world were expected, and to cope with them, special press rooms were established, with banks of telephones to pass their copy back to newsrooms. The trial would be reported verbatim; the world was hungry for news about the exotic doctor and the gruesome murder of his bubbly wife and their maid.

The Crown were calling 115 witnesses who would be accommodated in a converted lumberyard near the court, with 209 Crown exhibits laid out in another specially converted room near the court. These included the bath from Dalton Square, sections of floor from the house and pieces of the staircase so carefully removed by Professor Glaister to his laboratory in Glasgow. There were numerous articles of clothing and hundreds of photographs, but by far the most gruesome articles were Dr Ruxton's surgical instruments – his Syme's knives, scalpels and even a small axe.

By the early spring of 1936, the most eagerly awaited trial of the century was set to begin. A local judge, Mr Justice Singleton had been appointed to preside, and the scene was set.

CHAPTER 16

REX v BUCK RUXTON

MONDAY, 2 MARCH 1936
SALFORD HUNDRED MANCHESTER ASSIZE COURTS

The High Court of Justice opened its Manchester winter assizes on Monday, 2 March 1936 to hear the case of Rex v Dr Buck Ruxton.

The Judge Mr Justice Singleton
Counsel for the Crown
Mr J.C. Jackson, KC
Mr Maxwell Fyfe, KC and
Mr Hartley Shawcross
Instructed by the Director of Public Prosecutions
Counsel for the Prisoner
Mr Norman Birkett, KC
Mr Philip Kershaw, KC
Instructed by Mr Edwin Slinger, Solicitor, Lancaster

Even the huge Assize Court at Manchester looked small as the cast of characters assembled for the start of what was a huge public event in the north of England. More than one hundred journalists were present, and by the time all the court officials were accommodated there were few seats available for the public. Access was on a first come, first served basis, so the crowds gathered from the early morning to get a place at the head of the queue. Police were on hand to prevent the disorder seen at the remand hearings, but they could not prevent places at the head of the queue changing hands for substantial sums of money. Local newspapers gleefully reported that many of the spectators on the public benches were women, fashionably dressed to attend the great public spectacle. The Assize Court was an old court, built at the same time as Strangeways Prison in the nineteenth century and its design added to the drama; the dock placed to be in plain view of the steeply tiered seating was encircled by spiked iron railings, as if to emphasise the danger of the wretched individuals doomed to occupy it.

At exactly 10.32 a.m. the trial opened and, after a brief formal statement from the Crown confirming their decision to drop the charges relating to Mary Rogerson, the court hushed as the prisoner was led up from the holding cells directly below the dock. A murmur of shock broke the silence as the crowd saw Ruxton for the first time. The many sketches and old photographs of him carried by the press since his arrest showed a fit and handsome man, immaculately dressed, with sleek black hair, but the man who stumbled up the stairs into the dock was very different – grey, shrunken and shabby in ill-fitting clothes.

In law, it is not necessary that there be a dead body in order to prefer a charge of murder, but in the absence of a body there must be evidence of a killing or that a person has been killed. Ruxton could therefore not be convicted unless it was proved beyond reasonable doubt that one of the bodies found at Gardenholme Linn was Bella Ruxton. Since the murder of Mary Rogerson did not appear on the indictment, evidence of her identification was only relevant in as much as it might assist in the identification of Bella and point to Ruxton as her murderer. Everyone involved in the case knew that the forensic evidence was key, and Crown Counsel knew that the evidence not only had to be convincing, it had to make sense to the jury.

The formalities of the court had to be respected so after the court rose as Mr Justice Singleton took the bench, the Clerk of Assize read out the formal charge in a form of words used for centuries.

Buck Ruxton, you are indicted and the charge against you is murder in that on a day between the 14th and 29th day of September 1935 at Lancaster, you murdered Isabella Ruxton. How say you, Buck Ruxton, are you guilty or not guilty?

The court strained to hear Ruxton's voice for the first time and after a pause he replied in a clear firm voice: 'I plead not guilty.' There was an almost audible sigh of relief from the public benches. There would be no last-minute capitulation. The evidence in all its gory detail would be heard; the verbal jousting of some of the finest legal minds in England was there to be relished.

A jury of local people was then empanelled and sworn in, twelve citizens of Manchester who, when all was said and done, would decide the fate of Dr Buck Ruxton based on some of the most complex and circumstantial evidence ever heard in an English court.

After the hubbub of the jury selection, the court settled, awaiting the first act of this long-awaited drama – the opening speech of the Crown.

This was the time when the leading counsel for the Crown laid out the case for the prosecution, the time to seize the attention of the jury, impress them with the quality and quantity of the evidence and leave such a lasting impression on their minds that no matter what evidence was produced to the contrary, that impression remained.

To a large extent, the course of any trial is unpredictable. Some witnesses are impressive, some are not; some witnesses do not repeat in the witness box what they said in their formal statements, and others become confused or are overcome by nerves. Counsel for both prosecution and defence know this and prepare themselves to adapt, but the set pieces of a trial are fixed, and both sides see them as crucial. The opening and closing speeches are key to success, and all leading counsel take great care to ensure they are polished and hard-hitting. If the evidence is the substance of the meal then the opening speeches are the menu, apt to leave a lasting impression on the jury for good or ill.

J.C. Jackson, leading for the Crown, was a highly regarded Kings Counsel. A craggy man with long experience, he knew the complexity of his case and the particular importance of his opening speech, and had carefully crafted this element of the trial. He was not going to miss this opportunity.

He began by painting a picture of the house at 2 Dalton Square and the Ruxton family that lived there, the sudden disappearance of the two women Bella and Mary on or about 14th September and the discovery at Gardenholme Linn on the 29th.

The Scottish Police were called and found in that ravine portions of two bodies wrapped in parcels. Parts of the flesh were missing, but the scientists who have been called for the prosecution were definitely able to come to the conclusion that they formed parts of

145

the bodies of two females. The bodies had been horribly mutilated and had been dismembered and the joints neatly cut through. The suggestion of the prosecution is that this disfigurement and dismemberment were done first, for the purpose of convenience in conveying the bodies from Lancaster to Moffat, and, second, to destroy any signs which might lead to their identification.

In these few words Jackson summarised weeks of exhausting and groundbreaking investigations at Moffat and Edinburgh, and while he referred to the horror of the dismemberment and disfigurement, he did all he could to spare the sensitivities of the jury. It was a delicate balance that he and his team had to strike throughout the trial. If one of the jury members fell ill or fell out, the trial would be halted and would have to start afresh with a new jury empanelled. The Crown team were very aware of the incredibly gruesome evidence that was to come. They did not want to burden the jury any more than was necessary.

Jackson went on to highlight Ruxton's unique qualification for the dismemberment of the two bodies – the ability to commit the crimes, or special knowledge.

It is suggested that both women died a violent death and the dismemberment was carried out by somebody with medical knowledge and surgical skill. I would remind you that the prisoner is a bachelor of both medicine and surgery.

Then came motive: Jackson described the household at 2 Dalton Square, how Ruxton and Bella had met, how they had set up home in Lancaster, how Ruxton had established a thriving medical practice and how, over time, Ruxton's jealous and possessive nature had emerged. It would be a crucial part of the evidence and one of the reasons the Crown has proceeded with the charge of killing Bella and not Mary.

Various witnesses will be called to prove that the prisoner was a man of violent temper and that he inflicted violence on Mrs Ruxton on several occasions, whilst on one occasion when Mrs Ruxton left with all her clothes he said, 'She will not come back alive. I will bring her back to the mortuary.' Which is tantamount to a threat of violence and probably of murder. They will tell of times when the doctor was seen with his hands on Mrs Ruxton's throat – and it is a significant fact that the cause of death of Mrs Ruxton was strangulation – and of threats with knives, of obscene abuse and other disruptions in that household.

It was a devastating passage laying out all the information known to local Lancaster Police about the domestic turmoil of the Ruxtons and about which they had done precisely nothing. But Jackson was by no means finished – this was his chance to convince the jury before the evidence was actually heard or the cross-examination considered. The opportunity was not to be wasted.

On 6 April 1934 Mrs Ruxton went to the police station and from what she told the detective sergeant it was necessary for him to go across to the Ruxtons' house. The police officer invited the doctor to come over to the police station, which he did, and when he saw his wife there he went into a violent temper, accused her of being unfaithful and said he would be justified in murdering her. The next day she again went to the police station and made a statement, after which the prisoner also arrived and again flew into a violent temper despite all efforts to placate him.

On each occasion of his two visits to the police station he used threats of murder.

And so it went on.

In May 1935, a policeman responding to a call to the house found the doctor in a very excited state: 'He was behaving like a madman and said he felt like murdering two persons in Dalton Square.'

This was the first mention of a second person and it wasn't Mary; the person referred to was Robert Edmondson, the young trainee solicitor whose family Bella was friendly with and who Ruxton had suspected was her lover. The Crown team surmised that Ruxton's defence would include blaming Edmondson, if not by formal impeachment, then by inference to muddy the waters and raise doubts in the minds of the jury. Jackson and his team would try to destroy this line of defence before it was even led:

At this time, he mentioned the name of Mr Edmondson as one of whom he was jealous, without I submit any justification whatsoever.

There is no justification for murder and the prosecution does not need to prove any motive, but I shall ask you to bear in mind the evidence of this jealousy of disposition and would suggest that the motive is clearly indicated and apparent in this case and that it followed on the great and foolish jealousy of the prisoner.

Jackson went on to describe Robert Edmondson as an upstanding young man and Bella's friendship with the Edmondsons as entirely innocent. Then he described the trip to Edinburgh on the weekend before the murders.

On Friday, 6 September, Mrs Ruxton called at the Edmondsons' house and arranged to go to Edinburgh the next day. A party was made up of Mrs Ruxton, Mrs and Miss Edmondson in the doctor's car and young Edmondson and his father in Edmondson's car, and they went to Edinburgh where they stayed in the Adelphi Hotel and returned the next day. Mr Edmondson and Mrs Ruxton each occupied separate rooms. It was a most innocent expedition and one which no reasonably minded man could possibly have objected to, but Dr Ruxton, with his jealous mind, knowing that they were going away, hired a strange car and followed the party to Edinburgh. It may well be that that trip to Edinburgh was one of the culminating points in his jealousy which led very shortly to the death of Mrs Ruxton.

The scene was set now, and Jackson came to the key weekend of Saturday, 14 September.

Ruxton sat slumped in the dock, dwarfed by the two large policemen flanking him, and as Jackson paused to adjust his papers, he saw to his satisfaction that the jury were craning forward on their benches, raptly anticipating his next words. Their body language said it all – in this most important part of the trial, when first impressions counted for so much, he had them in the palm of his hand.

The weekend of 14–15 September was laid out carefully: Bella's trip to Blackpool to see her sisters; her later-than-expected departure; her failure to contact or communicate with her family and friends; her beloved motor car, so symbolic of her independence, abandoned at 2 Dalton Square; and her sudden unexplained disappearance alongside her faithful maid, apparently deserting her three young children without a word or a note or a goodbye. Bizarre and suspicious behaviour for two women devoted to the children and who were in touch with them daily, even when away from home. And why abandon her beloved car? Surely if she had run off she would have taken it with her.

What could explain this abrupt disappearance and behaviour so out of character for Bella Ruxton and Mary Rogerson?

Then came the hammer blow: Jackson described the sleeping arrangements on the top floor of the house, the three bedrooms occupied by Bella and the children, Mary and Dr Ruxton himself.

You will hear that Mrs Ruxton had received before her death violent blows in the face and that she was strangled. The suggestion of the prosecution is that her death and that of the girl Mary took place outside these rooms on the landing at the top of the staircase outside the maid's bedroom, because from there down the staircase right into the bathroom there are tracks of enormous quantities of blood. I suggest that when she went up to bed a violent quarrel took place; that he strangled his wife and that Mary Rogerson caught him in the act and so had to die also. Mary's skull was fractured; she had some blows on the top of her head which would render her unconscious, and then was killed by some other means, probably a knife, because of all the blood that was found down these stairs.

There was a gasp from the public gallery; the brutal nature of the murders had been guessed at, the speculation running wild for weeks, but this concise summary delivered in such cold legal language shocked the assembled crowd. The Crown team scanned the jury carefully for signs of response. Was anyone going to faint or break down? But no, the jury's faces were grim, as if set in stone. They had taken it all in and were waiting for more.

Jackson's tactics had been carefully planned; he had sewn in the minds of the jurors the presumption that the bodies found were those of Bella and Mary. Later this would be hotly contested by the defence, but for now the positive identification of the bodies was implanted in the minds of the twelve jurors who would decide guilt or innocence.

Next came a summary of the next phase of the Crown case – the cover-up. The three charwomen with regular access to the house would tell of Ruxton's highly unusual behaviour over that weekend:

locked rooms and straw littering the floors; blood-soaked clothing and carpets, and the purchase of a large quantity of cotton wool; midnight fires in the yard behind 2 Dalton Square and conflicting accounts of the two women's disappearance. Then there was the swapping of cars, unexplained journeys north, the serious cut on Dr Ruxton's right hand explained as the result of opening a tin of fruit but which medical experts said was more likely the result of a straight sharp blade.

It was going well, but Jackson was very aware of jury fatigue; he had already spoken for an hour and didn't want the jury to become bored or distracted. He moved round the well of the court, moving closer to the jury benches as he spoke, established eye contact with individual jurors, raised and lowered his voice and paused to emphasise key points – everything to hold the attention of the ordinary folk who made up the jury.

From time to time he saw the jury members glance over to the dock where Ruxton sat. Jackson was painting a picture of a violent, powerful and brutal man and it concerned him that the jury were seeing anything but. Instead Ruxton cut a pathetic figure – nervous, agitated and occasionally gibbering incoherently to himself, seemingly on the edge of collapse.

But there was a lot more to cover. Jackson next detailed the strange goings-on at 2 Dalton Square over the crucial weekend and accurately described Ruxton's dilemma:

What is his position? He has on his hands two bodies that must be got rid of, and they must be got rid of so that they cannot be traced to Lancaster and, if possible, be unrecognisable and unidentifiable; he has to get rid of bloodstains in that house; he has to allay the suspicions of the relatives of both his victims and he has to cut up and dismember the bodies so that they may be carried the more easily and run less risk of identification.

The prosecutor then moved to the issue of the newspapers so important to the evidence trail and the delivery of the *Sunday Graphic* to Dr Ruxton's home on the morning of 15 September – no ordinary newspaper but the special slip edition issued in such limited numbers and later recovered and preserved by Sergeant Robert Sloan at Moffat.

Pausing to let this strange fact sink into the jurors' consciousness,

Jackson deliberately tried to lighten the mood by musing why, when there were no less than three charwomen employed in his house, Dr Ruxton himself had undertaken so much domestic work.

Can there be any reason, unless to conceal murder, why a doctor with a maid living on the premises and three charwomen coming to his house should do all this active work with the carpets and place them outside in the yard where it was raining and throw Lux over them.

The cut on Ruxton's hand was next to be explored:

When the girl with the milk arrived (Sunday 15th) she noticed that his hand was heavily bandaged, and he told her he had jammed it. Many times after the prisoner has said that he cut it while opening a tin of peaches, but this wound is a clean-cut wound and a medical man will tell you that in his opinion it could not be so cut. I suggest to you that he either cut it when dismembering the bodies – and a knife gets slippery when soaked in blood – or he deliberately cut his own hand to have some explanation for the bloodstained carpets and the blood marks on the various articles in the house.

Jackson was deliberately introducing the idea that Ruxton was a cold and calculating man, suggesting that he may have deliberately cut his own hand. It was an understandable tactic but logically flawed. Ruxton would not have deliberately inflicted such a debilitating wound on his master hand when he needed it so badly. Jackson's first suggestion was the correct one: fatigue and stress had caused the slip, carelessness that Ruxton found inexcusable.

The opening speech had now gone on for two hours and the Crown team were very aware of the limits of the jury's stamina. It would have been possible to ask for an adjournment, but Jackson signalled that he would rather not break the spell he had cast over the jurors. His opening speech had been carefully constructed to deliver a powerful message, the tempo and tone carefully rehearsed – there should be no interruption unless members of the jury were seen to be flagging. As he scanned the individual jurors, meeting them each eye to eye, he detected no glazed eyes or listlessness; they were alert and they were hooked.

Next, Jackson went on to describe more of Ruxton's strange behaviour – the purchase of two cans of petrol, despite just having filled up his car.

The case for the prosecution is that the tins of petrol were used for the purpose of burning and destroying carpets, clothing and certain portions of the bodies.

It is a strange thing to destroy in your own backyard, up till midnight, carpets and your maid's clothing.

Then Ruxton's changing accounts of Bella and Mary's disappearance. Had they gone to Scotland? Blackpool? Were they together or had they run off separately?

Jackson was feeding suspicious fact after suspicious fact to the jury, all of which he promised would be supported by witnesses' evidence shortly to follow. Then came the account of Ruxton's missing hours, where there was little fact but a strong theory that Jackson was keen to propose.

At 9.30 p.m. that night (Monday 16th) he left the Andersons' house (where he left his children) in his car. From that time no one can give any assistance as to where he was – Moffat, where the bodies were found is 100 miles exactly from the prisoner's house. He had a Hillman Minx and the journey can be done in 2¾ hours by day with an extra half hour at night. The case here is that the bodies at this time were lying at 2 Dalton Square, either to be parcelled up or already parcelled.

One of the charwomen had called at Dalton Square early the next morning but no one was at home. Jackson had a hypothesis:

The prisoner had left at 9.30 p.m. at night and was not back at 7.40 a.m. the next morning. Had he gone to Moffat with these bodies or portions of these bodies?

And so Jackson continued with the facts: Ruxton's swapping of his car for a hire car, when there was nothing wrong with his own Hillman; the strange visits to the Rogerson family when Ruxton had tried to pacify them, suggesting Bella and Mary may have gone touring for a fortnight, or that Mary may have had a boyfriend and was pregnant; his desperate attempts to delay the Rogersons reporting Mary missing.

Having set the scene, Jackson then moved on to describe the discovery of the body parts at Gardenholme Linn. He had been speaking for over three hours and though the jury were captivated, he knew they would be reaching the extent of their stamina. He had to be brief, but the next part of his summary was vital.

The bodies had been dismembered by a man of surgical skill. The prisoner is such a man. All the parts were not there but there were sufficient portions of these two bodies for the eminent scientists that I am going to call before you to come to the conclusion that they were the bodies of two women. They have been able to piece these bodies together in a remarkable way.

Jackson went on to describe the similarities of the two reconstructed bodies to Bella and Mary, the identifiable marks and features of the two women, all of which had been removed from the body parts. Then he moved to the fingerprint identification of Mary.

If you accept that evidence as identifying that body as that of Mary Rogerson, then it may help you to identify the other as that of Mrs Ruxton because they lived together, were last seen at 2 Dalton Square the same night together and portions of the body, which we say is that of Mary Rogerson, were found in the same parcel as portions of the body which we say is that of Mrs Ruxton.

It was a strange move by the Crown; they had not charged Ruxton with the murder of Mary but were going to use the evidence of her death to support the charge of murdering Bella.

Finally, after over four hours, Jackson was coming to the end of his opening speech with the most important evidence of all – the identification of Bella. Knowing that the jury must be nearing exhaustion, he moved closer to them and spoke slowly, as if to emphasise the importance of his final words. He stressed the physical similarities of one of the bodies to Bella, then summarised again the suspicious behaviour of Ruxton from the day of the disappearance: the lies, the deceit and the attempts to persuade witnesses, before concluding:

You are only trying him for the murder of Mrs Ruxton, but the incidents connected with the death of the girl Mary Rogerson may help you considerably in deciding whether the prisoner is guilty of the charge that is brought against him.

I have spared you a great deal of detail which it will be necessary to call before you, but there you have a brief outline of the incidents on which the prosecution in this case ask you to say that the prisoner is guilty of the murder of Mrs Ruxton. With the assistance of my learned friends I will call the evidence before you.

Jackson had finished with a theatrical flourish but in fact he had spared the jury very little of the evidence and sought to emphasise that, overwhelming though the evidence he had described was, there would be even more when the witnesses gave their testimony.

The opening speech from the Crown had lasted over four and a half hours and Jackson had delivered a masterclass: he had described the fine mesh net of circumstantial evidence that had clearly impressed the jury with its range and depth. The defence team could only sit in silent admiration; even Norman Birkett, the master orator, realised just what a fight he had on his hands. And in the dock, Dr Ruxton sat slumped as the full weight of the evidence against him was revealed to him for the first time.

The jury adjourned for lunch late on the first day of the trial. Mr Justice Singleton had accepted that the Crown team had the right to make their opening speech uninterrupted and they had timed it precisely – the jurors would now hungrily eat lunch in the jury room while also digesting the well-chosen words of J.C. Jackson, KC.

After lunch, the Crown team opened the evidence for the prosecution, but now the defence had a role in cross-examination. Norman Birkett would be able to unleash his formidable skills in the defence of the prisoner. Now with a part to play Ruxton perked up, sitting erect in the dock and scribbling copious notes which he frequently tore off to pass to his defence team. As each witness took the stand Ruxton stared hard at them as if checking some internal reference. The Crown team, aware of jury fatigue, tried to keep the remainder of the first day light. The opening speech had been the important part.

To set the scene, the first witnesses described the layout of the house at 2 Dalton Square, the drainage system and the crucial distances –

100 miles to Moffat, 156.3 miles to Edinburgh, 21 miles to Kendal.

The next witness was more important: Detective Lieutenant Bertie Hammond, the Glasgow detective who had done so much to identify the dermal prints of Mary Rogerson. But fingerprints were not the subject of his evidence; it was the examination of the house and the crime-scene photographs he had meticulously taken. Now, for the first time, Norman Birkett got to his feet, carefully cross-examining with his usual courtesy every aspect of the lieutenant's evidence, particularly the evidence of burnt debris found in the yard behind the house.

The last witness of the day was Jeannie Nelson, Bella's older sister and head of the family. She gave the antecedent history essential to paint a picture of Bella and her life: her childhood and early marriage to the bigamous Dutchman Van Erns; her meeting with Captain Hakim (Ruxton) and the birth in 1929 of their daughter Elizabeth; then the move to Lancaster and the emerging picture of domestic violence and what we now recognise as coercive control. It was important evidence of a course of unreasonable conduct by Ruxton.

Nelson described how over the years since 1932 Bella had come to stay with her on a number of occasions, to get away from Ruxton, and how she was always persuaded to return to Lancaster. Finally, she described the family trip to Blackpool on 14 September. It was the last time she had seen her sister and the account of that time obviously distressed her.

Sensing her anguish, the judge attempted to comfort the witness, asking: 'You were always very friendly, you and your sister?'

Nelson drew herself up and, with tears running down her face, said, in a strong defiant voice, 'Friendly! I loved my sister.'

A murmur of sympathy ran around the court and several members of the jury began to look distressed.

Mr Justice Singleton knew that it was enough for the day and, thanking Jeannie Nelson kindly, he asked her to return to continue her evidence the next day and adjourned the court.

It had been a day packed with information, with a masterful opening speech and an ending filled with emotion and drama. And it had been a very good day for the Crown.

The second day of the trial was delayed in starting due to the rush to access the public galleries. The morning newspapers had reported the first day's proceedings in detail, especially the Crown's opening speech, but the headline came from Bella's sister – her emotional cry of, 'I loved my sister', was made for newspaper headlines.

Once the public benches had been packed full, leaving hundreds disappointed outside, the Crown and defence teams took their place, the jury filed into their benches and, once the court had settled, Buck Ruxton himself was brought up the internal staircase to take his place in the dock. A hush descended as all eyes turned to him, a wretched-looking figure in an ill-fitting suit. It looked as if he had shrunk overnight, his skin a sickly yellow-brown colour, his manner nervous and agitated. Finally, the court was called to order by the clerk and all rose as Mr Justice Singleton took the bench. After a moment's delay, Jeannie Nelson was recalled to the witness box, staring hard at Ruxton before she resumed her evidence.

She described her sister's relationship with Ruxton as happy at first but then troubled. Bella was impulsive, and Ruxton excitable and controlling, but while Bella had left home on a number of occasions, she always returned, and both were, in their own way, devoted parents. They found it difficult to live with each other but impossible to live without.

Gradually a picture was emerging of the underlying passions and violence that had defined their relationship.

As she finished her evidence, she described Ruxton's parting words the last time she'd seen him on 9 October: 'If anybody comes to the house do not say a word.' He had been calm but appeared distracted.

The next witnesses were the police officers from Lancaster who had attended the various domestic disputes at Dalton Square over the years. It was a familiar pattern – the doctor in a highly agitated state, Bella terrified and threatening to leave – but, in the end, they made up and no police action was taken.

Then came the various servants who had worked in the house since 1930. The arguments and domestic tensions were described in detail.

The highlight of the second day's evidence came when young Robert Edmondson took the stand. Ruxton glowered at the man he believed was his wife's lover as he took the oath and was questioned by J.C. Jackson.

Their friendship had been purely platonic, their visit to Edinburgh a family trip, and the young man was adamant they had never been romantically involved. He had last seen Bella in passing, on her way to Blackpool on 14 September, and heard nothing since.

Edmondson was the first witness that the defence could really get their teeth into and Birkett tried his best. This was the man Ruxton was suggesting was behind the disappearance of Bella and Mary, but try as he might, the young trainee solicitor stood his ground, presenting himself as honest and straightforward.

The second day was concluded by evidence of the newspapers' delivery, the strange swapping of cars and purchase of petrol and lastly the Anderson family, friends of the Ruxtons who had looked after the children following Bella and Mary's disappearance.

The day's evidence had been successful, if unspectacular, for the Crown, but the defence had failed to make an impression on young Robert Edmondson. It was one of their big opportunities to contradict the Crown's version of events, to cast doubt and hope it would stick in the minds of the jury. In this they had failed; the case was building.

On the third and fourth day, to a packed court, the Crown continued to build its case through the evidence of the charladies, ex-patients and tradesmen who helped in the house, the most important of whom, Mrs Oxley, spoke of Ruxton's strange behaviour on the weekend of 14 September, the blood-soaked carpet and suit of clothes. These were such bizarre and suspicious incidents that the defence had to do its absolute best to offer alternative explanations or at least minimise the impact. Mrs Oxley spent almost two days in the witness box being examined and cross-examined but, in the end, her obvious honesty gave the defence team little leverage.

FIFTH DAY: FRIDAY, 6 MARCH

By the fifth day, the Crown team were very aware of jury fatigue. The court would sit on Saturday, giving the jury just one day's rest. Jackson observed the jury members carefully; so far so good, but he would have to do his best not to overtax them. He estimated that the trial would last two weeks, depending on what the defence team had planned, but this duration was unprecedented, and there was always the threat that if one of the jurors fell out, a mistrial would be declared, and they would have to start again.

With all this in mind, Jackson entered the fifth day as he had the previous four, with one or two main witnesses and a number of background witnesses, non-controversial and non-taxing on the jury.

Beginning the fifth day was Mrs Curwen, the cook and servant at Dalton Square. Like Mrs Oxley, she spoke to the conditions inside the house at Dalton Square on the weekend of 14 September – the blood-soaked carpets, the locked rooms, the strange, 'musty' smells.

During Mrs Curwen's and Mrs Oxley's evidence Ruxton became visibly agitated, jabbering to himself and scribbling notes to his defence team. It was obvious that he felt betrayed by these witnesses; towards the end of Mrs Curwen's evidence, he slumped forward in the dock as if in despair.

Following the charwomen came Jessie and James Rogerson, Mary's parents. With all the dignity they could muster, the couple described their worry and heartbreak over their missing daughter. As they described her distinguishing features, and her vaccination scars, their distress was evident – they knew they would never see her again.

Then, at last, at the end of the day came one of the star witnesses, Sergeant Robert Sloan of Dumfriesshire Constabulary.

Immaculate in his uniform, as smart as the guardsman he had once been, he made an immediate impression on the court. Carefully, Hartley Shawcross for the Crown led the evidence of the finding of the body parts on 29 September – the discovery, removal, examination at the makeshift mortuary and, crucially, the removal of the fragments of newspapers that wrapped the putrefied flesh and the finding of the woollen romper suit wrapped round a human head.

It was obvious to all that the sergeant was a meticulous man in every respect, his notebook carefully prepared, his recall exact. The recovery of the body parts was an obvious opportunity to find irregularities, establish reasonable doubt, but even the razor-sharp mind of Norman Birkett could not shake the immaculately prepared Sloan. His evidence and cross-examination were over in an hour, but it left a lasting impression on the jury.

It was exactly as the Crown team had planned. Each day's evidence was configured to start with important witnesses and end with a bang, something for the jury to remember as they went home, and Sergeant Sloan had certainly provided that.

SIXTH DAY: SATURDAY, 7 MARCH

The jury were tired; this was the sixth day in a row they had sat listening to the most detailed of evidence, but elsewhere the press and public galleries were in a febrile mood. There were Sunday newspapers to fill, and the pressmen hoped for a particularly juicy testimony to provide a new storyline – a dramatic 'splash'. The timing was tight but achievable; the court would adjourn before 5 p.m., leaving three hours to file the copy. In Sunday paper newsrooms across Britain, the front and several inside pages had been set aside. The public appetite for news of the trial was insatiable, and Sunday, 8 March would be a record day for circulation if they got it right.

The evidence opened with Inspector Strath from Dumfriesshire describing the transportation of the body parts to Edinburgh

159

University, followed by dentists speaking to the state and peculiarities of Bella and Mary's teeth.

After the lunch break, the first witness speaking to the forensic evidence was called, and from the press benches came a murmur of anticipation. There was a public fascination with forensic science, and in the well of the court, and the press and public galleries, all knew that this was the nub of the case. Even Ruxton, who had been sitting looking tired and listless, sat forward and took notice. The head of the testing house of the Manchester Chamber of Commerce testified that a piece of bed sheet found wrapped round one of the body parts was identical to the single bed sheet left on Bella Ruxton's bed.

The court was adjourned early on the Saturday, but before it rose the Crown called a number of Lancaster Police witnesses, speaking to Ruxton's behaviour in the days following the disappearance and his eventual arrest.

The day finished on high drama.

Detective Sergeant Staunton of Lancaster Police had described the long night's interview of Ruxton and Norman Birkett, concluding his cross-examination, suggested the length of time was unfair to the accused.

That means that from 9.30 the previous evening until somewhere about 6 o'clock the next morning he was answering questions and being questioned? He made a statement and then he answered these questions?

But the detective sergeant was equal to him, replying: 'A very great ordeal? I should not say so; he is a very active man is the doctor.'

A murmur of appreciation rose from the public gallery.

There was another great sound bite, perfect for the Sundays' headlines.

The court adjourned with a sense of anticipation, for on the witness list to give evidence on Monday was Chief Constable Vann and the great men of Scottish forensic science, Professors Glaister, Brash and Smith.

SEVENTH DAY: MONDAY, 9 MARCH

Captain Henry Vann, Chief Constable of Lancaster Borough Police, took the witness stand in a packed courtroom on the seventh day of the trial. Even more journalists had managed to pack themselves into the press benches, and a large crowd of disappointed citizens who had failed to get a place in the public benches gathered outside the court. The queue had started in the early hours of the morning with hundreds desperate to witness some of the most dramatic days of evidence ever heard in a British court. Vann stood immaculate in his chief constable's dress uniform, a stark contrast to the dishevelled and miserable countenance of Ruxton, once his social equal in Lancaster society.

The chief constable was spared questions about the long history of domestic abuse in the Ruxton household and his force's inaction in dealing with it; his subordinates had already had that discomfort. Vann was only there to testify about 11 and 12 October. The former being when Ruxton had handed over a photograph of Bella for publication in the newspapers and begged Vann to take action to stop press speculation, and the latter the night of the fateful night-long interview at Lancaster Police headquarters. Cross-examined about the interview, Vann was adamant that Ruxton had been cautioned appropriately and that at no time did he ask to leave or have a rest.

The document 'My Movements', prepared by Ruxton, was received into evidence and read aloud to a highly attentive court. But the circumstances of the long night's interview were causing problems, and after consideration Mr Justice Singleton decided that the questions put to Ruxton during the long night should not be admitted as evidence. Although Ruxton was not formally arrested till the early hours, he had been de facto in custody throughout and therefore should not have been questioned. It was a reversal for the chief constable, but as the older detectives present could have told him, utterly predictable.

It was also the first small victory for the defence team, though Norman Birkett knew he still had a mountain to climb; the weight of evidence was still stacked against his client and worse was yet to come.

The next phase of evidence was key to the Crown as it concerned the identification of one of the bodies as Bella Ruxton. Without that identification, there was no case to answer. Birkett and his defence team had had slim pickings up to that point, but this was their best chance.

First came the portrait photographer who had taken the striking picture of Bella, then Detective Constable Stobie, the Edinburgh photographic specialist who had photographed the skulls for superimposition. But this was just the prelude to the main event; just before lunchtime Professor John Glaister was called to give evidence. Everyone knew he was the most important witness in the Crown case, but although eminent in Scotland, he was virtually unknown to the English courts and newspapers. The drama in the courtroom was about to increase, yet behind the scenes there had already been drama aplenty.

The previous evening, the Crown team had met Glaister for the first time and run through his evidence to iron out any inconsistencies and establish a rapport. The question of time of death arose. Glaister described this conversation in his memoir:

> I've something to add, I told them, and explained about the maggot evidence. 'No, not under any circumstances' was their unanimous verdict. 'You mustn't put that forward, Professor Glaister.' I didn't understand. But it is definite, positive.
>
> That wasn't what worried them. Their major concern was the possible impact on the reactions of the jury!
>
> Senior Counsel Mr J.C. Jackson put the issue before me. The jury and laymen, for a week now they've been exposed to evidence and exhibits which, to them, constitute horror and strain. So far, they've stood up to it remarkably well.

But at that time English law laid down that if a member of the jury fell ill the case couldn't proceed with less than the full number of jurors empanelled. The maggots might be too much for some of them, and the result might have meant the need for a complete retrial, a risk the Crown was not willing to take.

> All right, I finally agreed, I won't volunteer this evidence. But I must reserve the right to use it if it is necessary to protect my professional opinion. If my first opinion on the time of death is destructively challenged, I will use the maggot evidence. It was left at that.

The Crown team had discovered that Professor Glaister was not to be pushed around. He was an independent expert witness in every sense of these words.

The next morning Glaister described his first impression of the Assize Court at Manchester.

After a few hours' sleep I was at court and in the witness box, looking out on benches crammed with a generous representation of members of the Bar, and to the curve of the gallery packed by an array of British and international pressmen. In the front seats medicolegal experts for both Crown and defence were arranged in almost equal number. At the distant rear those members of the public who had managed to obtain what accommodation was left waited expectantly.

It is a vivid picture and is notable for what it includes and what it does not – there is no mention of the accused, Dr Ruxton himself, and little wonder; now a shrunken shadow of himself, he cowered in the dock, all his worst fears having come true. Here to give evidence against him was one of the great men of forensic science. The court may not have been familiar with Professor Glaister's reputation for excellence, but Ruxton, who had attended his lectures and avidly read his publications over the years, certainly was. In some part of his mind he must have realised that here in the shape of a man he most admired was his nemesis.

Professor Glaister was to spend nearly two days in the witness box, for the first day being led through the Crown evidence by Maxwell Fyfe. It was an unavoidably gruesome account of the body parts and Glaister's meticulous examination, detailing how the various body parts had been disfigured to hide identifiable birthmarks and abnormalities. The removal of the teeth, eyes, lips, noses and scalps. The disarticulation of the bodies, cutting and separating the joints rather than sawing through them – the heads from the trunks, the pelvic girdles from the trunks and legs. Then the cause of death, asphyxia and head injuries in Body No. 1 (Mary) and strangulation in Body No. 2 (Bella). Glaister had found the hyoid bone fractured.

In the hyoid bone – a little horseshoe-shaped bone with two joints situated in the region of the neck more or less just below the level of the floor of the mouth – the joint on one side showed signs of a patch of bone formation, and through that bone formation there had been a fracture – by that I mean that patch of bone had been broken. The bone is placed in a very protected position as a rule, and when it is found fractured it not infrequently has been fractured as the result of the application of local violence. Strangulation is one such method of violence.

Glaister went on to describe the unusually small amount of blood in Body No. 2. Mr Justice Singleton intervened:

May I take it that your view is, as in the case of Body No. 1 that the blood must have been drained from the body within a few hours of death and that the body must have been disarticulated within a few hours of death?

Glaister replied simply: 'That is my view.'
Some of the jury were looking uneasy, as were the Crown team, but the judge continued:

Suppose a skilled man, a man of experience in these matters, had to disarticulate a human body in the manner in which these are done. Can you give any idea as to how long it would be likely to take the man who had knowledge of the human frame?

Glaister paused to consider his response carefully.

The best way I can put it would be to apply such a question to the case of Body No. 2 [Bella] because the parts available are more extensive than in the case of Body No. 1 [Mary]. Provided the individual could proceed without interruption and undue fatigue, was dexterous and had proper light and sharpened instruments, I should think he would probably be able to effect that degree of mutilation somewhere in the region of four hours.

The judge sought clarification: 'That is including the taking of the flesh off the bones?'
Glaister replied: 'Yes, I would put that figure as a minimum. Some of the disarticulation would be rather difficult and some relatively

simple.'

It was a telling moment in the trial and the Crown team were quietly pleased. The judge was doing their job for them. The logic was inescapable – the dismemberment of the bodies had been done by someone with the expertise, the knowledge and the tools, and there was one person who had all these attributes. The jury's eyes turned to the dishevelled figure cowering in the dock.

Ruxton's demeanour had changed at the start of the forensic evidence; he looked haunted, transfixed as men he had idolised lined up to deliver damning evidence against him. It was his worst nightmare, being condemned by men whose approval he craved.

On it went. Once the evidence of the bodies was completed, Glaister's attention turned to the house at 2 Dalton Square. The stains on the stairs, which were brought into the courtroom, the carpet rods, the drainpipes from the bath all tested positive for mammalian blood. Next, the bath was brought into the court; once again blood had been found in the water outlet. Then there were the eighty blood spots on the woodwork behind the toilet near the bath and on the carpets and the blue suit of Ruxton's – 'very extensive staining of human blood'.

As the seventh day of the trial concluded, the Crown had almost completed its evidence with Glaister. Maxwell Fyfe finished with two important questions.

Firstly, he asked: 'Generally, with regard to the stains we have been discussing today, can you state the age accurately?'

Glaister responded: 'All one can say in such a case as this is that it is unlikely that the blood is very old.'

Fyfe concluded by asking: 'Would you say a little blood or a considerable amount of blood has gone to the making of this staining?'

'I would say an appreciable amount of blood has been deposited,' Glaister replied.

The jury had heard a masterly performance from Glaister and Fyfe. The next day it would be Norman Birkett for the defence who would have the opportunity to cross-examine Professor Glaister. In the meantime, the jury had more food for thought.

EIGHTH DAY: TUESDAY, 10 MARCH

On the morning of the eighth day, the packed courtroom knew that it was make or break for the defence. This fact was not lost on Norman Birkett either, and his confidence had not grown listening to Professor Glaister's evidence in chief. He had not encountered Glaister before but had researched his background and watched his courtroom demeanour carefully. It would be a challenge. Glaister was confident but without blustering or posturing. Careful and considered in his language, seemingly utterly fair and balanced in his opinions, he cut an authoritative figure in the witness box, every inch the expert.

Birkett started carefully, taking Glaister back to the shambles at Moffat on 1 October 1935: 'When you saw these remains at the Moffat mortuary what state were they in?'

Glaister replied candidly:

The majority of the portions were in a heap on one mortuary table and in the same apartment was a trestle table containing debris. The debris consisted of twigs, leaves and certain forms of animal life that had developed on the remains.

Birkett then went for a pre-planned gambit: 'In these remains there were 43 parts, mainly soft parts which remain unassigned to either body.'

The reply was straightforward – 'Yes.'

'Included in these parts was there a cyclops eye?'

Again, Glaister responded: 'There was a portion which we thought was a cyclops eye.'

An audible gasp rose from the jury and the public benches. What new horror was this? Perhaps this was not quite as neat and tidy as the Crown had suggested!

Birkett probed the cyclops eye at length, knowing it was just the kind of detail that could sow doubt in the minds of the jury. Was it human? Unlikely. Can it be tested further? Unlikely.

Eventually, having questioned Glaister at length about the eye, Birkett concluded: 'It was, in any event, a most startling and remarkable thing to find.'

Glaister responded: 'It was very unexpected, but of course, in our view, after consideration, we could speculate as to a cause of it being there – a reason.'

Birkett cut him short; he did not want to hear an explanation, especially one which may negatively impact his client. Better to leave it a mystery.

Birkett continued his cross-examination of Glaister, probing him in depth and with a preparation and expertise obvious to everyone in the court. Every major part of evidence was challenged; the body parts, the bloodstains. Could they be from shaving cuts, surgical procedures carried out by the doctor? And the bath – how old were the bloodstains? Could they date from a miscarriage Bella had suffered four years earlier?

And despite Birkett's reputation for courtesy and detail, there were moments when he ran into trouble. When questioning the bloodstains on the carpet he asked: 'Might a good deal of blood come from a man going downstairs with a hand bleeding profusely?'

Glaister replied testily: 'You yourself pointed out that twenty buckets of water were used to eradicate the blood, so it becomes less likely than ever.'

The professor was not to be trifled with.

Concluding his cross-examination, Birkett saved a powerful question till last: 'Did you at any time hold the view that the remains that were found in the ravine at Moffat were those of a man and a woman?'

With his usual candour Glaister replied:

Yes, quite definitely, we first of all thought that Head No. 2 [Bella] was a male. On 11 October we had pretty well satisfied ourselves that taking the sexual characteristics of the head and limbs of Body No. 2 we were probably dealing with a female.

Birkett came back: 'There was a stage when you entered positive doubt, that is to say, you were of the opinion that one was a male and one was a female.'

Glaister responded: 'More than one stage, I must confess quite openly.'

It had been one of the most detailed and exacting cross-examinations ever seen in an English court and yet the estimated time of death was hardly mentioned.

Later Glaister commented ruefully: 'It was touched on only briefly and in passing, during cross-examination. The jury never had to hear about the life cycle of the bluebottle maggot.'

No doubt the Crown team were deeply relieved.

His encounter with Norman Birkett left a deep impression on Professor Glaister as he later recalled: 'I'll always remember an experience with a master in the art of cross-examination, a man who could combine skilled probing with courtesy and scrupulous fairness.'

The two men, though adversaries in the most confrontational situation, had taken an instant liking to each other, and it is no surprise. They were very similar, masters of their respective arts; they were both meticulous, professional and fair. They became firm friends and, once Glaister's evidence was complete, dined together, talking and exchanging stories late into the night.

But in terms of the case, the cross-examination of Glaister had been a disaster – Birkett had not revealed a major flaw in the professor's evidence and neither could his array of forensic consultants find fault. Glaister's evidence had been compelling but measured; he had never stretched a point or overreached himself, and judge and jury had been visibly impressed.

Dr Gilbert Millar corroborated Glaister's evidence, then came Professor Brash, the anatomist. It was Birkett's last best chance to attack the forensic evidence and particularly the identification of Bella.

Professor Brash, although eminent in his field, had not much court experience in Scotland or England. Unlike pathologists, anatomists were rarely called as witnesses. Jackson for the Crown knew this and wanted to get any controversial business out of the way rather than let Norman Birkett have the advantage.

Jackson went straight to the cyclops eye so as to remove the doubts he knew the defence would try to infer. 'That, it has been suggested, is the eye of some monstrosity which I understand it is suggested was born to Mary Rogerson?'

Mr Justice Singleton intervened but allowed the line of questioning to continue.

Jackson: 'Was it in your opinion the eye of a human being at all?'

Brash replied: 'No, I did not think it was human.'

A red herring hopefully eliminated, Jackson moved on.

Again, the judge intervened, requesting that Brash explain to the jury exactly how he pieced the bodies together. The anatomist took some time to explain the procedure he used to assemble the partial

Body No. 1 (Mary) and the almost complete Body No. 2 (Bella).

The questioning then moved to the sex, age and approximate height of the two bodies, the casts of the feet and hands recovered and the match that was made to Bella and Mary's shoes and gloves. The defence team had been sitting silently all this time, but when Jackson moved to the superimposed photographs of Bella and the skull of Body No. 2, Birkett jumped to his feet and said:

Perhaps it would be a convenient moment to raise an objection which I indicated before that I might raise upon this matter. My Lord, my learned friend is now leading to the matter of the superimposed photographs and I submit that the evidence ought not to be allowed.

It was the major legal ploy of the trial for the defence. The identification of Bella was key to the case; if the powerful visible evidence of the superimposed photographs was excluded, Ruxton still had a chance.

Justice Singleton pondered and asked the basis of the defence objection.

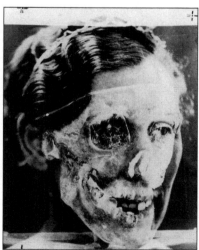

Killer evidence – the image of skull no. 2 superimposed on the photograph of Bella

The defence waffled: 'It is difficult to put it on an exact legal basis.' Unusually the judge then turned to Professor Brash and sought

169

his view on the relevance of the photograph. Unsurprisingly Brash stressed the importance of the evidence, the threat passed and the objection was dismissed, the judge saying that the evidence 'may be of use in some way.'

The spectral image of Bella's portrait photograph superimposed on the skull of Body No. 2 was shown to the jury, made more ghostly by the still-visible tiara, and drew gasps from the twelve members who had already seen so much.

While the legal value may have been limited, the impact on the jury was immediate. Any doubts they may have had as to the identity of Body No. 2 were dismissed. It was clear to all that this was the skull of Bella Ruxton. Despite all the legal caveats and qualifications, the image was burned into the consciousness of the jury, just as Detective Constable Stobie and Professor Brash had foreseen.

By the time Brash was cross-examined by Birkett, most of the salient features of the testimony had been well covered, but doggedly Birkett returned to the cyclops eye again, suggesting it was human. Brash played a straight bat – in his and at least five other experts' opinions the eye was not human – but as his testimony ended Judge Justice Singleton returned to the topic once more, asking: 'Have you any reason to doubt that that is an animal and not a human cyclops eye?'

Brash responded: 'I myself have no reason to doubt, but I do not claim expert knowledge of comparative anatomy of the cyclops eye.'

It was a carefully considered response in a thoughtful and balanced testimony. Like Glaister, Brash had been masterful in his evidence, never stretching a point; the superimposed photographs of Bella had been admitted into evidence and the cyclops eye successfully explained, as far as was possible. Another expert witness had given evidence without the best efforts of the defence making a mark.

Only the famous pathologist Sydney Smith was still to testify.

Smith was a superbly confident witness, veteran of numerous court appearances in the UK and abroad. His role in this case was one of quality oversight, confirming the findings of Professors Glaister and Brash. He glided through the Crown evidence effortlessly then faced Birkett, who knew this was his last chance to make a mark on the forensic evidence. In a familiar tactic, he decided on a concentrated challenge to one seemingly unimportant piece of evidence – the fingernails on the hands of Body No. 1 (Mary). It was a last attempt to confuse and raise doubts in the mind of the jury.

Birkett strongly suggested that the photographs showed the fingernails of a lady, not a working woman – well manicured, undamaged. But Smith could see the trap; he was not going to overextend himself and find himself cornered.

> I am not prepared to give any opinion on the difference between the nails of a mistress and a maid, but in reply to your question I say, from my examination of the nails, that they belong to a person who has been in the habit of doing manual labour.

It was a final throw of the dice and Smith had played it perfectly. He was too wily to be trapped into professing expertise in fingernails only to be clinically dissected in the witness box by Norman Birkett.

The long eighth day of evidence had come to a close. The court had heard testimony from three of the titans of twentieth-century forensic science, and though the assembled spectators could not know it, they had witnessed a confluence of expertise unprecedented in British legal history.

And for Buck Ruxton, sitting mesmerised in the dock, it was a special kind of torture, watching men he idolised – one after the other – build the scaffold steps that he would eventually climb.

NINTH DAY: WEDNESDAY, 11 MARCH

Learned observers expected the ninth day of the trial to be turned over to the defence, and speculation was rife in the law chambers and public bars about what tactic the great Norman Birkett would take. He had a number of options, including calling Bernard Spilsbury to attempt to refute the Crown's forensic evidence, but Birkett was wise and pragmatic. The standard of the Crown's expert witnesses had been outstanding, the best he had seen in his long career. He had tried his best to attack their testimony with little result and further attempts were unlikely to be fruitful.

But as he was mulling over his options there was a surprise. The Crown were calling one last witness, or at least recalling Detective Lieutenant Bertie Hammond. At the last minute, the Crown had

171

decided to call Hammond and introduce the dermal fingerprint evidence identifying Mary Rogerson. It was evidence they had initially rejected on the advice of Scotland Yard, resulting in Mary's name being removed from the indictment. Now, however, since it was only supporting evidence in the murder of Bella, they could take the chance. The logic was simple: if they could prove that Body No. 1 was Mary and Mary went missing with Bella, then it was further evidence, if any were needed, that Body No. 2 was indeed Bella Ruxton.

Maxwell Fyfe led Hammond through his evidence – how the ridges and whorls from the dead hands recovered at Gardenholme Linn positively matched the finger impressions recovered from Mary's bedroom and the kitchen at Dalton Square.

For his part Birkett could only try to minimise the fingerprint evidence – Hammond was not from Scotland Yard, was he certain of his professional opinion? It was all he could do, but the Glasgow fingerprint evidence had been powerful and inclusive.

As Hammond left the witness box, the Crown closed its case, having presented one of the most comprehensive and complex prosecution cases heard in an English court. Now it was the turn of the defence.

Birkett and his defence team had only three options: call a variety of expert witnesses to counter the Crown's forensic witnesses (though given the quality of the Crown evidence this was unlikely to succeed); offer no defence evidence which would leave an impression of weakness; or, lastly, call the accused to give evidence on his own behalf. This last option was high risk and the defence team knew it. Birkett had been watching his client carefully throughout the trial, noting his agitation, his sullen moods, his histrionics; he was anything but predictable, and of course the downside of giving evidence on his own behalf was that he would expose himself to cross-examination by the Crown. Birkett knew it could all easily unravel, but the Crown case had been compelling and his client faced the gallows – what was there to lose?

A hush descended on the packed court as Birkett rose to address Judge Justice Singleton: 'My Lord, I call the prisoner.'

A murmur of approval ran around the packed court. It was what they had all hoped for – a last act in what had been the most spectacular, melodramatic and widely reported trial in English criminal history.

It was the most dramatic moment of the trial when Ruxton, a

striking figure, entered the witness box. Sensing that this was his moment, he had drawn himself up, and, wearing his best clothes, he rose to take the oath and fight for his life.

Birkett led him gently through his evidence – his medical-surgical experience, of which he was hugely proud, his relationship with Bella, the children, his practice in Lancaster – but as he spoke his resolve cracked, leaving him sobbing hysterically or lapsing into gibberish, as if speaking to himself. As one contemporary commentator put it: 'He smiled, wept and stormed as he passionately protested his innocence.'

For over seven hours Birkett coaxed Ruxton through his lapses but inevitably he had to come to the point. Did he kill Bella?

Ruxton burst into tears and, spluttering incoherently, said: 'It is a deliberate and fantastic story. You might as well say the sun was rising in the west and setting in the east.'

And to the accusation that he killed little Mary he replied: 'It is bunkum with a capital B.'

While he flatly denied everything, some observers thought his later responses opaque; perhaps sensing that he would soon meet his god, he was trying to choose his words carefully.

Norman Birkett concluded his examination by asking again about the weekend of 14 September 1935.

Apart from what you have told My Lord and the jury of their departure on the morning of 15 September, do you know anything else about their disappearance?'

Ruxton replied strongly: 'No, I do not know anything about their disappearance apart from their going.'

Birkett sat down. He would have the last word, but his job was completed; now it was the turn of Jackson for the Crown.

He started on an unusual tack – Mary Rogerson: 'Was Mary the sort of girl who would stand by her mistress and defend her if she was attacked?'

Ruxton replied weakly: 'Yes, and would have stood by her master as well, or the children.'

His words hung in the air as members of the jury imagined the horror of that night in Dalton Square and realised that in this final response, at least, Ruxton was telling the truth.

On the tenth day Ruxton was recalled to continue with the cross-examination. He looked tired as he entered the witness box, and the packed court was quiet, sombre, as if they knew they were watching the last moments of a dying man – which, in a very real sense, they were.

Birkett and his team were aware this was a dangerous time for their client. He was a man used to being in control and now he was not. All the flaws in his personality would be revealed; there was no hiding place. The longer he stayed in the witness box, the more exposed he was, the more chance of a catastrophic meltdown. And eventually it came: the implausible responses, the hysteria, and all the time Jackson continued reprising the Crown evidence, taking the opportunity to re-emphasise to the jury the strengths of the prosecution case and seldom commenting on Ruxton's replies.

Since the defence had called only the accused, they had reserved the right to conclude, and so finally, Norman Birkett got to his feet and, as was his right, had the last word, offering last-minute explanations for the blood-soaked suit and carpets. But they rang hollow now as the court anticipated the closing speeches – the last dramatic chapter for Crown and defence teams.

Jackson for the Crown spoke simply and earnestly to the jury, once again running through the main parts of evidence. He concluded by emphasising the strength of the forensic evidence:

Only one further thing do I want to say to you. You are not to decide this case on anything that I have said; you will not decide it on anything that my learned friend says, however eloquent he may be; you will decide it on the facts that have been proved in this case. You will decide medical questions on the medical evidence that has been called in this case, which has not been challenged by any witness coming into the box to refute it. You will deal with it on the evidence that has been called and on the facts that have been proved, and on the evidence, I ask you to find a verdict of guilty of murder against the prisoner.

Birkett also summarised the long days of evidence, emphasising doubt and uncertainties about the identity of the bodies. He concluded:

> It is a collective verdict, but in the deepest and highest sense it is an individual verdict. Each man must answer for himself. If you have a doubt, speak it now, and I submit to you that on a full, dispassionate and impartial consideration of all the evidence in this case, this remains true: the Crown have failed to prove this case beyond all reasonable doubt, and that your verdict for Dr Ruxton must be a verdict of not guilty.

With that the court adjourned. The next day would bring the climax, the judge's charge to the jury and hopefully the verdict. The omens for Ruxton were not good. It would be Friday the 13th, but for all that the prisoner looked relieved, the inquisition was over; his fate was now out of his hands.

ELEVENTH DAY: FRIDAY, 13 MARCH

The judge's charge to the jury is one of the most important parts of any trial and the one that is most often the subject of appeal. The misdirection of a jury can result from the smallest imbalance, subjectivity or inaccuracy by the judge. Judges always choose their words carefully but never more so than when charging the jury, the purpose of which is to once and for all summarise the salient features of a case, rehearse the key points of evidence and pose the key questions that the jury must seek answers to, and finally direct the jury as to the options.

Judge Justice Singleton posed a number of questions. Is it likely that the blood-soaked carpets in the house at Dalton Square were the result of Ruxton's cut hand, and a miscarriage suffered by Bella in 1932? Is it likely that two women like Bella and Mary, so obviously devoted to the three young children, would disappear without a trace or a word to these much-loved children? And so on.

Eventually, he came to the forensic evidence and, bearing in mind the need for the strictest impartiality, his comments were remarkable:

> You have had a distinguished body of evidence from Professor Glaister, Professor Brash, Professor Sydney Smith and others, and you will not think that in any way I am pre-judging the matter

when I say this, that in my experience in this place, which is but short, and in my experience at the Bar too, never have I seen expert witnesses more careful and more eager not to strain a point against an accused person. No one could sit in this court and listen to the evidence of Professor Glaister, either in examination-in-chief or in cross-examination, without feeling that there is a man who is not only master of his profession, but who is scrupulously fair and most anxious that his opinion, however strongly he may hold it, shall not be put unduly against the person on his trial and the same applies to the others. Again, I should like to say that I find it difficult to imagine greater care and greater skill being used than was used by these distinguished professors of Edinburgh and Glasgow Universities in the putting together of these pieces, in their examination and in arriving at their conclusions.

Mr Justice Singleton paused to let his remarks sink in and a hush descended on the court. Neither the Crown nor defence teams could quite believe it; while the Crown team glanced at each other, wondering if the judge had gone too far, Norman Birkett sat staring at his feet.

And there was more. The judge went on to draw attention to the fact that, despite the considerable forensic expertise available to the defence, no witness had been called to refute the evidence of the Scottish professors and that therefore:

The evidence of Professor Glaister and Professor Brash and the others remains, apart from the cross-examination, undisputed. There is no evidence to contradict it apart from the prisoner himself so far as that could be said to be so.

It was a devastating passage – not only were the Scottish forensic experts of the highest imaginable calibre – their version of events was undisputed!

And so it went on. If the bodies were those of Bella and Mary, who else could have killed them and had the anatomical skill to disarticulate them in the way they had been?

Finally, after two hours of carefully weighted words, Judge Singleton concluded:

Members of the jury I have finished. I have been a long time, but I dare say you do not grudge me the time. You are told a heavy responsibility is thrust upon you, that the fate of this man is in your hands. It is a heavy responsibility, no one can deny that, but it is really no heavier than the responsibility which falls on every jury. It is most important, as Mr Birkett said to you, that no innocent man should suffer – most important. It is equally important that the principles of justice as administered in this country should be carried out and that juries shall not shrink from doing their duty when a case is proved. If it is proved, you will say so. Let me end as I began by saying, if there is any doubt on it, he must have the benefit of this doubt. If there be none, let your verdict be equally clear and let justice be carried out. Will you consider your verdict?'

It was a dramatic conclusion to the spellbinding eleven days of the longest criminal trial in English legal history. There was only the final act to come. The jury filed out silently. It was already 4 p.m. when the court rose, and the crowd of spectators and press emptied into the public assembly area at the front of the Assize Court while Justice Singleton and the legal teams retired to their chambers.

The pressmen were in a dilemma – would they go to the press area and file their reports, or would they wait in case the jury returned quickly? Most hung around, chatting to colleagues, some taking bets on how long the jury would take.

At 5 p.m. the crowd was starting to give up hope. The court would be adjourned till the next day and the jury would surely be sent home for the night, or perhaps lodged in a hotel to prevent jury interference.

But it wasn't necessary. At two minutes past five the foreman of the jury indicated that they had reached a verdict. The word went out like wildfire, the press and public flocking back into the court, in an attempt to regain their seats. After a few minutes hubbub, the legal teams took their places, Ruxton was brought up from the cells and the jury filed silently back to their benches before all rose when Mr Justice Singleton entered and took the bench.

The defence team knew it was bad news – a short deliberation by a jury in such a complex case usually was – but Ruxton himself seemed cheerful. He hated the loneliness of the holding cell, and in the court he was the centre of attention, just like the old days.

When the court had settled the Clerk of Assize rose and asked the foreman of the jury, 'Members of the jury are you all agreed upon your verdict?'

The foreman replied, 'Yes.'

The clerk then asked, 'Do you find Buck Ruxton guilty of murder or not guilty?'

After a moment's pause the foreman replied in a clear voice, 'Guilty.'

A gasp ran around the court. The Clerk went on, 'You find Buck Ruxton guilty of murder, and that is the verdict of you all?'

'Yes,' replied the foreman.

Then the Clerk of Assize posed the last of his formal questions before the sentence was passed.

Buck Ruxton, you have been convicted of murder upon the verdict of the jury. Have you anything to say why sentence of death should not be passed according to the law?

There was a pause – what would Ruxton's response be? In the course of the trial he had wept, jabbered and sunk into silent morosity. Now, though, he looked strangely fresh and seemed to have regained some of his vitality. He stood up smartly and spoke in a clear voice:

Subject to the point that I be allowed to appeal – in the administration of justice. I submit that to your lordship and the jury, I want to thank everybody for the patience and fairness of my trial. I have never attempted to pass any special restrictions. I should like to hear whatever his Lordship has to say about it.

Desperate to fit in and be accepted by English society, even at this time, Ruxton was playing out his role as an English gentleman to the end.

Mr Justice Singleton cleared his throat and reached below the bench to take out a small, square piece of black cloth and placed it on his bewigged head. It was a nervous time even for the judge, for this was the first time he had passed a death sentence.

Buck Ruxton, you have been convicted on evidence which can leave no doubt upon the minds of anyone. The law knows but one

178

sentence for the terrible crime which you have committed. The sentence of the court upon you is that you be taken from this place to a lawful prison and thence to a place of execution, and that you be there hanged by the neck until you are dead, and that your body be afterwards buried within the precincts of the prison in which you shall have been last confined before your execution; and may the Lord have mercy upon your soul.

A prison chaplain had quietly entered the well of the court and now added a firm 'Amen'.

It was over; the fine mesh net of circumstantial evidence so carefully woven by police and scientists had finally closed round Dr Buck Ruxton.

Mr Justice Singleton concluded by thanking police and scientists for their role, once again expressing his admiration for the manner in which the scientists had carried out their examinations and given their evidence.

He also made strong comment about the decision to switch the trial from Lancaster to Manchester, 'throwing very heavy duties on jurors in another part of the country'. Finally, he thanked the jury for their, 'very heavy duty', excusing them from further jury duties.

But the case was far from over – the newspapers on the following weekend, now free from legal constraint, carried extensive and lurid coverage, including wild speculation as to the fate of little Mary Rogerson, while in the pubs and polite drawing rooms of northern England, the Ruxton case was the main topic of conversation.

And in his cell at Strangeways Prison, Ruxton was planning his appeal. On balance, he had enjoyed the limelight of his trial. His nature and character dictated that he would play it out to the very end.

CHAPTER 17

APPEAL AND PETITIONS

No one could accuse Ruxton of giving up easily; at the end of his trial he had promised to appeal, and now, together with his legal team, he set about the task with renewed vigour. His confidence was buoyed by news of his rising popularity, especially among the working people of Lancaster.

The press coverage of the trial and the background of the key personalities had been extensive, and so as to vary the storylines and take their own tack, local Lancaster papers had carried numerous tales about the doctor's professional brilliance, his incredible record in delivering 250 babies without loss and particularly his philanthropic work, often waiving charges for poorer patients – in pre-NHS days unusual and particularly appreciated. As the trial ended and the death sentence was passed, the mood in Lancaster became impassioned, and in the warm spring evenings large crowds would spontaneously gather in Dalton Square to discuss the merits of the case and the sentence. Some were supporters of their doctor, some were part of a growing anti-capital-punishment movement and some came to argue for justice for Mary Rogerson, who many felt had been given a very raw deal indeed.

Within a few days, a petition seeking a reprieve for Ruxton had been raised, attracting six thousand signatures. It would be delivered to the Home Office, along with numerous other appeals for clemency, in the weeks between the end of the trial and the appeal. Meanwhile the enormous publicity surrounding the trial had attracted the full attention of the anti-capital-punishment movement and its formidable champion, Mrs Violet Van der Elst.

Van der Elst was a self-made businesswoman who had invented the first brushless shaving cream Shavex and made a huge personal fortune, which she used to campaign on social issues, particularly the abolition of the death penalty. A coal porter's daughter, she ran her campaigns from her recently acquired manor house in Lincolnshire. From there, she directed her resources to organise demonstrations, publish pamphlets and had trained herself to be a highly effective, rabble-rousing public speaker. She also had a deft touch for publicity and public relations, often hiring aircraft to tow banners emblazoned with her campaign slogans over venues considered most embarrassing to the government and particularly the Home Office. Officials shuddered at her name, and now she threw herself wholeheartedly into the campaign to save Dr Buck Ruxton.

While appreciating the public support and the growing campaign in support of their client, Ruxton's legal team had to have more than public support to take to the appeal court. To appeal against sentence was fruitless; if the conviction stood, then the death penalty was the appropriate disposal under the penal code. The appeal must be against the conviction itself but on what grounds?

Norman Birkett and the local solicitors beavered frantically to find new and compelling evidence that might throw doubt on the conviction, but there was little to find – the Crown case had been as comprehensive as it had been immaculately presented.

Birkett decided on a twin-track approach. First, he would appeal on the grounds that the guilty verdict was against the weight of evidence – though he himself believed this was more in hope than expectation. Secondly, he would appeal on the grounds of misdirection of the jury. Although Mr Justice Singleton's charge to the jury had been scrupulously fair, it had been incredibly detailed. Surely there would be some small error to pick out, one that might just be enough to convince the appeal court?

Ruxton, knowing the last act in his personal drama was to be played out, requested a personal appearance at the Court of Criminal Appeal. His request was granted, and he was transferred from Strangeways to Pentonville, and the cell previously occupied by another doctor sentenced to death – Dr Crippen.

With great relish, the guards made a point of recounting the story of Crippen and the London Cellar Murder of 1910, particularly that twenty-five years earlier Crippen had slept in the very same bed on the night before his execution.

It wasn't the talk of the haunted cell that upset Ruxton but the very fact that he could be compared in any way to Crippin, a common murderer and a quack doctor into the bargain. How could anyone see them in the same light?

The court heard the appeal in the case of Rex v Ruxton on 27 April 1936, just six weeks after the end of the trial. Outside the court, Mrs Van der Elst was conducting a noisy protest, which probably did little to improve the temper of the three judges who were to hear the appeal. Ruxton, Birkett and his team had appreciated the value of public support and the publicity generated by Van der Elst, but there was a time and place, and upsetting the solemn dignity of the highest court of appeal wasn't helpful.

The case had attracted such publicity, the public outcry so sustained, that it was almost as if the English justice system itself was on trial. Sensing the importance of the case and this appeal, Lord Hewart – the Lord Chief Justice himself – chaired the bench with Mr Justice du Parcq and Mr Justice Goddard (later a Lord Chief Justice).

It was a weighty bench of the most senior judges, as befitted the appeal they were about to hear.

For Norman Birkett, it was the biggest test of his illustrious career. He had carved out a reputation for professional excellence; now was the time he had to work his magic. The weight of evidence was stacked against his client and he knew it.

Birkett began by laying out his case. He accepted that there was a 'strong prima facie case that the remains found in the ravine were portions of the bodies of the two women' but said that the proof of murder was inadequate. Particularly he emphasised small discrepancies in the evidence of Mrs Hampshire, one of the domestic helps at Dalton Square, but it was thin stuff.

Moving to the alleged misdirection of the jury, Birkett drew attention to the judge's direction of evidence relating to the blood-soaked blue suit; his failure to impress upon the jury that the blood may have come 'from innocent sources'.

Summing up, he appealed to the judges: 'It is extraordinary how much of that evidence is mere surmise, and very dangerous surmise at that. It is sheer speculation that somebody was killed in that house.'

Given the detailed forensic evidence about numerous heavy bloodstains in the house, this statement stretched credibility, and the raised eyebrows of the Lord Chief Justice clearly indicated that the appeal court knew it.

Birkett then told the court that he wished to call further witnesses, two professors from English universities. He had hoped to throw doubt on the identification of the remains and the age of various bloodstains, but the Lord Chief Justice cut him short.

'Was that evidence available at the trial?' he asked.

It was a fateful moment. Birkett replied: 'I am bound to say that it was. I am specially requested by the appellant to make this application.'

These last words said it all. Birkett had gambled by not calling defence witnesses at the trial and had lost; the Court of Appeal would not hear the evidence and did not even require the Crown to speak.

Delivering his judgement, the Lord Chief Justice strongly supported the conduct of the original trial and the judge's direction to the jury.

There is nothing in it that can be said even faintly to resemble misdirection. On the contrary, as one reads it one is impressed by the care, thoroughness, patience and discernment which it shows.

The judge at the trial has said that the appellant was convicted on evidence which could leave no doubt in the minds of anyone. That was a perfectly correct statement.

The appeal must be dismissed.

It was the end of the road for Ruxton and his legal team. The only higher court was the House of Lords, sitting in its capacity as the highest court in the land, but the Lords only adjudicated on points of law which were of 'public interest'. The Ruxton case did not meet that criterion. All that Ruxton and his team could do now was petition for clemency, have the death sentence commuted to life imprisonment.

In the two weeks between the dismissal of the appeal and the date of execution, the clamour in support of Ruxton grew. Orchestrated by his solicitors in Lancaster and the tireless Violet Van der Elst, who threw herself into the campaign, large crowds gathered nightly in Lancaster, and the newspapers continued their wall-to-wall coverage, adding tens of thousands to their circulations.

But it was all to no effect; the horror of the crimes and Ruxton's lack of contrition gave the Home Secretary little option. Perhaps the high-profile activism of Mrs Van der Elst didn't help either; it was a time when authority did not respond well to public demonstration and criticism.

Returned to Manchester's Strangeways Prison, Ruxton was moved from the cell he had been held in since his arrest over five months previously. It wasn't a good move. As a condemned man with an execution date set, he was entitled to the privileges of the condemned cell – a more comfortable bed, better food, books and writing materials. In an odd contradiction, the life of a condemned man was made as comfortable as possible in the days leading up to his execution. Visitors were also allowed – the lawyer, priest, close friends or family – but the visits were strictly supervised. Even food brought to the prisoner was carefully examined. The hangman was not to be cheated.

In the days before his execution, Ruxton wrote many letters to his solicitor, some complaining about disputed legal points, others pleading for clemency, but in his final hours he began to focus on the reality that he faced and the well-being of his children. At midnight on the night before his execution he wrote a final letter to his solicitor Frederick Gardner. In the end, he was not protesting his innocence or pleading for mercy.

Please do your utmost for my three children. I am sure you will, wont you? Try to swell funds by all sorts of ways, and do not let bargain hunters rob my children. Remember, I die happy in the thought you are my administrator of my estate, and the trustee of my children. Please, do be good to them, and I will bless from above all of you.

I am sure you will not let every Tom, Dick and Harry know my children's name. You know what people are. I don't want them taunted by anybody. Never let my children separate. They must always be brought up under one roof. They must never be adopted individually by separate parties. Remember, it is my dying wish and I have full faith in you.

These were the last verified words of Dr Buck Ruxton. Undoubtedly a brutal murderer, his last words were full of concern for his children.

It had been a warm spring but the day of the execution, 12 May 1936, dawned dull and overcast in Manchester. A huge crowd gathered outside Strangeways Prison, the place of execution. There was nothing to see and it was a cold morning, but people felt compelled to come anyway, to witness the last act in a drama they had been part of for months. When Mrs Van der Elst arrived with her placards and loudspeaker vans blaring strident hymns, some of the crowd were hostile, perhaps sensing that despite her best intentions, in the end her campaigning had done Ruxton's fight for life no favours.

As usual she was arrested and charged with breach of the peace and traffic offences. It was the usual well-rehearsed attempt to silence the campaigner that did nothing to deter her in the slightest.

At the appointed time, following a restful night and a hearty breakfast, Ruxton said a polite farewell to his guards and delivered himself to the hangman's party without protest.

The execution followed the procedure laid down for judicial killing. The executioner Thomas Pierrepoint and his assistant Robert Wilson filled out the requisite forms LPC4. The prisoner was 5ft 7½in tall and weighed 137lbs – a drop of 7ft 11in was calculated to cause an instant fracture or dislocation of the second and third cervical vertebrae. Ruxton's arms were pinioned behind his back and he was walked briskly through an adjoining door from the condemned cell to the execution chamber itself. There he was positioned above the trapdoor. The noose was placed round his neck and a white cap placed on his head. The carefully choreographed procedure took less than a minute before Pierrepoint pulled the lever and Dr Buck Ruxton was pitched into eternity. According to the record he went to his death quietly and with dignity. At the end, the model of the perfect English gentleman he had always aspired to be.

Outside the prison, the loudspeaker vans fell silent and the crowds drifted away. In a final anti-climax the four aeroplanes chartered to fly towing banners of protest over the prison failed to arrive, grounded by the overcast weather. Having lost this battle but not her private war, Mrs Van der Elst moved on to the next campaign.

CHAPTER 18

SPIRITUALISTS, CHARLATANS AND TROLLS

The 1920s and 1930s saw a huge rise in religious and spiritualist interest in Britain. The awful toll taken by the Great War left tens of thousands of people grieving and desperate for answers. They had seen their loved ones, sons, brothers, sweethearts, husbands leave in the bloom of their youth for a short patriotic war never to return, and many did not know where they lay. The British policy of not returning the bodies of the dead for the rituals of funeral did not help, and the nagging questions recurred. Were they dead at all? Where were they? There had to be answers!

Most of the bereaved turned to the old comfort of the established religions. Across the combatant nations, churches of all denominations thrived and expanded. New churches were built, but congregations quickly outgrew them and annexes were opened with multiple services held as the churches did their best to give comfort where none was possible.

But for many it wasn't enough. There had to be more; there had to be a way to reach their loved ones even across the grave. It was a yearning answered by an unprecedented growth of spiritualism. It was hugely appealing, promising, 'human survival by demonstrating the fact of communication after death of the physical body – the indestructability of the spirit consciousness'. Across the country, widely publicised public meetings were organised by clairvoyants, séances were held and mediums were much in demand, becoming rich and famous in the process.

People of all classes took solace from this new answer to their grief and bewilderment, and it was contagious – even senior politicians claimed to receive messages from the other side, and many a mother and sweetheart felt their heartbreak relieved when they were sure they had communicated with their lost loved one. Some of the spiritualists offering their services were genuine members of spiritualist societies;

others were amateurs drawn to the drama. Then there were the unscrupulous, the confidence tricksters who took large fees to give access to those beyond the veil and tell desperate, grieving folk exactly what they wanted to hear. The Ruxton investigation and trial had attracted so much publicity and left so many unanswered questions, particularly about Mary Rogerson, that it was inevitable that spiritualists and mediums would be drawn to the drama.

Unfortunately, some who answered the call represented the worst excesses of the spiritualist movement. One so-called medium from Blackpool plagued the Rogerson family with numerous letters claiming contact with their daughter. Her messages included general prophecies of doom, warnings to the League of Nations as well as messages direct from Mary:

> I am writing this message from the sun and heaven. I would not be writing this only for the wavelengths from the sun. The rays make me into a human wireless in touch with the sun and all the planets.
>
> Dr Ruxton and Bruno Hauptmann (executed for the kidnapping and murder of the infant son of Charles Lindbergh in 1935) are here. They arrived in heaven in six days just like me because they are innocent. I see great trouble for those who were against Dr Ruxton. I have given information about the very place our trunks, fingers and toes will be found. We are buried underneath the floor of a house. There are also heads, legs and trunks there of 100 bodies.

This macabre letter concluded with a personal message about a coat worn by Mary's stepmother: 'It is too dark for you, Mother – wear blue!'

Hundreds of letters and postcards were sent to the Rogersons, many from people obviously profoundly affected by the murders and desperate to help. Some tried to comfort:

> I have been permitted to see through the veil. I saw the River of Jordan and the doves. I saw Mrs Ruxton's face and then Mary's, which was lovely with a halo round her head. Poor Mary's murderer is still at large.

There were also mawkish poems, prophecies and maps showing where the bodies really lay, even forwarding addresses in South

America for Bella and Mary, but worst of all letters purporting to be from Mary herself written in infantile block capitals and with a Morecambe postmark. One read:

Dear Mum and Dad

Don't bury these remains, we are not dead. I only saw a paper for the first time on Sunday.

We have dyed our hair, no one knows us. I cannot see the doctor hang. He was good to me. We are far away from England. Forgive me. I wish I was home.

Mary

It is impossible to imagine the hurt and pain caused to the Rogersons by these cruel messages, for all the interventions by spiritualists and mediums had common themes – that Ruxton wasn't guilty of the murders or that Mary wasn't dead at all.

The Rogersons were a very ordinary family grieving for their beloved Mary, overwhelmed and bewildered by the legal process, and uncertain of the exact fate of their daughter. They had buried a few body parts under her name but knew that they would never see justice done for her.

We tend to think that trolling is a very modern cruelty made possible by the anonymity of social media; the experience of the Rogerson family proves different.

But it was not only spiritualists and mediums who saw a business opportunity from the fascination with the Ruxton case. In Blackpool and Morecambe, the end-of-the-pier shows did their best to capitalise on the horror of the crimes. There were exhibitions of 'the actual bed' Bella Ruxton was murdered in, the 'table' the bodies were dismembered on, the bath the bodies were bled in, and numerous other hideous artefacts displayed in the most gruesome fashion. Two pence entry was charged, half price for children. All were fake; none of the furniture from Dalton Square was released by the police for fear of its misuse, and even the bath was kept and eventually used as a horse trough at Lancashire Constabulary headquarters until the 1970s. Nevertheless, as late as 1939, Blackpool Police had to intervene and close down yet another macabre sideshow claiming to display weapons used in the murders.

Following the trial, numerous books were written, some weighty academic texts, others lighter, semi-fictional accounts, and the case had enduring appeal. As late as 1975, a stage play was performed in Lancaster. It took a decidedly sympathetic view of Dr Ruxton, and while local people felt it was biased and unbalanced, national critics thought otherwise.

One critic from the *Daily Mail* was hugely impressed:

His [Ruxton's] death has left the town with a strong sense of guilt but fortunately this play succeeds in escaping from mere local conscience. On top of race prejudice against a black doctor, he overlaps class prejudice of a town hall set, jealousy from other doctors and the blind envy of small town people incapable of understanding the brilliance of a man, made alien to them as much by his intellect as the colour of his skin.

Forty years after the actual crimes, this was an insulting and grossly distorted account of the facts. Ruxton was very much a member of the so-called 'town hall set', which almost certainly protected him from police action over his ongoing domestic violence. Far from shunning Ruxton because of his colour, the people of Lancaster took him to their hearts as 'exotic' and very much appreciated his professional skill and generous nature. But it was typical of much of the coverage after the murders, the continued fascination with the case forcing journalists and playwrights to find new angles, new conspiracies – anything to keep the story going.

The Ruxton Murders had been the biggest press story for a generation; it had put tens of thousands on circulations and made the already wealthy press barons even richer. So embedded in the public consciousness had the story become that even after the execution the fascination continued. But why – what was so special about this case?

One of the reasons was that the nature of the crimes was much nearer to fiction than fact. In fiction, murders are usually carefully planned, while in reality this is very rare. Though the murders of Bella and Mary were certainly spontaneous, considerable planning and deception went into the disposal of the bodies and the attempt to escape justice.

In fiction, murder mysteries usually have attractive participants, prominent in the community. This is seldom true in the real world, but in the Ruxton case, both the doctor and Bella were well known and decidedly middle class.

In fiction, murder investigations always have twisting, complex narratives to build the mystery. In reality, this is unusual. Real murders are usually chaotic and messy but straightforward to investigate; the Ruxton case was complicated.

Lastly, in fiction the story is always populated by bold characters, to hold the reader's attention, but in reality, this is seldom the case. Most victims and perpetrators of murder are very ordinary people, yet Ruxton and Bella – both well known, colourful characters – were anything but.

For all these reasons, the Ruxton Murders were extraordinary, more akin to fiction than fact, perfect for the newspapers of the day and holding the fascination of readers for decades to come.

The story therefore had to be kept alive, and one of the mysteries that gave it legs surrounded Ruxton's alleged confession.

Despite all the evidence and the verdict of the court, there was still a suspicion that there was more to the Ruxton Murders than met the eye. It's common in high-profile crimes. The simple explanations are difficult to accept; there must be more and the conflicting accounts of Ruxton's confession fuelled the conspiracies.

Immediately after the execution, the *News of the World* carried an exclusive 'confession of a killer.' It read:

I killed Mrs Ruxton in a fit of temper because I thought she had been with a man. I was mad at the time. Mary Rogerson was present at the time. I had to kill her.

The 'confession' was dated 14 October 1935, two days after Ruxton's arrest and had allegedly been given to a *News of the World* reporter in exchange for £3,000 on the promise that it would not be published until after his death.

About the same time and perhaps in response, the last letter written by Ruxton came to light. It had been written in the death cell at Strangeways a short time before his execution. In this letter, he denied, 'in the last hours of my life, doing any harm to Mary Rogerson. In years to come God will unfold the mystery of their disappearance.'

Both these letters are worthy of examination. The 'confession' was contrary to Ruxton's continued denials throughout the arrest and trial. From the time of his arrest, his behaviour had swung wildly between depression and agitation, but at no time had he come near to admitting his guilt. Equally, the death-cell letter, if it was genuine, would have to have been smuggled out of the prison by one of the condemned man's visitors. Suspicion fell on Ruxton's close friend, the dentist Herbert Anderson, one of the last people to see Ruxton, but he firmly denied any involvement.

Whoever was responsible for smuggling out the last letter from Ruxton, it was almost certainly genuine and the *News of the World* confession almost certainly false. The last denial was written in a similar way to other correspondence known to be written by the doctor, while the language used in the 'confession' letter was entirely wrong for Ruxton, who wrote as he spoke, with flourishes and considerable verbosity.

The 'confession' letter, on the other hand, was sparse and stilted, exactly how a false confession would look if it had been written by an inexperienced hand or a desperate journalist. It was almost certainly an early example of 'fake news' by the *News of the World*, and there was no clue as to what had happened to the £3,000 allegedly paid to Ruxton. There was no large sum of money in his personal effects or his estate, further suggesting that the 'confession' and the huge fee were both the products of a fertile imagination in the paper's newsroom.

By the end of the trial and execution of Buck Ruxton, the facts and legends of the murders had become entwined and the case had developed a life of its own. Like the original Whitechapel Ripper Murders or the later assassination of JFK, conspiracy theories thrived regardless of the cold hard facts. Even 40 years later new crackpot theories were still emerging: Buck Ruxton was innocent; Bella and Mary weren't dead; the body parts were a medical student's prank; there were many more bodies found at Gardenholme Linn, but it was hushed up to prevent panic, and, of course, the cyclops eye provided a rich seam for many conspiracies all on its own.

In the final proof that the case had transcended the bounds of any ordinary criminal investigation, popular music hall songs were parodied. A romantic pop ballad with the lyrics, 'when I grow too old to dream I'll have you to remember,' was the hit song from the 1935

Romberg and Hammerstein musical film *The Night is Young*. A street version, sung loudly and tunelessly by urchins all over the land, was a direct reference to the Ruxton case: 'When you grow too old to scream, I'll have you to dismember.'

And there were more.

Buck Ruxton was a man with a strong sense of destiny. It drove him to succeed in his chosen profession and made him desperately seek acceptance in the British society he so admired. He had been sure that greatness and fame lay before him when his achievements were eventually recognised; certain that in time he would be famous and make a significant contribution to medical science.

In a supreme irony that may just have occurred to him as he mounted the gallows, he had achieved the first of his goals: he had become famous and his name would live on, but not in the way he would ever have hoped for or imagined.

CHAPTER 19

MONSTERS AND VICTIMS

Following a brief formal inquest, Ruxton's body was buried within the precincts of the prison, as directed by the sentence of the court. In the 1990s, building work at Strangeways led to the exhumation of the remains of all executed prisoners from the prison grounds to be reinterred in a mass grave at Blackely Cemetery, Manchester. There, in an unmarked grave, lies Dr Buck Ruxton, mixed with the remains of nearly one hundred executed men and women from a century of judicial killings. For a man of no little self-regard, he would certainly have been displeased at his companions in death.

The pitiful remains of Mary Rogerson's body were released to her family after the trial, with the notable exception of her head. In a final ignominy, and unbeknown to her family, her skull was retained by the Department of Anatomy at Edinburgh University. There it remains beside the skull of her beloved mistress, Bella Ruxton. Her death certificate had been granted by Justice Singleton, acting as coroner at the conclusion of Ruxton's trial. Accepting the fingerprint evidence of her identification, permission was granted for her to be buried.

Little Mary's funeral took place on a sunny 2 May at the churchyard of the ancient parish church of Saint Helen's, Overton, a tiny village a few miles from Morecambe. The press stayed away, respecting a family request for privacy. Her coffin was carried to her grave by her four uncles in the presence of friends and neighbours from the village. Her coffin plate bore the simple inscription:

Mary Rogerson September 1935
In the twentieth year of her age

To avoid further intrusion, no headstone was erected over Mary's grave, but it can still be found among the graves of her family, who have lived in Overton for generations. Mary's torso and spine were never found.

This simple but loving funeral should have brought the start of some closure for the Rogersons, but worse was to come.

On 5 May 1936, Jeannie Nelson, Bella's sister, received a letter at her home in Bothwell Street, Edinburgh. A small stiff envelope bordered in black contained a black bordered card from the Salford Hundred Assize Courts, Manchester. Dated 4 May, the handwritten note bore a stark official message:

Dear Madam

Herewith I enclose Burial Order in respect of your sister, known as Isabella Ruxton.

Yours truly – Clerk of Assize

And that was it – with these few words the case was over, the body parts identified as Bella's – minus her skull and a number of other bones, which were retained by Edinburgh University – were released to a local undertaker for burial. Mrs Nelson, elderly and already traumatised by the murder of her sister, was now faced with the organisation of her funeral. Fortunately, Edinburgh City Police had kept in touch with the family and DI John Sheed once again stepped in to help.

The remains of Bella Ruxton were laid to rest in a local Edinburgh cemetery. To avoid publicity, only close family and police officers attended the funeral. Her three children were considered too young to be told of their mother's death, let alone attend the funeral.

MONSTERS

In all the numerous texts written on the Ruxton case, few have focussed on the mind and motivation of the murderer. Ruxton has instead entered the pantheon of British criminal history as 'The Savage Surgeon' who murdered, a hideous perversion of a man, a Jekyll and Hyde character who, as a doctor, perpetrated the ultimate betrayal. Any anthology of famous British crimes carries the story of the killer doctor, with gruesome detail of the crimes and the triumph of forensic science that brought him to justice. It is the shocking yet comforting story of the triumph of good over evil, a moral tale to titillate and satisfy the reader. But when considered objectively, the story is more complicated and more familiar than that. The murders of Bella and Mary in fact reveal an all-too-common picture of domestic murder, the most depressingly common kind of homicide both in the 1930s and in the present day.

The murders of Bella and Mary were not sadistic or premeditated; the victims were not tortured or sexually abused. Instead they were killed in a moment of blind fury, jealousy and a catastrophic loss of control, all too familiar circumstances in the history of homicide. The Ruxton Murders were very ordinary crimes; it was the disposal of the bodies that was shocking and extraordinary.

But what else was Ruxton to do? On the night of 14th September, he was faced with the dilemma of two dead bodies to deal with and he had only a few hours of darkness to respond. Once he had decided to cover his tracks – and his nature, character and heroic self-image could not have allowed him to do otherwise – his options were limited. In that panicked and immediate situation he naturally fell back on his expertise – surgery!

He dissected the bodies of his 'beloved' Bella and little Mary not from a desire to inflict further indignity on their corpses or out of some perverted pleasure but out of expediency, a purely pragmatic response to his situation. Evading justice was always his only priority. He could not have admitted his guilt, even to save his life; the very core of his being craved acceptance from the society he so admired and the medical profession he'd worked so hard to conquer. Yet something in his desperation made it impossible for him to achieve his ambition. Despite the public support he enjoyed in Lancaster, he had always felt like the outsider with something to prove. He had never really fitted in.

Many years later, another murderer, Lee Harvey Oswald, was described as being, 'an utterly displaced creature without roots in nation, region, class.'

This perfectly describes Buck Ruxton and helps to explain his motives and his actions after the murders. He was jealous and possessive in nature, immensely narcissistic and controlling, and in a classic escalation of his coercive control, his behaviour had deteriorated over five years to the point where he had lost all objectivity and control. In September 1935, he was an unexploded bomb on a hair trigger. The prospect, no matter how irrational, of his wife having an extramarital affair did more than threaten his marriage and family – it threatened his status, his fragile self-esteem, his very being.

By the time Bella left to meet her sisters at Blackpool on 14 September he was on the edge, her return in the early hours the trigger. In his exhausted, paranoid state her late return was proof positive of her infidelity and of his humiliation, and in such a heightened state, the flashpoint can be for the most insignificant reasons. Had Bella not taken her sisters for a last drive along the promenade to see the Blackpool illuminations, disaster may have been averted. We will never know.

Even so, had Ruxton admitted his crimes at the outset, pleaded insanity at the time of the crime and not embarked on his gruesome cover-up, he may have escaped the death sentence. But that was never an option – his ambition, desire to be accepted and his sense of worth would never have allowed it.

Buck Ruxton was a brutal double murderer and a deeply flawed man, but he was not a monster and does not deserve to be placed among the many real monsters that have stalked our country in the last century. Even Sydney Smith believed the murders to have been unpremeditated.

I do not think Ruxton meant to kill. He was jealous and suspicious of Mrs Ruxton's relationship with another man, and I have no doubt that when she returned from Blackpool a quarrel broke out and he killed her in a fit of rage.

In considering why Ruxton has been so demonised, there are three obvious factors:

First, the investigation, the subsequent trial and execution were carried out in an unprecedented blaze of publicity. Never had an investigation been subject to such media coverage. As such, it defined a generation's memory and became embedded in criminal folklore.

Second, Ruxton was a doctor who killed – the ultimate horror, the ultimate betrayal.

Lastly, the macabre brutality of the dissection and disposal of the bodies was as titillating as it was shocking, the fact that one of the victims was a fashionable middle-class lady adding a special sexual frisson.

It was the perfect combination of power, sex and bloody horror with a little bit of race thrown in that ensured Buck Ruxton achieved the notoriety that he hardly deserved.

VICTIMS: BELLA RUXTON

If Buck Ruxton had much in common with many perpetrators of domestic murder, then Bella was also typical of the most common kind of victim.

Bella was vivacious, headstrong and full of energy and ambition, but the very facets of her character that magnetically attracted Ruxton eventually played on his deepest insecurities. When they met, he was immediately smitten by her, falling head over heels for her, but lovesick wooing is sometimes confused with stalking. Ruxton wanted to possess Bella not have her as a partner.

For Bella, Ruxton was an attractive proposition. Handsome, charming, exotic and generous, he also offered her the key to a comfortable middle-class life complete with the status of a doctor's wife. For a working-class girl with a bad marriage behind her but many ambitions and plans, it seemed a dream come true. And so it was until the three children came along. Bella was a loving and attentive mother, but as is often the case with insecure men, Ruxton resented what he saw as Bella's lack of attention to his needs. Ruxton loved his children in the somewhat distant way that was typical of the time, but he was also jealous of them and the obvious devotion of their mother.

From the birth of Elizabeth in 1929, Ruxton began to practise what we now recognise as coercive control over Bella and every aspect of her life. Every compliment had a caveat, the faintest praise had a double edge and cold water was poured on any ambition of Bella's other than her domestic duties. He frequently spoke of her profligate spending, her flirting and inappropriate relationships, her hare-brained business schemes, although there is no evidence to support any of these slurs.

In an all too familiar pattern, his wish to control her, restrain her and keep her entirely for himself escalated out of control. Although Bella could not have foreseen the ultimate catastrophe, she did bridle at his controlling behaviour and left him on a number of occasions, only to be persuaded to return by the same forceful passions that had won her in the first place. In a common misjudgement, Bella thought she could control the situation, and living with it every day perhaps did not detect the gradual heightening of tension that led to her death.

Could Bella have survived the relationship? Perhaps, but only if she had removed herself and managed to stay away, or if Lancaster Police had done a professional job to intervene in what they should have recognised as a violent course of conduct that could only end one way. As it was, Bella stayed too long and failed to read her madly jealous partner. Like many victims of domestic murder, female and male, she paid for her miscalculation with her life.

MARY ROGERSON

Many victims have been let down by the justice system over the years, but few have been as ill-used as little Mary Rogerson and her family.

Despite the fact that there was ample evidence to charge Ruxton with Mary's death, no charges were ever brought. Instead, the evidence of her identification by fingerprint was used to support the charges relating to Bella. The Crown were understandably reluctant to do anything to jeopardise such a high-profile case, but it seems odd that a substantial amount of supporting evidence regarding Mary was led by the Crown, including evidence by her parents, yet her name was not included in the indictment. Certainly, the evidence of motive in Mary's case was not as strong as Bella's, given the long history of domestic violence and threats, but the physical evidence, even excluding the fingerprints, was just as strong.

Once Ruxton was convicted and sentenced to death, the Crown's approach to Mary's death was purely pragmatic, if unfeeling, and best summed up by a director of public prosecutions who, when asked about Mary's death after the trial, said simply, 'You can't hang a man twice.'

But perhaps there was another dimension. Now, when studying the details of the case so many years later, one is left with the feeling that perhaps class and status played a part in decisions about Mary's case.

Mary Rogerson was a quiet, undemonstrative girl from a very ordinary, working-class family. She was sometimes described as plain, had a cast or glide in her eye and lived very much in the shadow of her extrovert mistress Bella. She had no social life of her own outside the Ruxton household, and the suggestions of her pregnancy were certainly false. She had worked for the Ruxtons in the early 1930s but had left their employment, disliking the tensions created by Dr Ruxton in the house. She was, however, completely devoted to the Ruxton children, Elizabeth, Diane and Billie, and was thus drawn back to the Ruxtons' employment.

As the situation deteriorated, Mary, the only live-in servant, was caught in the middle of the warring Ruxtons, becoming Bella's friend and confidante as much as servant. Frequently of an evening, Bella would sit chatting in Mary's tiny room on the top floor of the house, which was infuriating to Ruxton's jealous, paranoid nature. On the night of the murder there can be little doubt that Mary came to Bella's assistance during Ruxton's murderous assault and laid down her life for her friend. Was Mary killed in cold blood to remove a vital witness or did she simply become involved in the fatal assault on Bella? It's much more likely to be the latter.

Mary's fierce loyalty would have made it impossible for her to ignore an assault on Bella, and Ruxton's rage and loss of control that night meant her intervention would be met with the same extreme violence as was visited on Bella.

As for the Rogerson family, with few resources and no access to the establishment, they did all they could to raise the alarm and report their daughter missing, only to be largely ignored by the police. Only their perseverance, writing letters to all national newspapers, drew any attention to the case, where, in a stroke of luck, the tiny infill story carried in the Scottish *Daily Record* was noticed by the Glasgow detectives.

After the trial and appeal, the authorities' casual cruelty towards the Rogersons continued with Mary's pitiful remains being released for burial without any form of help or financial assistance. It could have been another body blow to this simple family, who had struggled for so long to deal with this tragedy. Fortunately, the citizens of Lancaster possessed a better moral compass than their 'betters'. Annoyed by a sense of the terrible injustice done to Mary and her family, a substantial sum of money was raised by public subscription to support the Rogersons and the Ruxtons' three young children. In tough financial times and in an area whose economy had been hard hit by the Great Depression, it is a tribute to the generosity of the ordinary folk of Lancashire, who took little Mary and the Ruxton children to their hearts.

THE RUXTON CHILDREN

Of the hundreds of thousands of words written about the Ruxton case, very few were expended on the Ruxton children, who arguably suffered most profoundly from the murders.

During the longest trial in English legal history to that point, they were hardly mentioned, other than in a passing reference to a child being in Ruxton's car when he was stopped in Milnthorpe on 17 September.

At the time of the killings, in the early hours of 15 September, Elizabeth, six years old, Diane, four, and Billie, two, were asleep in the nursery they usually shared with their mother on the top floor of 2 Dalton Square. Despite being a few feet from the murderous assault on their mother and nursemaid, it seems the children slept through the disturbance that must have taken place that night. One can only speculate on what might have happened if the older children had woken and disturbed their father during his deadly attack.

The next morning, the three children were farmed out to friends, and over the next four weeks until Ruxton's arrest, they came home infrequently, while their father juggled his professional and personal life, desperately covering his tracks and trying in vain to destroy all the incriminating evidence. After the arrest, the decision was taken to tell the children nothing about their mother and nursemaid's deaths or their father's arrest. They were simply told that their parents and beloved nursemaid had gone on holiday. One can only imagine the hurt and bewilderment of the older children at the thought of being abandoned by the three people who meant the most to them.

After the trial, the deception was continued, and it is not recorded when, if ever, the children learned the truth. Without parents, the three Ruxton children were treated as any other orphans, and since it was believed that Bella's sisters in Edinburgh were too old to care for young children and there was no other family, the three became the responsibility of Lancaster' public assistance institution, successor to the poor house. The substantial sum of money raised to support them helped care for them, but apart from that, the only substantial asset left by the Ruxtons was the house at 2 Dalton Square.

It was a dubious asset; the interior of the house had been substantially dismantled by Professor Glaister and his team, but in any case, the house was notorious – many believed haunted. It lay derelict for years after the case and was eventually bought for a pittance by the cinema next door.

Perhaps to protect them from the salacious publicity that continued to follow the Ruxton case, the fate of the Ruxton children was kept a closely guarded secret. Whether Ruxton's dying wish that they be brought up together was respected is unknown.

What is certain is that Elizabeth, Diane and Billie Ruxton joined that vast group of secondary victims – mostly unrecognised, their lives shattered – who continue to suffer in silence.

CHAPTER 20

CONSEQUENCES

The Ruxton murder investigation was arguably the most important criminal case of the first half of the 20th century, but not because of the crimes themselves, the forensics that solved the case or even the myths and legends that grew around it. It is largely remembered today as a bloody murder or a forensic triumph, but that misses the most important point.

The Ruxton case was important because of its legacy – it changed everything. It was this case that first established scientific methods as central to criminal investigation. It was the first modern murder, the landmark case that marked the line between the past and the present.

Such was the publicity surrounding the trial and the extensive coverage of the forensic evidence that it caught the imagination of the public and the establishment alike. It was compared with Sherlock Holmes come to life, and there was a new fascination with the scientific methods of the pathologists reflected by the growing interest in crime novels and the adventures of the great fictional detectives of the age. It was the era of Hercule Poirot and Miss Marple, the golden age of detective fiction where Agatha Christie's mysteries captivated and sold in millions.

Here were the heroes of fiction come to life, real-life detectives and scientists to admire and wonder at. Professors Glaister, Brash and Smith were lionised. They were already public figures in Scotland, but even they must have been bewildered by the avalanche of publicity that crashed over them. Hundreds of fan letters were received at Edinburgh and Glasgow Universities, together with numerous job offers, applications for jobs and countless requests to lecture and write about their experiences. Glaister in particular was picked out for praise; so impressive had his investigation and evidence been that he gained enormous personal prestige, so much so that the esteemed Lord Trenchard, then Commissioner of the Metropolitan Police, invited him to head a new medical directorship at the police college in Hendon. It was a tempting offer, an immensely powerful position with the opportunity to champion his aim of embedding scientific methods in criminal investigation, but on balance he decided to decline. He later explained his reasoning:

> It is still my belief that a university is the best place for a medicolegal institute to be located for the proper pursuance of forensic medicine. Such an institute is in turn embedded in the heart of a larger institution, the periphery of which holds representative specialists in the various fields and branches of science which from time to time may be required to give aid and assistance. In this way it is possible always to have a 'standing army' of experts with full facilities in their several fields without, to put it bluntly from a tax payer's point of view, the need to keep them on a separate strength.

It is a typically diplomatic explanation from Glaister, but there was more to it. The main reason for refusing the post at Hendon was independence. Neither Glaister nor any of his colleagues wanted to jeopardise the absolute independence that gave their evidence such weight and credibility, but the lessons from Ruxton stuck and it is interesting to examine the reasons why.

The police service is notoriously poor at remembering and learning the lessons of the past. Careers are short and there is no institutional memory. As a new generation rises to the most senior ranks, an amnesia sets in, and there is an overwhelming 'macho' tendency (women can be macho too) to sweep away all that went before as old-fashioned or obsolete. Then, over the decades that follow, they are condemned to relearn the lessons, often replicating exactly what they discarded in the first place. As a famous criminologist once said, 'The only new ideas are those which have already been forgotten.'

It is a tiresome and expensive process with the wheel usually coming full circle every thirty years or so. Yet the lessons from the Ruxton case were learned and entered the mainstream mainly because the pathologists came from a different culture, one of continuous improvement and academic rigour. They quickly recorded their findings, taking the learning from the case.

Though many of the 'new' forensic techniques developed during the investigation were not presented as evidence in court, they were fully described by Glaister and Brash in a technical textbook which won the Swiney Prize. (Another Swiney Prize would come to Glaister in 1949 for a new edition of his textbook *Medical Jurisprudence and Toxicology*.)

Never before had one investigation brought forward so many new forensic innovations. It had been a brilliant episode. At no time before or since has Scottish forensic science enjoyed such international credit or prestige.

The effects were profound. As Glaister put it:

> In the months and years that followed, case after case of murder at home and abroad was solved by application of the methods developed by the Ruxton team – often we received requests for information from some of these medicolegal men in other countries and were glad to answer.

In the truest sense, Ruxton was a turning point.

Throughout the UK and Europe, the publicity surrounding the case, and the academic papers and textbooks that followed, attracted the attention of police forces and, just as importantly, the police authorities that funded them. The old non-scientific methods of policing were archaic; any police force worth the name had to adopt scientific methods and should not have to depend on bigger forces for help.

It became a badge of honour for even the smallest forces to have their own detective branches equipped to use the latest scientific and forensic techniques. Even the lofty Home Office took notice; it was no coincidence that, shortly after the trial, a number of regional Home Office forensic laboratories were opened, fully equipped to provide the best of scientific assistance in the investigation of crime. Dedicated detective training courses were established with emphasis on crime scenes, fingerprints and the preservation of evidence – for the first time, detectives would be more than just constables out of uniform; they would be specialists specifically trained to work with the new laboratories and the new sciences.

As the City of Glasgow had discovered when Sillitoe brought science to detection five years earlier, the effects were spectacular – detection rose across the country and there was a new confidence in the professionalism of the police.

For the leading men in the investigation, the fame brought by the trial led to huge change and opportunity. For Glaister, Brash and Smith there was international recognition, further burnishing their already stellar reputations and bringing huge credit to their universities. Students from across the world flocked to study under these famous men.

Bertie Hammond, the Glasgow fingerprint expert, was seconded to Lancashire Constabulary to set up their first fingerprint bureau. Lieutenant Ewing, the other senior Glasgow detective, was also much in demand, advising police forces all over England on the investigation of serious crimes and the duties of detectives. Scotland Yard, once the sole custodians of such expertise, had lost the primacy they had enjoyed for over a hundred years, ever since the modern police service was formed.

Back in Scotland, the huge success of the case gave further impetus to Percy Sillitoe's drive to modernise and improve Scotland's forces. Once he had returned from his various secondments, Hammond continued to build the City of Glasgow Police's fingerprint bureau to be second only to Scotland Yard's in size and reputation. Eventually the Glasgow fingerprint bureau became the national Scottish Criminal Records Office and remains serving police in Scotland to the present day.

In Edinburgh, the reforming Chief Constable, William Morren, used the prestige of the case and the tide of support for scientific methods to get funding from the usually parsimonious Police Watch Committee to build and improve Edinburgh's small identification branch. While Glasgow specialised in fingerprints, and Edinburgh had its own local fingerprint bureau, it concentrated on photography, handwriting and crime-scene management. The work done in Edinburgh on the photographic superimposition of Bella Ruxton had particularly caught the imagination, and it brought funding for equipment, training and more specialist officers.

Forensic science and specialised policing gained traction across Scotland in the aftermath of the Ruxton case, with police laboratories established in Edinburgh, Glasgow, Dundee and Aberdeen. And throughout the UK the best and brightest were attracted to work in the police and Home Office laboratories, either as civilian scientists or police officers specialising in fingerprints or photography. Chemistry and biology were the main disciplines, with specialisms in bloodstains, hairs, fibres and ballistics.

It was an expensive and lengthy process. The capital set-up costs were huge, and with seven years' training before gaining expert status it was a long time before fingerprint or handwriting experts could be used in the field. Such was the confidence in new scientific methods.

During the decades that followed, the range and proficiency of the identification branches and the crime laboratories grew. The detection of serious crime now depended more on science than the old methods, and juries became educated, expecting to hear evidence from forensic experts. Defence lawyers rushed to catch up, calling their own experts to throw doubt on the prosecution's. Even the judges had to educate themselves to become familiar with blood-splash patterns and the comparison of hairs and fibres. As the generation of men who had led the Ruxton investigation retired, new young officers took over to take the new techniques on. In Edinburgh, a young visionary named David Kerr introduced the first crime-scene vehicles, mobile laboratories fully equipped to recover and preserve evidence from crime scenes. It was another step forward, and many were to follow, each improving gradually the proficiency and range of scientific methods.

30 years after the Ruxton investigation, a network of forensic services covered the country. The police generation of the 1970s, my generation, took it for granted that such expertise was available, and it was sorely needed as the late 1970s and 1980s brought unprecedented challenges from the serial killers Robert Black, Peter Tobin and Angus Sinclair, who stalked the central belt of Scotland. Never before had Scottish policing faced such a task – organised killers who left little forensic evidence.

Yet on the early morning of 16 October 1977, a young biologist from the Lothian and Borders Police forensic laboratory attended a murder scene in East Lothian. Lester Knibb approached the deposition sites of teenagers Christine Eadie and Helen Scott using the same fastidious care that Glaister had used at Moffat forty years earlier and a mobile crime-scene vehicle – a successor to the one David Kerr had introduced 30 years earlier.

And in the end, it paid off – after a remarkable gap of 37 years, the evidence gathered and preserved in 1977 was instrumental in convicting Angus Sinclair for the double murder of Christine and Helen all those years before. It was an outstanding example of the professional recovery and care of forensic evidence and, like many other major crimes across the UK in the late 20th century, it was solved directly because of the legacy left by the Ruxton case – the first modern murder.

In death and infamy, Dr Buck Ruxton had in a perverse way achieved his second great ambition: a notable contribution to the development of medical science.

CHAPTER 21

WHO SOLVED THE RUXTON MURDERS?

The dust had hardly settled when the speculation began. Who had solved the Ruxton Murders? Who should take the credit and who should take the blame for things that went wrong?

As the case was seen as a triumph, there was little criticism, but who would take the credit? The prime witnesses, the scientists, the master detectives, the skilful lawyers or even the press.

THE SCIENTISTS

The scientists took the early laurels; their role had been groundbreaking and their evidence both spellbinding and macabre. Professors Glaister and Brash in particular were lauded for their meticulous work. Natural modesty prevented these brilliant men from claiming credit for themselves or basking in the adulation that followed the trial, but they were worldly enough to recognise the benefits to their departments and universities resulting from the trial's high profile.

Unlike most of the other players, they also quickly recorded their actions in both academic papers and books. Later, both Glaister and Sydney Smith wrote bestselling autobiographies, devoting considerable chapters to the Ruxton Murders. History has judged that the scientists take the credit for the case because it was the scientists who wrote the history. That said, Glaister, Brash and Smith do deserve much credit for the success of the case. Glaister particularly was visionary in the way he approached the investigation and interpreted his findings. His presentation of evidence in the court was nothing short of brilliant, his balance and fairness setting the standard for expert evidence from thereon.

LANCASTER POLICE

The police officers involved did not write their memoirs but in the aftermath of the trial shared much of the credit. Chief Constable Captain Vann of Lancaster Borough Police came in for special praise. His career prospered after the case and he went on to serve as Chief Constable of Maidstone in Kent.

This was a generous assessment which does not stand up to scrutiny. Vann had acted decisively once the overwhelming evidence had been laid before him, but his force had been very slow to join the dots or act professionally to help the Rogersons in their search for little Mary. But none of that was as critical as their abject failure to act on the long-established and ongoing domestic violence in the Ruxton household. Time and again Lancaster Police were called or learned of the threats and violence against Bella yet effectively did nothing to intercede, protect Bella or prevent further violence.

Of course, it is dubious to judge these actions against the norms of the present day, but even by the low standards of the 1930s, the actions – or rather lack of them – by Lancaster Police were lamentable. The Ruxton case has many victims, unlucky by virtue of time and place, yet Captain Vann and the rest of the force were fortunate indeed to avoid severe criticism, let alone come out of it all with their reputations enhanced.

THE GLASGOW DETECTIVES

The Glasgow detectives Ewing and Hammond were also credited with cracking the case, not least by an enthusiastic and partisan Scottish press. These plaudits were better deserved than those of Captain Vann. Ewing had lent all his considerable experience of serious and violent crime in Glasgow to supervise a professional murder investigation in Moffat and Lancaster. In both these difficult and unfamiliar environments, it was to his huge credit that he managed to bring together disparate teams of mixed experience and ability to complete a complex case. So highly regarded was he that he was asked to remain in Lancaster after the better-equipped Lancashire Constabulary took the case over. On completion of his secondment, he was presented with a magnificent silver bowl, purchased by his colleagues, in admiration and gratitude for the valuable work he had done.

Detective Lieutenant Hammond's brilliant fingerprint and photographic work had attracted the attention of police forces throughout the UK. He was seconded to a number of areas after the trial, Chief Constable Sillitoe only too pleased to loan out his prodigy in order to advance his crusade to modernise. Neither of these outstanding officers ever claimed credit for solving the Ruxton murder during their lifetime – they were far too modest for that – but years after their deaths, various publications hailed them as the master detectives who solved 'the crime of the century'.

As usual with such 'great man' theories, this is overly simplistic. It is, however, indisputable that Ewing and Hammond, with their team of Glasgow detectives, contributed significantly to the successful investigation of the case.

But no examination of Glasgow's contribution is complete without reference to Chief Constable Sillitoe. He sent his best men to help Dumfries without hesitation, though he could hardly spare them. It may have suited his greater purpose, but even so it was a generous gesture.

On completion of the enquiry, once his men had eventually returned from the far-flung parts the investigation had taken them, Sillitoe declined to send a bill to Dumfries, Lancaster or anywhere else. He considered the expert help he had given as simple assistance in a common cause. It won him many friends among the small police forces in Scotland, always wary of the big city forces.

THE LAWYERS

Although the lawyers could never have been credited with actually solving the case, the brilliance of their court performances, played out word for word in the national press, won many admirers. The skill of J.C. Jackson in piecing together such a complex circumstantial prosecution, his obvious mastery of highly specialist forensic evidence, and the support of Maxwell Fyfe and Hartley Shawcross all deserved credit, and their work had come to the notice of the legal hierarchy far away in London. They had been provincial northern figures before Ruxton, but now they were known nationally, their reputations gilded by the case.

Likewise, the defence team of Norman Birkett and Philip Kershaw were much admired for the stoic manner in which they had defended their client. It was obvious that they had done their utmost in a scrupulously fair and honest manner.

Even the judge, Mr Justice Singleton, won praise; his handling of the trial, his summing up, had all been flawless. It was the highlight of his career, but Maxwell Fyfe, Hartley Shawcross and Norman Birkett all went on to greater things. And in Scotland, the young Advocate Depute, Jock Cameron, was destined to become one of Scotland's greatest and longest-serving judges of the 20th century.

DUMFRIESSHIRE CONSTABULARY

Even with perfect hindsight and all the knowledge of the developments of the intervening eighty years, it is impossible not to credit Dumfriesshire Constabulary with a magnificent effort during the initial stages of the Ruxton investigation.

With absolutely no specialist resources, no detectives and little training or experience, this tiny force responded in textbook fashion. Certainly, they were fortunate to be led by an able chief constable, who had friends in all the right places and the realism to know when to contact them for help.

Not for Chief Constable Black the reluctance to seek help and apparently show weakness, so prevalent in small forces in later years. His experience as a Glasgow detective had given him the skill to lead a serious criminal investigation, he knew his force's strengths and weaknesses and did not hesitate to seek help to compensate for them. Without delay he'd sought help from his three larger neighbouring forces, and in turn those big forces had responded – Lanarkshire with its search teams, police-firemen and bloodhounds, and Glasgow and Edinburgh, with the best and most experienced detectives in the land – all without hesitation or charge.

Chief Constable Black's next great achievement was to harness this disparate group of officers and scientists to focus on the crucial early stages of the investigation. Working from a tiny rural police station, in the centre of a media storm, he avoided all the red herrings and distractions that attend big cases. Quickly assessing that the bodies and the crimes

211

were not local, he did everything in his power to communicate with all other forces in the UK. It certainly wasn't his fault that police in Lancaster and Lancashire just a hundred miles south failed to notice or appreciate the significance of the special notices alerting forces to the finds near Moffat.

Black was a highly competent officer and leader, but he was also fortunate to have a uniquely able group of men to help him. Sergeant Robert Sloan and Inspector Strath, without specialist training or experience in investigating serious crime, proved exceptionally able. Even taking the most critical retrospective view, it is hard to fault them.

Likewise, it was fortunate indeed that three giants of twentieth-century forensic science were nearby and able to assist the investigation. Every investigation needs some luck but the stars that aligned Professors Glaister, Brash and Smith, three visionaries of forensic science, was beyond good fortune.

Once the investigation moved south, Dumfriesshire withdrew as the focus shifted to 2 Dalton Square and the pathology laboratory at Edinburgh University. Dumfriesshire officers gave evidence at the trial, but it was routine testimony which attracted little press attention. Yet the actions in Dumfriesshire on 29 and 30 September 1935 had, in a very real sense, been the difference between success and failure.

Black was a naturally modest man who sought no limelight, wrote no memoirs and claimed no personal credit, but realising the importance of the case, he was hugely proud of his force's vital contribution. When, after the trial, the forensic experts were publicly acclaimed and credited with solving the case, he was forced to speak out, but only in the most confidential police circles. A short time after the trial, he spoke to a group of Scottish police officers:

So much has been said and written about the part science played in the elucidation of what became known as the 'Moffat Ravine Murders' and afterwards as the 'Ruxton Murders' that the police methods employed, and the result of these in establishing facts upon which the scientists were enabled to work are in danger of being lost sight of.

An eminent medical jurist said to me shortly after the case was disposed of that the application of science to the detection of crime is like a glass to the eye – an aid: and just as it is the case that if there is no sight behind the eye, the glass can be of no service, so is it, in criminal investigation, if there is not a good ground work of ordinary police inquiry, science, in the generally accepted sense, cannot alone achieve success.

It was and remains a fundamental truth: get it right at the crime scene and all is possible; get it wrong and no amount of scientific brilliance can compensate.

Still today that hard lesson is being learned, and many a historic or cold case remains undetected because of sloppy crime-scene management or poor evidence retention at the time of the crime. But Black and Dumfriesshire Constabulary knew the truth and the limitations that all police forces, particularly small ones, face.

Black concluded his comments with a pragmatic reminder of the realities of policing:

In calling for the assistance of experts in crime investigation from the cities we are not admitting that there are better police brains in the cities than in the county districts. We merely acknowledge the obvious, that in the large city forces the staff have more experience and better facilities in such work than we can possibly have. Moreover, by asking for that help we satisfy the public – our employers – that everything is being done that can be done to solve the crime.

I cannot conclude these remarks without acknowledging the energy and efficiency with which the members of my own force carried out the tasks assigned to them, the very able collaboration of the senior detectives and the ready and valuable co-operation of our colleagues in other forces.

In these few words Black established a pragmatic doctrine for his force that remained central to its ethos till it disappeared through amalgamation 78 years later. It enabled Dumfriesshire, later Dumfries and Galloway Constabulary, always the smallest police force in Scotland, to consistently punch above its weight, and when Pan Am 103 crashed into the small Dumfriesshire town of Lockerbie in December 1988, they once again, assisted by their larger neighbours, rose magnificently to the challenge.

But if credit has to be given for individuals' performance then it has to be Professor Glaister and Sergeant Robert Sloan – Glaister for his vision and forensic brilliance and Sloan for his magnificent performance at Gardenholme Linn and Moffat in the first crucial forty-eight hours of the investigation.

Both men's futures would be defined by their part in the Ruxton murder investigation. Glaister would go on with Smith to establish many of the principles of forensic detection that we know today, though the life of Sergeant Sloan, the hero of Gardenholme Linn, took a different trajectory.

Although they would never have claimed it, Chief Constable Black and Dumfriesshire Constabulary had most justification to take credit for solving the Ruxton Murders. But of course, it is seldom as simple as that; few major crimes are solved by one man or one agency, and the Ruxton Murders were no exception. In the final analysis, they were solved by seamless teamwork of an extraordinary high standard. It was exceptional by the standards of the day and Professor Glaister recognised the significance:

> In the Ruxton case I had realised for the first time what I had always envisaged – absolute teamwork towards a common objective, a collective effort in which both scientists and police worked side by side.
>
> It made a refreshing contrast with an older outlook, which sometimes left one man sitting on a case on his own, guarding it against all comers like a dog savouring a juicy bone.

It was a dream come true for Glaister and the model of joint working that he, Smith and Chief Constables Sillitoe and Morren would promote as best practice from then on.

But it was far from plain sailing. Often over the years police forces reverted to the older outlook, with forces reluctant to share information or show weakness by calling for help.

The Ruxton Murders were investigated in the most difficult and complicated of circumstances, requiring groundbreaking forensic techniques and involving not only different force areas but different jurisdictions, different legal systems and the active cooperation of very different disciplines – policing, science and the law, each of which had their own champions, priorities and egos.

What was the vital ingredient that in 1935 brought these different men and disciplines together in such a remarkable way? I believe a major factor was the time and place. Most of the key players – police, scientists and lawyers – had one thing in common: they had all served in the Great War, many with considerable distinction.

That sense of a shared extraordinary experience gave them a feeling of common brotherhood. They had worked under pressure, seen death close at hand and appreciated the true value of life. They felt blessed to be alive and were imbued with a sense of purpose and tenacity. They were also used to working in teams of different skills and abilities, and above all they knew the value of synergy in a common cause. They would not have described or perhaps even recognised it but that was the glue that bound the survivors of that great generation together in respect, humility and common understanding.

Even a man of Dr Buck Ruxton's guile and resolve stood little chance.

CHAPTER 22

DRAMATIS PERSONAE

The Ruxton case had a profound effect on its principle players; for some it was a springboard to fame and success, for others a disaster.

The house at 2 Dalton Square stood derelict for years. Although the staircase and other parts removed by Professor Glaister and his forensic team were reinstalled, it was a patch up, and aside from its terrible reputation, many felt it simply wasn't structurally safe. Proposals to demolish it were rejected as it formed part of a terrace of houses. Attempts to turn it into a 'Black Museum' (a museum housing criminal memorabilia) were also firmly repulsed – the good people of Lancaster had had enough of the ghouls and voyeurs that now came to gawp at Lancaster's 'house of horrors'.

One of the big problems with the house was its ownership. It formed the main part of Ruxton's estate, which was bequeathed to his children, but since they were not of age, the responsibility fell on Ruxton's executor, his solicitor. No one could decide what was to happen to the place and eventually the bright interiors that Ruxton was so proud of faded, the antiques he had so lovingly gathered disappearing piece by piece.

After years of wrangling, the house was eventually sold for a pittance to the adjacent cinema, but by the 1970s both house and cinema had fallen into disrepair. Finally, the local council stepped in and compulsorily purchased the house, intending to renovate it, but plans to turn it into a nightclub came to nothing and in the end it was converted to a council planning office.

Even today it is a dark building with a forbidding sense of menace. Paint and décor cannot disguise what happened there, and this theme of mixed fortunes is also present for many of the other players in the tale.

The legal teams on both sides came out with their reputations greatly enhanced; the long public exposure made them not only household names but stars in the closed world of barristers and King's Counsels.

The judge, **Lord Justice Singleton**, went on to become one of Lancashire's most distinguished judges. He died in 1957, the Ruxton trial being the highlight of his long legal career.

J.C. Jackson, KC, who led for the Crown, already had a formidable reputation. In 1934, he had defended Jackie Brown, the world flyweight boxing champion when he was convicted of biting a piece of a man's ear off during a street fight. But the Ruxton prosecution was his masterpiece. His carefully woven net of circumstantial evidence would be studied by law students for decades to come.

Norman Birkett, KC, who led the defence, eventually accepted appointment to the bench, becoming a judge in 1941 and later serving as one of the British judges at the Nuremberg war trials in 1945. Although he disliked judicial work, preferring the specialism of contract law, he was an excellent judge and considered one of the most brilliant legal minds of his era – 'the Lord Chancellor that never was'. He died in 1962.

David Maxwell Fyfe, Jackson's understudy for the Crown, was knighted in 1942 and served as Solicitor General, Attorney General, Home Secretary and eventually Lord High Chancellor of Great Britain. He was raised to the peerage and died in 1967 the 1st Earl of Kilmuir.

Hartley Shawcross, the other understudy in the Crown team, was the lead British prosecutor in the Nuremberg trials. Knighted in 1945, he became Britain's principal delegate to the United Nations after the Second World War. He subsequently became Attorney General, succeeding Maxwell Fyfe, and President of the Board of Trade. He lived to be over a hundred years of age and died in 2003 as Baron Shawcross.

Philip Kershaw, KC, and the instructing solicitor for the defence did not enjoy such stellar careers, but in the north of England their names were always positively associated with the stalwart defence of Buck Ruxton.

In Scotland, the young **Advocate Depute, Jock Cameron,** went on to become one of Scotland's finest and longest-serving judges. Having served in the Royal Navy as a boy sailor during the Great War, he re-joined in the Second World War, winning a Distinguished Service Cross on convoy duties. In his later years, he served on numerous

Royal Commissions and enquiries, his legal knowledge and common sense making him indispensable when awkward problems had to be resolved. Lord Cameron died at ninety-six years of age and was considered by many the finest Scottish judge of the 20th century.

The scientists, not distracted by fame, continued their work in Edinburgh and Glasgow Universities.

Professor Sydney Smith was knighted in 1949 and served as rector of Edinburgh University. In 1959, he wrote an autobiography, *Mostly Murder*, which became a standard text and bestseller, being reprinted many times. He died in 1969.

Professor James Couper Brash became one of the pre-eminent anatomists in the UK, writing extensively on the Ruxton case and many others. He edited the *Manual of Practical Anatomy* for many years and died in 1958.

Professor John Glaister remained at Glasgow University till 1962, regularly writing and broadcasting on forensic science. He died in 1971, having, with Sydney Smith, helped lay the foundations of practical forensic science and crime-scene management that is still practised throughout the UK today.

For the police officers involved in the investigation, however, it was a mixed bag.

The Glasgow detectives **Ewing and Hammond** went on to lead Glasgow's CID during its golden post-war period, Ewing becoming one of the legendary detective chief superintendents who headed the CID.

As previously mentioned, **Captain Henry Vann**, Lancaster's lucky chief constable, received great credit for the success of the Ruxton investigation and, being an ambitious man, took full advantage of his new-found reputation by securing funding with which to modernise his tiny force. Having established himself as a successful reformer, he then applied for a number of senior chief constable's positions, including Blackpool and Stoke-on-Trent, before eventually being appointed as Chief of Maidstone in Kent.

Percy Sillitoe, the architect of the modern police service in Scotland, resisted invitations to apply for senior positions in England and remained in Glasgow till 1944, when he eventually accepted the appointment of Chief Constable of Kent County. There he continued his reforming ways, being the first chief constable to appoint a large force of female officers, as well as radio communications and a fleet of fast response vehicles. But few realise the full extent of his influence as the father of Scotland's modern police service.

In 1945, he was knighted and appointed head of MI5, a remarkable testimony to the high regard in which he was held. It was an unhappy chapter for Sillitoe; MI6, the foreign intelligence service, was riddled with double agents, the Cambridge spies, and Sillitoe's MI5 took undeserved blame for failing to detect them.

Following his retirement, Sir Percy fulfilled a lifelong ambition and opened a sweet shop in Eastbourne. The business failed. He died in 1962 one of the most influential and far-sighted police officers the UK has ever seen. Police officers throughout the world still wear the black-and-white chequered hat band – 'Sillitoe tartan' – that he introduced to Glasgow in 1931.

In Edinburgh, Sillitoe's young disciple **William Morren** remained in post till the 1950s. He was knighted and left the legacy of a thoroughly modernised police force. He lived to a great age, and even in the late 1960s he could be seen running the line at police rugby matches, setting an example and encouraging young officers to the end.

Detective Superintendent Berry remained in service during the Second World War, retiring as Assistant Chief Constable in 1951. His legacy was an Edinburgh CID staffed by first-class thief-takers, including my father. Generations later, the foundation Berry had so painstakingly laid could still be seen.

Detective Inspector John Sheed was promoted to lieutenant, postponed his retiral for the duration of the Second World War and remained Berry's strong right arm throughout. He lived on to the 1970s and in great old age he gifted all his personal papers to Lothian and Borders Police, successor to Edinburgh City Police. These papers are the basis for significant chapters of this book.

'Dr' Howard Campbell, the fake doctor who had come so close to being arrested for the murders did not appear on the files of Edinburgh Police again. Perhaps his close encounter with The Edinburgh CID had taught him the error of his ways. More likely he learned a different lesson and adapted his behaviour to avoid further scrapes with the law. It is unlikely that this scoundrel even realised just how lucky he'd been.

If Chief Constable Vann took advantage of his role in the Ruxton case, his worthier colleague, **Chief Constable William Black** of Dumfriesshire, did not. Black was a modest man who eschewed fame and never claimed personal credit for the investigation, even though his leadership during the initial stages had been outstanding by the standards of any day. He remained Chief Constable of Dumfriesshire until 1948 when the merged force of Dumfries and Galloway was formed. His legacy was a police force, small but confident in its own ability always to punch above its weight.

For **Sergeant Robert Sloan**, however, the Ruxton case brought both triumph and disaster. Though largely eclipsed in the media by the forensic scientists, he was recognised within his own community for the incredible contribution he'd made. The local hero was promoted to inspector ahead of a number of rivals in 1938 and posted to Thornhill, over thirty miles from his beloved Moffat.

But the knives were already out. In the police service success and a high profile always brings admiration and jealousy in equal measure, and the new Inspector Sloan was no exception.

On arrival at Thornhill he had established his own high standards quickly, gaining the enmity of several of his more laid-back juniors, who resented his celebrity and his authority. Wisely, Sloan never socialised near his home station but frequently travelled back to Moffat, where he could relax in the company of old friends.

On 27 December 1938, just ten months after his promotion, he travelled by bus to Moffat to enjoy a late Christmas meal at the Star Hotel. He missed the last bus back so borrowed the car of the owner of the Star and made his way back to Thornhill in time for his period of duty the next day. It turned out to be a quiet day, so Sloan took the opportunity to return the car to Moffat during his working shift, but it was a stupid mistake; he knew he had enemies and now they pounced, reporting his absence to the chief constable himself.

Any kind of social relationship with publicans was strictly forbidden under the discipline code; borrowing a publican's car and leaving his place of duty were serious transgressions. It seems harsh now, but Chief Constable Black had little choice – Sloan was reduced in rank back to sergeant less than a year after his promotion.

It was a devastating blow to the proud and intensely private Robert Sloan, and his subsequent transfer to Dumfries headquarters and non-job was a further humiliation from which he never recovered.

His war service had left him with stomach problems and his health failed alongside his spirit. He developed severe gastric ulcers and, on 21 December 1940, he died following a failed operation to treat a perforated ulcer. He was 44 years of age. His death certificate gives the cause of death as, 'gastric perforation operation and myocardial degeneration.'

His son Robert junior, just nine years of age at the time of the Ruxton Murders, would later follow his father into Dumfries and Galloway Constabulary.

Sloan has now been largely forgotten, his role in the Ruxton investigation seldom described in the numerous accounts of the case, but not in Dumfries and Galloway, where former officers and local historians still remember the hero of Gardenholme Linn as one of their own, the ordinary county police sergeant who, on 29 September 1935, did extraordinary duty and played a key role in solving one of the major crimes of the 20th century.

The redoubtable **Violet Van der Elst** continued her campaign against the death penalty for the rest of her life. In the face of continued persecution and institutional brickbats, she never wavered in her determination to see an end to hanging. Time and time again she and her supporters took direct action at prisons, courts and the Home Office, and time and time again she was arrested on spurious charges, but nothing deterred her. She stood for parliament on a number of occasions, each time unsuccessfully, and wrote a well-received book, *On the Gallows*, in 1937. In the same year, she published a series of ghost stories, all with a theme aimed at swaying public opinion against the death penalty.

The word indefatigable was made for this lady, but eventually her campaigning and failed political runs depleted even her vast fortune. She was forced to sell her country estate and move to a small flat in London. Even then she did not stand aside, continuing to agitate and campaign until her health failed. She must have been quietly satisfied when, in August 1964, Gwynne Owen Evans and Peter Allen became the last men to be hanged in Britain. Ironically Evans's execution took place in Strangeways Prison on the very gallows that Ruxton had met his end on thirty years before.

Van der Elst died in a nursing home in 1966, secure in the knowledge that hanging in Britain had been discontinued – eventually to be outlawed. Throughout her long life campaigning against the death penalty, she had been subject to every legal sanction and institutional discrimination, her behaviour and direct action considered unladylike, but what really upset the powers that be was her confrontational style, her power to embarrass and her success.

Even in death she was snubbed – given no credit for her role – when the death penalty was eventually abolished, and today she is largely forgotten. There are no statues of her, no plaques to commemorate her life, no institutions in her name. But as new generations of independent young women search history for role models, it is hoped that they rediscover Violet; they would do well to study the life and resolve of this formidable woman. She deserves to be remembered.

Following Mary's death, the curse of the **Rogerson family** seemed never-ending. As well as being exposed to years of trolling and the cruellest of hoaxes, they lost another child, a son, in an accident two years later. He was buried in the same grave as his sister. Later, in 1937, another son was seriously injured after being set on fire while playing near a bonfire. Thankfully, he survived.

Over time the Rogersons slipped from the headlines and it is hoped that this simple and upstanding family, so marked by tragedy, lived out their lives in peaceful obscurity and without further suffering.

But bad luck seemed to dog some who were close to the case.

Herbert Anderson, the dentist who was Ruxton's close friend and who was suspected of smuggling his last letters out of prison, never recovered his health after the execution of his friend. There was poisonous local gossip that he had known of the murders, had even helped to cover them up, and deny it as he might, Anderson never shook the stigma of association with the murders.

Further tragedy struck when his 21-year-old daughter died suddenly. He suffered from insomnia and failing eyesight, always seeming deeply troubled, and in the November following the trial he committed suicide, found by his housemaid with his head in the gas oven. We will never know the full extent of his knowledge or of any complicity in the murders or of his part in smuggling the last letters from the prison, but what is almost certain is that the respectable small-town dentist was another secondary victim caught up in the Ruxton Murders.

At the time of their mother's and father's deaths, the **Ruxton children, Elizabeth, Diane and Billie**, were six, four and two years old. They had been in the house at Dalton Square on the night of the murders – asleep in the nursery adjacent to the top stair landing where their mother and beloved nursemaid were brutally murdered. In the days following the murders, they were farmed out to various friends and Billie, the youngest, even accompanied his father on one of his runs north to dump the body parts. After their father's arrest, they were told simply that their parents and nursemaid had gone on holiday without them and were sheltered from the enormous publicity that engulfed Lancaster.

After the trial and execution, the three children were placed in the public assistance institution at Lancaster, the successor of the workhouse, and thereafter faded from the picture. Were they kept together as a family unit, per their father's last wishes? Did they keep the name Ruxton or were they adopted together or separately, taking the surnames of their new families? Were they ever told the truth about their mother and father? And what happened to them as they rebuilt their lives, so cruelly shattered that night in September 1935? Of all the millions of words written about the Ruxton case, the children are hardly mentioned at all. In the cold, emotionless legal world of 1936, they were seen only as collateral damage, an administrative inconvenience.

When researching this book, I became fascinated by Elizabeth, Diane and Billie. I wanted to know how their lives had gone and how their story had ended. Perhaps they had large successful families of their own? It was even possible that they were still alive in great old age.

So I determined to track them down to find out, but second thoughts prevented me. If they knew their family history, then all I would do is reopen old wounds, and if they didn't know then I was set to re-victimise them and their families all over again, eighty years on. I couldn't take that chance. They deserved to be left in peace.

Tom Wood
2020

LIST OF ILLUSTRATIONS

	Page
1. Dr Buck Ruxton	2
2. Bella Ruxton	13
3. Mary Rogerson	14
4. Sergeant Robert Sloan	21
5. Percy Sillitoe	30
6. Professor John Glaister Jnr	42
7. Professor Sydney Smith	42
8. Professor James Brash	42
9. The Reassembled Body No. 2 (Bella Ruxton)	95
10. Skull No. 2 superimposed on photo of Bella	169

BIBLIOGRAPHY

Black, W., notes and speeches on The Ruxton Murders (unpublished)

Blundell, R.H. and Wilson, G.H. (1937) *Trial of Buck Ruxton* (London: W. Hodge)

Edinburgh City Police, statements, photographs, telephone messages and case documents relating to the Ruxton Murders (unpublished)

Glaister, J. (1964) *Final Diagnosis* (London: Hutchinson & Co.)

Glaister, J. and Brash, J.C. (1937) *Medico-Legal Aspects of the Ruxton Case* (Edinburgh: Livingstone)

Potter, T.F. (1984) *The Deadly Doctor Ruxton* (Preston: Carnegie)

Sheed, J., papers relating to the Ruxton Murders (unpublished)

Smith, S. (1959) *Mostly Murder* (Whitefish: Kessinger Publishing.

ABOUT THE AUTHOR

Tom Wood was one of Scotland's most senior and experienced police officers.

He is an authority on serious violent crime, the policing of large-scale events, and a noted authority on police perspectives on drugs and alcohol.

He is a graduate of Edinburgh University and the FBI Academy, Quantico, Virginia.

In 1994, he was appointed Commander of the Royal Norwegian Order of Merit and in 1995 was awarded the Queen's Police Medal.

Latterly he was Deputy Chief Constable and Director of Operations of Lothian and Borders Police. He was Officer in Overall Command of the linked murder investigation into the deaths of a number of young women including Helen Scott and Christine Eadie (the World's End Murders).

Since leaving the police he has worked in the fields of alcohol and drug strategy, adult and child protection and has undertaken a number of independent serious case and homicide reviews.

He lives in Edinburgh.

ACKNOWLEDGEMENTS

Researching and writing this book has been a privilege, particularly the rediscovery of the forgotten heroes who contributed so much to this story and laid the foundations of modern science-based investigation.

The generations of detectives and scientists that followed are in their debt.

I am grateful to my family, friends and many former colleagues who helped and encouraged during the process. I am particularly grateful to the great Val McDermid for her unfailing support and to my friend Peter Ritchie for his time and expertise.

I would also like to record my thanks to the late Bob Ovens QPM, former Deputy Chief Constable, and to Joe Craig, custodian of Dumfries and Galloway Constabulary historical records.

Many people have contributed to this book and deserve recognition – my tireless agent Claire Scott, my friend and artist Stella Fulton for the cover artwork, Jim Mackintosh for the photographic images and Anna Jones for her usual meticulous editorial work.

Lastly, I could not have completed this work without the help of my friend and long-suffering ex-secretary Jeanette Shiells who once again has made sense of my scribblings.

This text is based on numerous documents, some previously published, but many from unpublished private family sources. Access to these private papers was given to me on the strict understanding that no one would be authorised to re-use them as source material without my written permission.

I am grateful for that trust.

The descriptions and interpretations of the various scenarios surrounding this crime are based on the evidence presented at the trial, the original statements, contemporary accounts and the behavioural characteristics common in serious crime and domestic homicide.

All opinions and any errors in the text are mine alone.

Tom Wood
2020

Other Titles from Ringwood

All titles are available from the Ringwood website in both print and ebook format, as well as from usual outlets.

www.ringwoodpublishing.com

mail@ringwoodpublishing.com

Cuddies Strip

Rob McInroy

Cuddies Strip is based on a true crime and faithfully follows the investigation and subsequent trial but it also examines the mores of the times and the insensitive treatment of women in a male-dominated society.

It is a highly absorbing period piece from 1930s Scotland, with strong contemporary resonances: both about the nature and responsiveness of police services and the ingrained misogyny of the whole criminal justice system.

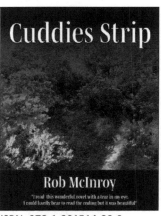

ISBN: 978-1-901514-88-9
£9.99

ISBN: 978-1-901514-43-8
£9.99

The Ten Percent

Simon McLean

An often hilarious, sometimes scary, always fascinating journey through the ranks of the Scottish police from his spell as a rookie constable in the hills and lochs of Argyll, through his career in Rothesay and to his ultimate goal: The Serious Crime Squad in Glasgow.

We get a unique glimpse of the turmoil caused when the rules are stretched to the limit, when the gloves come off and and when some of their number decide that enough is enough. A very rare insight into the world of our plain clothes officers who infiltrate and suppress the very worst among us.

Murder at the Mela

Leela Soma

Newly appointed as Glasgow's first Asian DI, Alok Patel's first assignment is the investigation of the brutal murder of Nadia, an Asian woman. Her body was discovered in the aftermath of the Mela festival in Kelvingrove Park. During the Mela, a small fight erupted between a BNP group and an Asian gang, but was quickly quelled by police.

This novel peels away the layers of Glasgow's Asian communities, while exploring the complicated relationships between Asian people and the city.

ISBN: 978-1-901514-90-2
£9.99

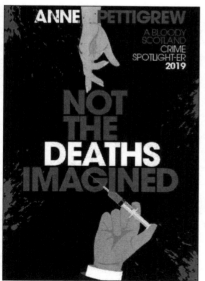

Not the Deaths Imagined

Anne Pettigrew

It's here, the medical noir novel you've been waiting for! The sequel to Anne Pettigrew's acclaimed debut, *Not the Life Imagined*.

In *Not the Deaths Imagined* we again follow Beth Semple, now a dedicated GP and mother in Milngavie, as she aims to navigate Glasgow's busy medical scene.

But when she starts asking questions about a series of local deaths, Beth finds her life – and that of her family – is about to be turned upside down.

ISBN: 978-1-901514-80-3
£9.99

Inference

Stephanie McDonald

Natalie Byron had a happy life in Glasgow. She had a steady job, supportive friends and a loving family. Or at least, she thought she did. The morning after a date, Natalie wakes up inside a strange house, in a strange bed, sleeping next to a man named Jamie who claims he is her boyfriend. .

But this isn't her life and Jamie certainly isn't her boyfriend. Fearing she's been kidnapped, Natalie flees, but not one person on the island will help her. But there is one thing Natalie is sure of. She needs to get off this island.

ISBN: 978-1-901514-68-1   £9.99

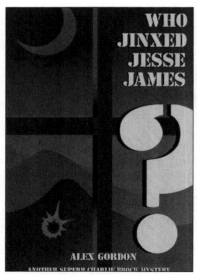

Who Jinxed Jesse James?

Alex Gordon

Jesse James – real name, Frank – shoots straight from the lip: the controversial gossip columnist makes a living sullying the reputations of the elite and, like his Wild West counterpart, is no stranger to infamy. He finds himself with no choice but to swallow his considerable ego and seek the help of his former colleague, freelance sports journalist and amateur sleuth, Charlie Brock. They soon becomes entangled in the mystery surrounding the identity of an enigmatic scribe - known locally as 'The Red Phantom'...

ISBN: 978-1-901514-71-1   £9.99